THE WILL TO BE HUMAN

THE WILL
TO BE
HUMAN

SILVANO ARIETI

QUADRANGLE BOOKS
A New York Times Company

ACKNOWLEDGMENTS

The author wishes to thank the following publishers for permission to reproduce excerpts from some of his previous works:

Basic Books © 1966 for excerpts from a chapter of the *American Handbook of Psychiatry* Vol. III, edited by Silvano Arieti, Basic Books © 1967 for excerpts from a chapter from *The Intrapsychic Self,* Grune and Stratton © 1972 for excerpts from "The Origin and Effect of Power" by Silvano Arieti in Masserman, J., Ed. *Science and Psychoanalysis* Vol. XX.

Library of Congress Card Number: 72-78504

Text design by Ruth Schmerechniak

PREFACE

OBSCURE SOCIAL FORCES, SEEMINGLY SIMPLE, CONVINCING, AND
clear, are seeking to endow man with a new image. They portray man as totally conditioned, programmed, and without any
role in determining his life. In an age like ours, when many
feel that they are drifting aimlessly, or are being used by others,
or are too afraid to resist, or too uncertain to choose, or too
weak to act, it is easy to accept that image. Few are the voices
which affirm man's initiative in directing his own steps and
building his own home. It is my hope that this book will be one
of those voices.

This book shows that man's will, freedom, and dignity can be
crushed by the ways people are raised, or by oppressive and deforming social conditions, or by those who accumulate power.
But this book will also show that will can be returned to the
people. It is true that especially critical times demand that man
be redefined, but any new definition must add to the variety
of his dimensions, and may not necessarily simplify his understanding.

Busy, noisy, and polluted Manhattan, where things happen, and Sardinia, the island where things do not happen, but where the calm sea, the silent rocks, and the blue sky are and always will be, have witnessed the labor of these pages. If one place has indicated to me the fever with which man wills each of his days, the other has made me sure that his search, too, is one of the eternals.

My gratitude to Jack and Jules Bemporad, who gave constructive criticism, to Robert Ackerman, who gave editorial assistance, and in particular to my son Jimmy, who, with filial affection and scholarly endurance, straightened the syntax and improved the diction.

Silvano Arieti

Contents

T O
Marianne

CHAPTER 1

The Cogent Issues

HOW MAN'S WILL BEGINS AND GROWS, HOW THE WINGS OF FREE-dom make it fly to unpredictable heights, and how the chains of adverse powers dissolve it into nullity or despair has long concerned the Western world.

Numerous studies have approached the problem with strictly philosophical arguments, aiming at establishing whether free initiative really exists in man or whether it is an illusion in a world where everything is determined by uncontrollable causes. Other studies have excluded the phenomenon will from the realm of science, although they have affirmed that actions can be controlled by men.

My approach, on the other hand, will consist of first consider-ing will within the realm of human, perhaps humanistic, psy-chology and psychoanalysis. Soon it will appear, however, that the inquiry must be at least of two kinds, for the freedom and adverse powers which affect the will may come from within and be predominantly psychological, or from without and be predominantly social. I shall examine the connection of the will with our basic biological nature, our actions, wishes, intentions, relations with peers, elders, society, the world in general, the forces of oppression and the forces of freedom, the forces which work for the attainment of our aspirations, and the obstacles which frustrate our efforts. I shall make psychological interpretations as a psychiatrist and a psychoanalyst. I shall discuss the sociological facts and events as a man who is involved with the problems of our time and who has tried to show how they are related to psychological phenomena.

In my opinion, will, as the capacity to make and implement choices, is the culmination of all psychol·ical functions. On the other hand, any function of will—that is, any action—produces a change in our relations with others and therefore becomes a social and even a political event. The same argument could be repeated in reverse order for any social event which affects our will.

Because of the various situations into which will enters, my exposition will not unfold in a single linear sequence. In different chapters, when I shall describe different social situations, I shall present now man ·he loser, now man the winner. I shall describe society now as the nourishing mother, now as the witch who twists and devours. My faith in man, I hope, will come through.

An observation made many years ago will open my presentation in a roundabout way. I was twenty-four years old when I left the country of my birth, in flight from tyranny and in search of freedom. When I arrived in the United States my attention was at first attracted by the things which reconnected me to the old country. I soon discovered that among the works of Italian literature competing with such classics as Dante, Boccaccio, and Machiavelli was *Pinocchio*, a little book for children, written by an otherwise obscure author named Collodi. This discovery had the savor of a pleasant surprise, since the book was associated in my memory with the tenderness of my mother, who sat next to me on the sofa and read to me the astounding story, when I was three or four.

Why was *Pinocchio* so well known in America, too? What was so enchanting about the tale of this puppet? Like all puppets, Pinocchio was made of wood, but unlike the others did not need a puppeteer to move his strings. He was capable of motions on his own, of *willed acts*.

What was the result? From the very first moment that his father, carpenter Geppetto, finishes making him, he gets into trouble. As soon as Geppetto gives the last touch to Pinocchio's hands, those hands grab Geppetto's wig and don't want to let it go. As soon as Geppetto makes the legs, the legs start to move and kick Geppetto. And from that time on, it is one naughty deed after another. Pinocchio goes through the stages of being a disobedient child, a juvenile delinquent, and a real psychopath.

In a leap of artistic imagination, Collodi bypassed the great evolutionary process of billions of years, which first gave autonomous movement to organic matter, then coordinated motion, finally voluntary acts and moral deeds. Collodi's story created a paradoxical situation: while Pinocchio must act as a moral human being, he is not qualified to do so. As the story evolves he becomes tamed, socialized, industrious, and acquires a conscience. When this gradual transformation is completed, he deserves to be changed into a child of flesh and blood, a regular member of the human race. But this, let us call it maturation, was not easy. Among the many spectacular adventures of the puppet, having to do with his own misdeeds and the misdeeds of the cruel world, is his turning up alive in the big belly of a whale. It is there that Pinocchio repents, finds again his father Geppetto, and there redemption occurs.

The similarity to the biblical book of Jonah is obvious. Consciously or unconsciously, Collodi was inspired by it and imitated it. The fact that the story is similar to Jonah is not coincidental, nor should it appear sacrilegious to the religious man who reveres the Bible, for eternal truths may also appear in myths and in children's tales. The Book of Jonah is indeed one of the greatest which has ever been written on moral issues. Its importance is revealed also by the fact that every year on Yom Kippur, the Day of Atonement, Jews read it again as part of the liturgy of the day. Jonah appears towards the middle of the Old Testament as one who dared to confront God. He seems the counterpart of another great biblical figure who appears at the beginning of the Old Testament—Abraham, who is submissive to God to the point of being willing to sacrifice his son Isaac.

Jonah escaped from what appeared to him the strict paternal figure of God, who had asked him to bring an important and terrifying message to the city of Nineveh. Like a demanding father, God expects Jonah to be active and to do daring things. But there is a strong streak of passivity and escapism in Jonah. He prefers to run away from the command. Instead of going to Nineveh, he boards a ship directed to Tarshish, probably

Tartessus in southwest Spain. On board he finds himself a niche at the bottom of the ship, probably to make himself inconspicuous since he feels that he must hide. While a hurricane rages, he falls asleep. The incredulous sailors go to him. How can he sleep while the storm roars and the ship is in extreme danger? Jonah eventually confesses his crime to the crew: he has disobeyed the order of God. In an attempt to save the others and to obtain deserved punishment, he asks the sailors to throw him into the sea. In the sea he is swallowed by a whale. According to the language of myth, the belly of the whale is the first and last refuge, a symbol of the maternal womb. It is worth noticing that in Hebrew the word *rachamim* means both "womb" and "mercy." Translated into ordinary language, the story tells us that Jonah attempted to escape from the demanding father and go for protection to the merciful mother.

In Collodi's tale Pinocchio had no mother. Collodi did not say so explicitly in the book, but in interpreting the story psychologically we may infer that the absence of a mother was the main reason why it was difficult for Pinocchio to be a good boy. He always had the paternal love of Geppetto, who was making demands on him and requesting commitments from him, but not the all-accepting, embracing love of a mother. Only at the end of the story does Pinocchio find a maternal figure, the Fairy with the Blue Hair, who will transform him into a real child.

One of the truths which seems implied in religious books as well as in myths and tales is that in the developmental journey which leads to independent will and to the ability to make the good and right choice, human beings need the assistance of two personal and older centers of will. One of them is symbolized as paternal, and generally individualized as the father, the chief, God. The other is symbolized as maternal, and generally individualized as the mother, Mother Earth, or the community. Both centers of will *will* to dispense wisdom and love. The paternal figure, however, is generally connected with wisdom; the maternal, with love. Both figures include authority: the paternal authority directs the individual to do a certain action because sooner or later that action will reveal itself to be the right or wise one from the point of view of the individual himself, of the community, or God. The maternal authority directs the individual to do a certain action (desired by either parental authority) because by doing so the individual will get maternal love or a substitute for maternal love. These two author ities are not infrequently seen in conflict. In the biblical story Jonah too felt this conflict. He finally obeyed God and went to Nineveh to announce the divine message: the city would be destroyed because of its sins. But contrary to the assurance made to the prophet that He would punish Nineveh, God became maternal, merciful, and forgave the sinful city.

What I have so far presented, in an apparently digressive manner, is a prologue to a prologue. Our main problem concerns the relation between free choice and authority. Can free and good choice develop without authority? If authority, parental, scholastic, or governmental, is necessary for the development of free choice, will such authority eventually impede that choice? How will such authority affect us, inside in our psyche, and outside in our social or individual actions? Many authors today write about a coming revolution; and yet although they clearly outline some changes which should take place in society, they do not stress enough that any innovating movement implies a change in the concept of authority. The change is not merely social or political but also psychological.

The relation between free choice and authority has always been recognized as a complicated one, but the social developments which have occurred in the last few years have increased the complication. Many persons today want to be in a state of constant confrontation with any and all authorities. They want to increase their individual freedom to an unprecedented extent. They also do not want to conform to the prevailing habits of the community, but instead want each person to follow his own inclination.

Let us give a first, and therefore elementary, look at each of these propositions. At first one may think that in spite of new aspects this confrontation with authority is the old one, repeated innumerable times since time immemorial: the search for freedom. That man repeatedly, if not constantly since ancient history, has tried to be free, is true. We must recognize, however, an additional characteristic in the search for freedom in which young people especially are engaged today. This additional characteristic appears evident if we compare current trends with some ideas expressed by Erich Fromm in *Man for Himself*.[1] This book, published in 1947, was a noteworthy contribution in its time but has been outgrown by recent developments. Fromm wrote that there are two types of authority: rational and irrational. People must follow rational authority but rebel against irrational authority. This is common sense. Few theorists have ever advocated obeying an authority recognized as irrational. Even when dictators want people to obey, they try to disguise their irrationality as rationality. Of course much irrationality still exists today which we must try to recognize in its hidden manifestations and eradicate. The problem, however, goes much further than that and extends to much more obscure matters. Many people today feel that confrontation must also be directed toward *rational* authority. It is authority *as authority* that must be challenged. At first this seems to be an absurd request, reminiscent of anarchist theories of the past, and easily dismissed. But these people who dislike the way things are do not advocate removal of obligations to the state, to the collectivity, or to the individual, but a change in such obligations for the betterment of everyone. Thus, instead of branding these ideas as old-fashioned anarchism we must study the problem more deeply, analyze the intricate and intriguing connections of the psychological and the social, and be fair to the group of intelligent, honest, and sincere people who, perhaps in unclear, awkward, and often unrestrained and maladroit ways, express dissent. We must hope to learn something new by studying how and why an increasing number of people today consider as an injury to the human spirit of any adult the act of being subjected or of complying to any will not their own. No wisdom of any would-be paternal figure, no love of any would-be mother should bend your will, when your will does not coincide with theirs. This feeling, directly or indirectly, seems to be a basic one in the revolutionary trends which today permeate several segments of our society. If this feeling is correct, what are we to do with the seeming truth, implied in Pinocchio's story, and corroborated by many psychologists and psychiatrists today, that to reach a mature personality and an independent will one must have been under the loving authority of mother and the wise authority of father? Moreover, if the feeling is correct, what are we to do with the seeming truth, so well represented in Jonah, that there are situations in life in which, in order to pursue a higher aim, we must surrender our will? We shall examine these problems later in this book.

The second proposition—that you should not conform to the habits of the community when you are inclined to act in another way—seems equally absurd—at first. In fact, it goes against the psychological economy of human life. Human life is so complicated and requires such specific actions in so many different circumstances that it is impossible to improvise new ways of facing every current situation. This economy of the psyche obliges you to follow the standard ways, at least in most instances. Moreover, in many given situations, our personal ways, although original, would have unpredictable and possibly disastrous results. It is indeed safer to remain within the already proven or beaten path. Although many of us can be original, only a few of us can be creative with our originality, whereas some of us can be destructive. We should not blur the distinctions between these possibilities. But if we accept authority and we conform when we do not feel like conforming, we give up part at least of our will. To the extent that part of our will has yielded to that of others—people or institutions—we increase the power of these people or institutions, and decrease our own. Finally, we feel the humiliation of the partial or total surrender. It is no longer possible to say that we willingly adopt the will of others, that we do not submit, but that we agree. This last rationalization is no longer possible for many young dissenters today, as we shall see in greater detail in later chapters.

The problem of individual will versus authority presupposes the knowledge of what will is. But do we know what will is? First of all, does such a thing as will exist? If it exists, one of the most important mysteries that confronts us is the appearance of will itself, in a cosmos which seems will-less. The will-lessness seems so universal that some religious people believe that will exists only in God. Many people who work in various fields of science say that the cosmos is regulated by ineluctable physico-chemical forces or mathematical rules, not by any will. Why must we believe in an exception for the human condition? Does not such a belief attribute to man a miraculous property? As a matter of fact, some (but by no means all or most) schools of philosophy, psychology, and even psychiatry maintain that will does not exist; it is only a pleasant fiction, like Santa Claus. We are either determined by chemico-physical forces to act in certain ways, or our actions—apparently free—are the results of conditioning or motivations, conscious or unconscious, originating either from within ourselves or from our environment.

Among the staunchest deniers of freedom today is Burrhus Frederic Skinner, the best-known living behaviorist. Skinner tells us repeatedly that will plays no role in our life; there is no such thing as autonomous man.[2] Man does not act; he responds. Hidden emotions, purposes, deliberations, values, personality, character, unconscious aspirations, goals, images, and imaginations are fictitious concepts. The only way by which man can better himself is by devising more adequate methods of control. Skinner thus advocates that we give up our illusion of freedom and get busy learning how to control our life by eliciting the conditioned reflexes which best fit our needs.

It is true that man is not *totally* autonomous. To become completely autonomous is an impossible task; but, as I shall try to demonstrate in this book, it is possible to increase our *margin of autonomy*. This has always been the aim of freedom-seeking man. In the complete denial of autonomous man, Skinner makes of man an automaton or, at best, an electronic computer. Now the point is that man can *come* very close to being an automaton or a computer. He may allow himself to fall into that state. One of the purposes of this book is to help him avoid that tragedy, to show that although our destiny is not totally in our hands, we ourselves are among the important forces which mold it. Although complete freedom is not realizable, the book will try to delineate that degree of freedom which is attainable to man.

The book will try to demonstrate how, in this will-less universe, will originates and develops as the most specifically human characteristic. It will also try to demonstrate in how many ways the capacity to will is thwarted and warped, so that few people are really capable of willing. The search for freedom is thus perennial. Even partial freedom can be retained only through sustained effort. At times free will is experienced or manifested only as a striving to achieve free will. Often free will is, to a large extent, taken away by various conditions, and whatever residue of initiative is left must be used to return will to the people. Will is an evolutionary process in the same sense that man in his totality is; not only because of his biology, but also because of his history.

But if free will exists, it opens new and unlimited horizons. One is that of the unpredictable. In a cosmos where everything can be predicted, once we discover the inviolable laws which govern the phenomena and their unbreakable chains of causes and effects, the unforeseeable emerges, the result only of man's choice. The unpredictable is not antiscientific, but yet it defies science. It makes the will of man the only dissenter in a cosmos unredeemably enslaved by the laws of nature. Only if free will exists can we speak of man's liberation or indeed of any liberation. The state of not being coerced by law, condition, or imposition permits one to be genuinely himself. He can be authentically in the world, and can experience the exhilaration of his authenticity. But if free will exists, man must also carry the heavy burden of this responsibility. If he is his own, any action of his is also his own and he is responsible for it. Man thus, if possessor of his will, is endowed with apparently mutually contradictory traits: to the extent that he is free, he is unpredictable, authentic, responsible. As we shall see, however, he is never completely free; therefore, he is to some extent predictable, not authentic, and not responsible.

CHAPTER 2

From
Spontaneous Movement
to
Responsible Action

BEFORE THE WILL

AMONG THE BILLIONS OF THINGS THAT MOVE, ONLY MAN MOVES to carry out his will. Solar systems and galaxies travel in interminable space for eons of time without knowing that they exist and without willing their movements. As animal life evolved, its movements became increasingly complicated until it reached its culmination in man's voluntary behavior.

The first movements in animal life occur in very low species. As described by Von Holst,[1] they are spontaneous and originate automatically as functions of a primitive nervous system, without the need of any stimulation or provocation from the external world. From these spontaneous movements, through long evolutionary processes, all the movements developed which permitted the animal organism to live, to adapt, to evolve. As important as they are, we shall not discuss them, as they are not part of the process of *choosing*, and therefore of *willing*.

The first glimmering of what will will be emerges in the

human baby in the forms of playful activity and imitation. Playful activity is a pleasant spontaneous behavior. Toward the fifth or sixth month of life the baby starts to grab a rattle or other objects which are within his reach. He does not reach for the rattle after considering whether to grab it or not; he is drawn toward it. His actions are directed by pleasure seeking and do not involve hesitation or conflict. On the other hand, they are not compulsive or impulsive in the usual meaning of these terms. They appear identical to acts of will, although they are not, in a mature sense.

Imitation should not be confused with those numerous patterns of behavior which are instinctive and not learned from experience. Until we reach the ranks of primates, animal behavior is to a large extent instinctive, and to a very small extent imitative.[2] Apes, however, do have the habit of imitating in a real sense. This notion about apes, which sounds like hearsay, has found scientific corroboration in the accurate works of Yerkes[3] and of Hayes and Hayes.[4]

The greatest imitator of all animals is not the ape, however, but his closest relative in the phyletic scale: man. He imitates from birth on; that is, he reproduces acts observed in others. As the psychologist Asch has clearly indicated,[5] we must be careful not to confuse imitation with pseudoimitation. For instance, when we observe a three-month-old baby smiling in response to the smile of his mother, can we say that he imitates? He sees the mother smiling, but his own smile is a pleasant automatic response. The baby does not know that by moving the muscles of his face, as he does, he will smile in a way similar to that of the mother. He does not see himself smile.

Many of the actions which the child copies from the surrounding adults take place almost unconsciously and are similar to the baby's smiling response. They require, however, learned movements and not congenital reactions. Many times they seem to be based not on a real determination to imitate but on what has been called an "osmotic" relation to the environment; that is, a readiness to observe, to absorb, to copy. This type of osmotic imitation is not directly or forcibly imposed by the adults. It is welcomed by them, however, and their approval has the value of a *reinforcement*. Reinforcement as used by psychologists means strengthening a learned way of behaving by means of some external or internal influences, such as approval or reward.[6] I shall point out that often what is meant to be a reinforcement is experienced by some individuals as an *enforce-*

ment; that is, something which is imposed by the will of another person. Often it is difficult to distinguish between the two. At times what is an enforcement is disguised as a reinforcement. We can also say that educating a child with methods of reinforcement means exerting will on the part of the attending adult.

THE BIRTH OF THE WILL

Will starts with a "no," a "no" that the little child is not able to say but is able to enact upon his own body. The child enacts a "no" when he stops the urine from flowing in spite of the urge to urinate, and the bowels from moving in spite of the urge to defecate. When this possibility of control appears with physio-psychological mechanisms in the human organism, will also appears for the first time in the cosmos. The individual has a choice. He may allow his organism to respond automatically in a primitive way or not.[7] He has developed a neurological mechanism of control over these functions.

It is important to be aware of the fact that although the child has developed neurologically the ability to inhibit these primitive movements and reactions, he still has the urge to allow them to occur. It is unpleasant to use these inhibitory mechanisms, and the child would not use them if other human beings did not train him to do so. For instance, when his rectum is distended by feces, it would be easier for the baby to relieve himself and defecate; but during toilet training he learns not to do so because he understands that another person (generally the mother) does not want him to. Thus, in early childhood, behavior acquires a new dimension when it becomes connected with the anticipation of how other people will respond to that behavior. Any activity ceases to be just a movement, a physiological function, or a pleasure-seeking mechanism on the part of the child: it acquires a social dimension and thereby becomes an action. Thus, even in the child's first volitional acts which imply choice, a new dimension, the interpersonal, enters. The first enacted "no" is also the first enacted "yes"; "yes" to mother, "no" to oneself.

From a philosophical point of view it seems a contradiction in terms that the first acts of real volition should not be real choices but acts of obedience, submission to the will of others, or at least devices which seek approval. Yet it is a fact that the portentous choosing that emerges with the human race cannot, in the earliest stages of human development, be exercised independently of others. *It almost denies itself in the act of emerging from involuntary activity.* To will, in its earliest forms, means to will what other people want. As a matter of fact, the child learns to will an increasingly large number of actions which are wanted by his mother. In other words, he learns "to choose" as mother and the other adults around him want him to choose. Mother tacitly and benevolently implies that the "no" she wants the child to enact is not a "no" to his self, but to his body. His self is not yet mature, and will mature more quickly by virtue of that "no."

The concept of action thus emerges at this early stage of childhood. At this point it is already possible to understand why Aristotle restricted the term "action" (*praxis*) to human operations. An event whose occurrence is necessary because of physical factors or biological antecedents is not an action. Action is a possibility, not a necessity. The baby may or may not inhibit the bowel movement. Thus the term "social action" as the sociologist Talcott Parsons has formulated it can be applied to the child also.[8]

Control of one's urge to defecate has the goal of remaining clean and maintaining a clean environment in spite of the act of defecation. But this is not the direct goal of the child, who cannot know the value of hygienic rules. The goal of the child is to please mother or at least to elicit in mother an attitude toward him which is pleasant and to avert an attitude in her which is unpleasant.

THE IMPERATIVE OTHER

In early childhood the human being is in a state of receptivity, imitativeness, and suggestibility which enables him to understand and introject to an incredibly large degree forms of behavior from the surrounding adults. The child, biologically equipped, is ready to receive. Without this equipment his psychological development would not continue.

The behavior of the adult has an implicit message which is never verbalized. If it were verbalized it would say, among other things, "Copy me; you will be one of us by doing what we are doing." It is because of the high development of the central nervous system that the child can introject complicated forms of behavior, often having a symbolic meaning. We are not referring now to spontaneous imitation, which, in its simplest types, is similar to that occurring to a limited degree in animals. We are referring now to a more complicated mechanism, much more important for us, which consists of adopting patterns of behavior that the child believes the adult wants him to reproduce. In these cases the child intuitively senses an attitude of "imperativeness" in the surrounding adults. The adult is experienced giving a command, using words not in the indicative mood but in the imperative. When he uses the indicative, an imperative is implied. The child of course does not know what the indicative and imperative moods are grammatically, but he experiences the moods psychologically. For instance, if the adult says, "This thing is dirty," these words mean, "Don't put that dirty thing in your mouth. Don't eat that thing."

This imperativeness is promptly perceived by the child. He senses that he has to obey in order to please or at least not to displease. But let us examine in greater detail the position of the baby who has the urge to defecate. He would like to move his bowels right away, but he has learned that if he allows himself to do that, mother will be displeased. He thus wants to please mother by delaying defecation, but in order to do so, he must endure the unpleasantness of the delay. The child is in a predicament: he must choose between two pains (delaying defecation or displeasing mother) and between two pleasures (immediate defecation or pleasing mother). He may develop automatic obedience and in a sort of conditioned reflex obey mother automatically. In a normal child, however, the mechanism is more complicated and means a conflict between the urge to defecate and the wish to please mother, between physiological pleasure and social pleasure. In addition to the conflict, the intuition of the imperativeness coming from the adult makes the phenomenon still more complex. This imperativeness has not yet been incorporated or internalized: it comes from the external world and is registered by the child. In other words, the child does not yet give a command to himself. The command comes from others.

This intuition of the imperative is a very important phenomenon which is at the basis of many more complicated notions and is the foundation of ethics. In his *Treatise of Human Nature* (Book 3, Part 1, Section 1) Hume describes the imperceptible changes that authors make when they pass from a descriptive to a prescriptive style. They talk of "ought" or "ought not," but they do not explain the transition from a language intended to describe and to explain, to one which prescribes norms of behavior. The leap from "is" to "ought" is enormous. Hume writes, "This change is imperceptible; but is however of the last consequence. For as this ought or ought not expresses some new relation or affirmation, it is necessary that it should be observed and explained; and at the same time that a reason should be given for what seems altogether inconceivable: how this new relation can be a deduction from others that are entirely different from it." Hume's perplexity about the transition from "is" to "ought" is understandable; he is definitely right in realizing that the change has profound consequences. We may start to throw light upon this huge problem if we understand that the ethical "ought" was preceded by a primitive imperative, not yet ethical in nature but interpersonal in origin. Moreover, the change is in the opposite direction of what Hume believed. It is from the imperative to the indicative, as we shall argue later in this chapter, when we shall discuss the origin of language. Thus the injunction, "Don't eat dirt" is eventually transformed into "Dirt is not edible." [9] This origin of the imperative is extremely important to understand, not only in order to uncover the origin of ethics and Hume's problem, but the origin of any command which comes from the external world. In other words, it is the origin of a process which may lead in several directions: to Kant's categorical imperative, or to a tyrannical authority, or to other possibilities.

The baby is confronted with the conflict between obtaining the *immediate* relief of defecating and suffering *subsequent* punishment, or *delaying* relief and enjoying *eventual* pleasure. When we phrase his situation in these words, especially those in italics, we become aware that the action of will acquires a new dimension: the temporal. The present must be sacrificed for the sake of the future. In this case the future is near future, but it still implies a delay. The child, at such an early age, must pass from a life regulated by what Freud called the pleasure principle to a life regulated by the reality principle. Reality requires that the child either renounce immediate pleasure or accept immediate displeasure (intrapsychic dimension); be considerate of others and relate his behavior to that of other human beings (interpersonal dimension); delay some course of action (temporal dimension).

Thus renunciation, interpersonality, and temporality are important elements in the development of the will.

This level of volition, represented by the example of bowel

control, is obviously primitive. In cases of abnormality, as in severe mental illness, there may be a return to a level of behavior in which even that minimal degree of volition is lost. Psychotic patients in acute or chronic regression become incontinent of feces and urine; they cannot repress the stimulus, cannot delay the response, and are not considerate of others. On a few occasions I have examined some patients who before they became obviously sick wanted to get away from civilization and return to an animal-like or "natural" state of existence. They lay naked on the floor, where they defecated and urinated and, to accelerate the process of regression, were taking high doses of heroin and amphetamine. When I came to see them for medical consultation they were psychotic and had to be hospitalized. The psychosis in these cases was at least partially induced by the drugs. But what I want to stress here is the prepsychotic desire to return to a primitive level where even body inhibition does not exist.

In infancy the child generally does not have a conflict for more than a short period of time. The adult is experienced as an imperative other who imposes his will and, in an apparently paradoxical way, teaches the child to will on his own. This imperative other, once introjected by the child, becomes somewhat similar, but by no means identical, to what Freud called the superego. The child obeys in order to obtain food, love, affection, approval, and to avoid discomfort and the disapproval or anger of the adult.

In normal conditions, the imperative attitude of the adult is lost or forgotten in the context of the other good qualities of the adult (her generosity, affection, tender care, smile, approval, fondling, body contact, companionship, etc.). As a matter of fact, soon the child does not remember that the habits acquired were impositions from others; he believes that he has willed them. All this is reminiscent of what occurs in hypnosis practiced on adults.[10]

The study of primordial men reveals phylogenetic equivalents of these early stages of volition in child development. Diamond [11] has advanced the plausible theory that the first words were used as verbs in the imperative mood. These primitive words conveyed a request-command for action or for participation in an action. The first words corresponded to our "Look! Hit! Kill! Run! Strike!" and were used by primitive men to obtain cooperation from other humans in overcoming the difficulties of the tasks. They contained a conative element, or sense of effort, trying, striving. According to Diamond the vocal sound was accompanied by an automatic movement of the arm. Of course, we have to take the designation of these primitive words as "verbs used in the imperative sense" with caution. These words did not have a universal meaning like verbs used later, nor a definite mood. Probably they were a mixture of exclamation, signal to action, command, and gesture. They referred to a specific concrete situation which required a given position or attitude of the body. It is important to recognize that the development was from an exclamation (expression of individual experience) to a call to action and imperative (interpersonal relation).

The imperativeness was probably understood by the listener before many other meanings were added to the word. In groups of prehominids vocal sounds were perhaps exclamations which expressed joy, pain, relief, etc. When the word ceased to be an exclamation or an individual expression of an experience and became interpersonal, it acquired first the meaning of a command or prescription. The change was from an experiential expressive stage to a prescriptive stage. The command, as a stimulus to obey, was reinforced by the individual's quick discovery that good results came about as a consequence of following the order.

A spirit of collaboration existed in early communities of men, exposed to the many dangers of an adverse environment and to the scarcity of food—something similar to the cooperative spirit prevailing among the Eskimos today.[12] Command and consequent obedience implied more spirit of collaboration than imperiousness or servitude.

If we compare the acquisition of the first words in the early stages of the development of the human race to that in the early stages of child development, we realize that today's children do not learn the first words as Diamond described. This is by no means a surprise. There is no reason to suppose that child development should mirror human race development in learning language. The central nervous system of a one- to two-year-old is probably quite different from that of primordial man. The infant has a genetic potential for language which will be fulfilled if maturation is unimpeded and the proper environmental stimuli are present. We cannot postulate that primordial man had a similar potential. In the former case the process is one of normal maturation, while in the latter it is one of emergent evolution. There are additional reasons why the two processes are not analogous. For at least a million years, generations of human babies have been in a situation completely different from that of primordial man when he first acquired the faculty of speech. When the baby has reached an age suitable for the acquisition of language, he is handed it "on a silver platter" as a tool ready to be used, a product of the largest part of human history. It is true that the baby is only gradually exposed to the complexities of language; nevertheless, we recognize that he is taking a very accelerated "course."

Diamond's theory of the origin of language is a plausible one, for which some additional evidence can be offered. Not being a neurologist, Diamond does not present the neurological facts that support his theory. For there is indeed a neurological connection between arm-hand and language functions.[13] It is unnecessary to elaborate here on the relation between the physiology of the language centers and that of the centers which regulate the movements of the hand. Language and hand become the two tools of the emerging will: language gives the command; the hand executes it.

THE SECOND DECISIVE NO

The child does not comply meekly or obey without protest. From the very first few weeks of life the baby may frustrate all the efforts to feed him, even by pursing his lips and clamping his jaws. After the age of seven months he refuses to be picked up by strangers, and allows only the mother to do so, for he individualizes her more and more as the person on whom he depends. He resents being separated from her. These and similar primitive resistances can be interpreted as a resistance to whatever disturbs his equilibrium, peace, and state of rest. It is especially from the age of eighteen months to the end of the third year that the child puts up active, willed resistance, as many mothers know very well. This attitude has been called stubborn, oppositional behavior, negativism, and has been compared to the behavior of very ill adults, suffering from catatonia.[14]

This stage is called negativistic. The child says "no" to many suggestions of mother. He does not want to eat, to be dressed, undressed, washed, etc. Mother often has to put up a battle. Some children show resistance with obvious outbursts of temper tantrums, but many others express resistance by refusing to comply.[15]

We must not look upon this almost universal phenomenon as a period of naughtiness children go through or a difficult stage parents have to tolerate. All the "no's" constitute a big "no" to extreme compliance, to the urge to be extremely submissive to the others or to accept the environment immediately. They constitute a big "yes" to the self. The submissive tendencies are always very strong because it is through them that the child becomes receptive to the environment and allows himself to experience influences which nourish him and make him grow. Negativism is a healthy correction. The no period is a decisive turn of the will. Control now no longer involves only body functions, like the inhibition of reflexes or elementary physiological behavior. It is interference with behavior willed by others and the beginning of a liberation from the influence or suggestion of others. It is the first spark of that attitude that later on will lead the mature man to fight for his independence or to protect himself from the authoritarian forces which try to engulf him.

It has been noted that children who have not gone through this period of stubbornness become much more dependent on the teacher's help than the others.[16] Children generally outgrow this period, but residues of negativism remain in some adults, who, for instance, refuse to wear overcoats, to carry umbrellas, procrastinate, always arrive late at parties and meetings. Adults who indulge in these habits are not necessarily motivated by hostility toward others. The negativistic residues have become habits, or ingrained mechanisms which no longer need specific motivation to be put into motion. Negativism is a useful preparation to asserting one's individuality and autonomy, but misses its target if it continues to be used for the purpose of opposing others.

THE BEGINNING OF THE SENSE OF RESPONSIBILITY AND GUILT

Let us go back to our primitive man who has learned to obey. As an independent doer, he tends to feel guilty very easily. He feels guilty about doing things on his own because, after all, in a primitive world who knows what will happen as a result of what you are doing? What you do may have an effect on the whole tribe; its repercussion might be enormous—an epidemic or a drought. The mythical flavor of primitive thinking magnifies the assumed effect of one's actions. As Kelsen has illustrated, to cause an event may often mean to the primitive to be guilty, if he causes the event on his own.[17] In order to diminish his feeling of guilt, primitive man refrains from acting freely; he performs only those actions which are accepted by the tribe. The tribe teaches the individual what act to perform for any desired effect. Ritualism and magic thus originate. By performing each act according to ritual or magic, primitive man removes the anxiety that arises from the expectation of possible evil effects. The ritual ensures that the effect will be good. Thus, imitation, conformity, ritual, and magic blend together.

But what about guilt? What is it, and where does it come from? If a primitive man acts freely and believes that a bad thing (such as an epidemic) has ensued, he may experience *anxiety* because he believes that the bad thing will affect him, too. But guilt is not merely anxiety or expectation of danger, or pain. Is the feeling of guilt the expectation of punishment? Certainly such expectation is an inherent part of this emotion. The individual cannot expect to be punished only because he too will be the victim of what he has caused. The more he has caused bad events to happen to others, too, the more he must be punished by men or the divinity. Feeling guilt, however, is not merely expectation of punishment. A political dissenter may expect to be punished by the government and not feel guilty at all. Feeling guilty is the feeling that one *deserves* to be punished. In other words, the punishing authority has been introjected, becomes part of the psychological inner life of the individual, and makes him feel guilty.

Regret for what one has done, expectation of punishment, and, most of all, the feeling one deserves the punishment are components of the guilt feeling. Guilt feeling is a very powerful emotion which reduces the activity of the tribe to conformism or to the magic of ritualism. But let us study now what happens in the life of the individual child raised in modern times. Here conformity and obedience occur at first almost exclusively in relations with one's parents.

Early in life the child develops the notion that whatever happens, happens because of the intervention of others. For instance, if he is put to the breast, or is fondled, or is placed on mother's lap with tenderness, it is because mother does these things. Although the very young child does not have a concept of will, he realizes that many things depend on the actions of others. The occurrence of events after other people have expressed the intention of doing things or have actually done these things does not enable the child to formulate an abstract concept of will. But he does develop the knowledge that things happen because people initiate actions which make these things happen. The child comes to attribute whatever happens to the intention of other people. They have the power to effect. He also learns that the intention of people who care for him is generally good. He can trust them. Mother will feed him when he is hungry, clean him when he is dirty, cover or embrace him when he is cold, etc. A feeling of basic trust, about which we shall speak more in Chapter 5, develops. This feeling of trust implies two elements. One is temporal: by trusting, the child unconsciously assumes that good things will happen in the future, too. The second is volitional: by trusting, the child recognizes that other people have the capacity to will; that is, to put things into effect.

Soon, however, the normal child acquires more and more autonomy. He gradually realizes that what is going to happen in his life is to an increasing extent the result of his own actions. The image that he will develop of himself is to some extent dependent on the way he feels the other people interpret his actions (good or bad). If his actions are good, he will get approval, tenderness, affection, and love. If his actions are bad, he will get disapproval, distance, scolding, anger. Actually he will consider good the actions which bring about approval and bad those which bring about disapproval. Between goodness and badness of actions and approval and disapproval from others a circular process is thus taking place which, from a logical point of view, is untenable, but which nevertheless is the beginning of values. The child soon realizes that the best way to obtain love and approval is to imitate or obey the parents. Obeying mother is the price he pays for love. But obedience to mother opens access to the world. The benefit is immediate even if what he has to do (be clean, quiet, compliant) requires deprivation, limitation of spontaneity, and loss of many residues of negativism. The child very much needs the love of mother. Moreover, by obeying he sees more and more that the results are good, and even more important, he builds up an image of himself which is satisfactory. It is not true that mother's love appears to the child unconditionally, or not requiring a price. It is certainly unconditional in the first few months of life if the mother is a normal person. But every mother soon expects something of her child. The demands of mother are relatively easy to fulfill; mother is also prone to forgive in case of transgression. Obedience to father is in most families somewhat different. Recently, at least in some Western countries, the role of the mother and the father have become more similar. By and large, however, the father remains the more demanding parent.

It is especially because of his relations with his parents that the child develops a sense of responsibility and gradually diminishes his extreme dependence on others. Responsibility implies the possibility of foreseeing the effects of one's actions and of correcting one's actions in accordance with such foresight. Although responsibility makes one diminish his dependence on others, it first consists of following the demands or instructions of one's parents or parent substitutes. But this is only the very beginning. Maturation of the individual and the progress of the human kind requires that the growing individual take into account many other factors. As we shall see in the following chapters, facing one's own instincts and wishes, relating to one's family and friends, to society as a whole, recognizing the ethical ideals and the need to be faithful to the emerging self will all weigh in the complicated balance of the will. But at this point we are still concerned with one's father and mother. We know that Freud has given a sexual meaning to this relation in the concept of the Oedipus complex. The little boy who has entered "the phallic phase" of development becomes passionately tied to his mother, wants to marry her, has great rivalry for his father, and would like to remove him from his mother's bed. Conversely, the little girl wishes to marry her father, has rivalry for her mother, whom she wants to displace and replace. Incest wishes for the parent of the opposite sex and death wishes for the parent of the same sex emerge as feelings and ideas which are strongly felt and strongly feared. According to Freud, it is at this point that the little child experiences a great fear of the punishing parents. The boy is afraid of being castrated and the little girl is afraid of losing her mother's love. For Freud the nucleus of morality is represented by the reaction to these incest and death wishes. The parental figures who are the inhibiting and forbidding adults are introjected and become part of what he called the superego.

There is no doubt that such drama occurs in the early childhood of many people. But, as many adherents to the neo-Freudian schools of psychoanalysis believe, it is doubtful that this sensuously passionate drama is universal. Even when it occurs, it is part of a general relationship with one's parents. It is this relationship, involving the various facets of the personality, that is universal. Among the most important aspects of this relationship is that of the emerging will, contrasting with or adhering to that of the parents. Is the child going to listen or not listen, to obey or not obey? He must learn to obey and to disobey, not only in childhood but throughout life. This lesson is difficult to learn for him as well as for his parents. At times he will be faithful to himself by obeying and at other times by disobeying. The drama of the will is as important as that of infantile sexuality.

We have seen that traditionally the father is the more demanding parent, and the one with whom clashes of the will are more likely to occur when the child approaches adolescence. Father is usually the punishing agent. Mother often says to the child, "If you don't behave, I'll tell Dad, and he will punish you." Moreover, although the father requires immediate obedience, he conveys the idea to the child that the benefit of this obedience will be experienced by him later on, perhaps when he will be an adult. Father, too, grants immediate approval, but his approval is not as sweet as mother's love. And what father wants often requires a sustained effort—for instance, scholastic achievement. It is more difficult to obey father than to obey mother. This is one of the hard facts of life that one of our symbolic characters, Pinocchio, had to face. We must now return to him and to Jonah.

BACK TO PINOCCHIO AND JONAH

As you remember, because Pinocchio had no mother from his very birth, he had to obey his father, Geppetto. But from the very beginning of his life he found it difficult to do so. He experienced simple requests as terrible impositions and finally ran away from home. He was thus deprived of father as well as of mother. The whole book can be interpreted as losing one's parents and eventually retrieving them. Later in the book a loving female figure appears, the Fairy with the Blue Hair. Because of his love for her, Pinocchio changed his way of living. He wanted to become a real boy as the Fairy had promised him that he would. It is obvious that this figure represents the Good Mother Pinocchio never had.

As we have already said in Chapter 1, Pinocchio first found both parents in a symbolic, unconscious way when he was in the belly of the whale (maternal womb) and rejoined his father.

between them, which kept them apart? We do not know. Was that distance existing only in his fantasy because of his unresolved Oedipal problems? Like Pinocchio he must have felt guilty for his own hostility and must have wished to reconcile himself with parental authority. Unlike Pinocchio, he was able to fulfill his hope only partially. The father died when Collodi was in his teens and had not yet been reconciled with him. Long after his father's death, Collodi went to live with his mother and assumed his father's financial responsibilities. Like Pinocchio he found mother late. He never married, but devoted himself to his mother. For her he did even more: he overcame the problem of alcoholism, but only temporarily.

In Chapter 1 we referred to the similarities between Pinocchio's story and the Book of Jonah. Both Pinocchio and Jonah find themselves in the stomach of a big whale—symbol of maternal womb and of mercy. There Pinocchio finds a father alive, in the flesh. Reconciliation occurs, and from now on Pinocchio and his father, Geppetto, will be on good terms. The Book of Jonah, of course, deals with this subject and others at a much more profound level. Inside the whale, Jonah finds the spirit of God, the Divine Father. He prays, invokes the Eternal Father, repents, and is forgiven. In Jonah a maternal figure is missing, and Jonah has to find refuge in the stomach of the whale, the symbol of a maternal womb. It is important to point out that in the Old Testament there is no important female figure comparable to those of the pagan Greco-Roman world or to the Virgin Mary of Christianity, and especially Catholicism. In the Hebrew cultural tradition, which makes no use of concrete or personal symbols, the female role is abstracted and attributed to the whole Jewish people or to the group, tribe, community, congregation, etc., which helps, nourishes, forgives, accepts. God is the absolute Divine Father, the community is a mother for the collectivity.[19]

Jonah finds God again and obeys Him. He now accepts doing the difficult task: to go to Nineveh and announce to the inhabitants that they will be destroyed. Jonah's confrontation with God is not finished. We shall examine the subsequent events of the story in a later chapter. Here it is important to point out that Jonah obeys; he recognizes the wisdom of God, but also God's ability to punish. But why should God punish Jonah? Why should Jonah obey God and do something abhorrent to himself? Because Jonah was and experienced himself as a prophet. For the man who hears the highest message, there is an implicit commitment: to transmit the message to others. Thus by obeying God Jonah was faithful to himself.

SKINNER'S SIMPLIFICATION

The mechanism which intervenes between the environment which impinges upon the child in a myriad of ways and his behavior becomes increasingly complicated. While the parents once towered as the only giants in the child's little world, big people and important events crowd more and more his enlarging vistas. At the same time the inner life of the child acquires new dimensions which enable him to change his responses into chosen and willed actions.

Some authors have devised easy schemes with which to solve or replace the complexity of this problem. Skinner, for instance, writes. "It is in the nature of an experimental analysis of human behavior that it should strip away the functions previously assigned to autonomous man and transfer them one by one to the controlling environment." [20]

According to Skinner the organism lives psychologically by responding to the stimuli which come from the environment. The stimulus and the response form a unity called a *reflex*. New reflexes can be developed through conditioning, as Pavlov taught. A more complicated form of conditioning called *operant conditioning* is the most effective. For instance, if an animal is hungry it eats, if possible. The eating is an operant conditioning, or positive reinforcer. In other words, the animal which has relieved hunger by eating will eat again in the future when it is hungry. Negative reinforcers are aversive, since they make the organism turn away from them. For instance, a child burns his finger by touching a hot radiator. He turns away from the radiator, is relieved from the burning sensation, and in the future will avoid the radiator. Reward and punishment are respectively the main positive and negative reinforcers in child training.

There is no doubt that animals and children behave in accordance with operant conditioning. But this type of functioning, which for Skinner is the beginning and end of the mechanism of behavior, is for us only a small part of the process by virtue of which the human being feels, thinks, and acts. It is true that children and adults repeat the behavior which follows positive reinforcers and turn away from negative reinforcers. To the extent that they do so, they use mechanisms they have in common with animals. For Skinner there are no other mechanisms. Only what can be observed and externally controlled exists. Feelings, emotions, attitudes, introjection, guilt, expectation, purpose, goal, inner self, personality, determination, choice, will, etc., are miraculous or imaginary entities. Since ideas, dreams, images, insights, and conflicts cannot be seen or observed, they do not count; nor can the existence of an inner life be inferred from them. Nor does Skinner follow the medical procedure, for a physician does not simply observe his patient's behavior, but makes inquiries about what goes on inside of him.

Behaviorism, as represented by Skinner, and my approach have, however, one aspect in common. For both of us what ultimately counts is man in motion, what he does. But for Skinner man in motion is matter activated by the environment, and his motion is *behavior*. For me, what man does represents the complicated influence of the external world, but it also represents his choice to the extent he has the possibility of making it, his creativity to the degree he is endowed with it, and his responsibility in the way he is able to experience it. Accordingly, what man does reveals implicitly or explicitly what he means and how he feels. It is true that what we mean and feel is often not at all clear and that we have to recapture feelings and thoughts from what we do—a difficult procedure leading to frequent error. But certain and even greater error lies in limiting our inquiry to our external behavior.

Skinner bypasses what goes on inside of man not only from the point of view of psychology but also from that of neurophysiology. Although he does not deny that the central nervous system has something to do with behavior, he pays no attention to what goes on inside of it and concentrates on observable bodily responses.

From bodily responses we cannot arrive at the concepts of reflection and contemplation as distinct from action, creativity as distinct from forced conditioning, value as distinct from reward. Inasmuch as the concepts of freedom and dignity are based on subjective states, they too are fictitious, according to Skinner, and should be abolished. As the title of his recent book states, we should go "beyond freedom and dignity" and try to reach a satisfactory life through subtle conditioning techniques that control behavior. Such subtle conditioning, effected by rewarding and not by punishing, would not coerce or tyrannize. I strongly feel that it *would* coerce and tyrannize because it would deprive people of freedom without their being aware of what had been perpetrated on them. For Skinner, man's struggle for freedom is not caused by a will to be free, but by certain behavioral processes, the chief effect of which is the avoidance of the "aversive" features of the environment.[21] Skinner takes into consideration only some forms of freedom (freedom from) and not others, the highest (freedom to), which we shall describe in Chapters 11 and 12.

It seems to me that what Skinner prescribes is not a state beyond freedom and dignity but one *preceding* freedom and dignity. Animal species which are compelled by their biological status to learn and behave only in accordance with simple conditioning and operant conditioning cannot be considered from the point of view of human freedom and dignity. There cannot be freedom, value, or creativity when the organism is tied to the immediacy of the desire and the unreflective nature of the response.

The search for simple formulas, like those of mathematics, with which to explain man is understandable. In this kind of attempt, however, authors often consider only some aspects of man, not his totality. This attempt cannot lead to a superior synthesis, but only to reductionism. Skinner is by no means the only reductionist. Even among the greatest thinkers we find those who have interpreted man only from the point of view of sex and rage and have made of him an animal at the mercy of its hypothalamus. We find those who have seen him involved only in lofty ideals and have castrated him, or those who have considered him only from an economic point of view and have materialized him.

When the human being, because of severe illness or extensive physical traumata, functions with mental processes similar to those of low animals, the Skinner method works. For instance, operant conditioning gives satisfactory results with defective and autistic children who are unable to learn in any other way. Some authors have reported fair results with regressed schizophrenics confined to mental institutions for many years by using a variety of the method of operant conditioning which they call "token economy." [22] By awarding tokens for such good behavior as work, grooming, bathing, toothbrushing, etc., these authors were able to make more likely the occurrence of good behavior.[23] Since nothing so far has been devised that would help these very sick patients, even such minimal results are to be welcomed.

In my experience, however, these methods do not work with

schizophrenic patients (fortunately now the majority) who do not reach such profound regression. As a matter of fact, according to my observations, when a not-so-sick schizophrenic has been treated with these methods, in most cases he becomes sicker, perhaps bcause he has experienced yet another attack on his freedom and dignity.

CHAPTER 3

The Wish
and the Will

CHOICE AND ERROR

THE INDIVIDUAL SAYS TO HIMSELF, "I WANT TO DO THIS," AND HE
does it. This apparent simplicity is deceptive since the person
is not aware of the many complicated mechanisms of which his
actions consist.

For the purpose of this book it is not necessary to describe
the major steps inherent in a voluntary action.[1] Strange as it
may seem, the mechanisms of some of these steps have not
been clarified or explained by modern science. We do not know
when neurology ends and psychology starts. In spite of intense
neurological research we do not know the nature of the intimate
mechanism which initiates a voluntary movement. What we
definitely know is that thinking is a prerequisite for mature
willing. Before the individual masters the determination to
carry out the chosen course of action, he must have evaluated
the several possibilities, must have chosen one, and planned
doing it. In other words, without thinking, no act of will is

possible. A willed action actually develops from a thought to an action. But from what kind of thought?

As we shall state more clearly later, thinking opens up an endless number of possibilities. The higher the level of culture, the larger is the number of possibilities. Whereas an animal is forever tied to the limited patterns of its instinctual behavior, man may be directed in infinite directions by an infinite variety of thoughts. Here actually resides the genesis of the rise and fall of man.

Man, alone among all creatures, finds himself in a state vaguely reminiscent of Pinocchio's paradoxical situation. He is not a piece of wood; but he is little and finite, just as the other animals are. Yet he has to face the infinity which his symbolic cognitive powers present to him in the form of thoughts. We may say that if his thinking offers him the understanding of an increasing part of the infinity, it also puts him in a position to make errors, whence man's fallibility.

The history of man is the history of his triumphs and his errors, both of which depend not only on his cognitive achievements but also on the choices he makes. Any choice has an effect, and therefore brings about an inherent reward or a punishment, according to whether the effect is good or bad. We can surely state that man grows as a result of his own choices more than for his intellectual achievements. This statement could be repeated about a specific society or culture, that it grows or fails to grow in certain directions because of the choices that its people or leaders make. At this point let us consider the individual's proclivity to error.

If we think of the infinity of choices open to him, we may be inclined to be compassionate toward man for erring so often. But man is conscious and very much afraid of his erring. No wonder that in his course toward mature volition he passively complies with mother, father, the tribe, the community. Let us examine a question which at first may seem ridiculously naive. Why does man err? Why does he not immediately choose the right possibility? After all, he hardly ever chooses at random, but after some reflection.

There are at least five major reasons for erring, which are not at all ridiculous and naive. The first reason for erring is limited knowledge of facts. Man never has complete knowledge about anything. How could he? His life span represents less than an atom of time in the life of the cosmos. In order to be sure of making the right choice he would have to know many things inaccessible to him. If some thinkers are correct in say-ing that all things which occur (even on other planets) are ultimately related and affect each other, complete knowledge is impossible even theoretically and is to be attributed only to the divinity. Man was not there to witness the creation of the world, and therefore he may have only an intuition or what he calls a revelation about it. Although science increases the areas of knowledge, it remains limited in comparison to the congeries of facts and events which have occurred in the billions and billions of years since the cosmos began.

As important as this reason is from the point of view of reach-ing ultimate truth or knowledge of the absolute, it is not the most important reason for error in the practice of everyday life. Of course, generally the more a man knows, the better is his position; but, as we shall see later, even with his limited knowledge he could avoid making many errors in the restricted area of his life.

The second reason for erring consists in making a logical mistake, or mistake in judgment. Either because the premises were wrong or because the deductive or inductive steps were not correctly stated or applied, an error is made and a wrong choice ensues. Books of logic are filled with such errors. Again, I must stress that, as important as this reason is, it is not the most common cause of error in everyday life. For the usual conditions of their life, normal men are generally capable of making good judgments. Moreover, if a person makes a logical mistake, often it is not because he is incapable of thinking logically, but because he is drawn by obscure forces toward making the mistake. The third, fourth, and fifth reasons for erring are more important. I shall devote most of the rest of this chapter to discusing the third and the fourth. The fifth reason will be discussed in Chapters 4 and 5.

The third cause of error is that *in choosing, man follows not his best judgment, but his wish.* The fourth reason is only a variation, although an extremely important one, of the third. Man believes that he chooses according to his best judgment, but he actually deceives himself: the wish lurks behind.[2] The wish has disguised itself; man no longer knows that he harbors it inside of himself and he becomes the victim of what in psychoanalysis is called *unconscious motivation*. The fifth cause is determined not by wish but by another strong emotion: fear. The direct or indirect fear of other people determines man's choice.

The importance of the wish reveals itself when we consider the third and fourth causes: to repeat, the individual who evaluates several possible courses of action and chooses one of them frequently is guided not by his best judgment but by his wish, conscious or unconscious.

THE WISH

Thus the tremendous role of the wish among the determinants of human action is obvious to every student of man. And yet this factor, wish, in spite of its importance, is one of the most difficult concepts to define or to study scientifically. Even in psychological, psychiatric, and psychoanalytic schools wish is often confused with appetite, need, tension, urge, tendency, drive, instinct, pleasure seeking, and with will itself. Some philosophical schools have equated will with what in Latin was called *appetitio*. According to this point of view, to will means to wish, or to choose the wished alternative. According to other schools of thought, and also to my own point of view, to will implies, among other things, the decision of whether to carry out the wished alternative. What then is a wish? We cannot resort to the circular dictionary definition that a wish is an object or expression of desire. In fact desire is also defined by the same dictionaries as any object or expression of wish. And yet we must really have some conception of this portentous fact to which we attribute such a major role in influencing human choices.

The difficulties are many and of various orders. Even psychoanalysis, the science which has stressed the importance of the wish in human motivation, is at a loss in explaining the phenomenon. Many psychoanalytic books and treatises which deal with wish fulfillment offer no definition of wish. Since a wish is such a common psychological event, its definition is taken for granted.

In my opinion the difficulty in psychoanalysis stems from the fact that the original Freudian theories have implied two different and in some respects incompatible concepts of wish. According to one psychoanalytic concept, wish is a *force*: the force that moves man to act. There is nothing wrong in considering wish a force toward the attainment of something if we use the word "force" in a metaphorical sense as something which exerts pressure on the human being to act in a certain way. However, psychoanalysis has used the concept of force literally, like a charge of electrical energy which gives man the physical power to act. On one hand, the origin of this confusion is to be found in the desire on the part of Freud to describe and interpret psychological phenomena with qualitative physico-chemical methods. On the other hand, the confusion results from the difficulty in distinguishing wish from appetite.[3] This is part of a general tendency in psychoanalysis, as well as in experimental psychology, to explain human functions with the simplest psychological mechanisms, occurring at the earliest stages of development. Most of the time an analogy can be reached between the lower and higher functions, but not a law which is applicable to all levels. Appetite in psychological language does not refer merely to an urge to eat, although it indicates that urge, too. The concept is applied to a larger category of tendencies of the animal organism to move toward, to grab, to incorporate. Something good, pleasant, and satisfying is expected by the animal as a result of this incorporation or contact. This expectancy refers to what occurs in the period of time which immediately follows the stimulus. For instance, an infant sees his mother and has the appetite for being nursed. Sexual urges stimulated by the proximity of the sexual object or by the state of the sexual organs are also included in the category of appetite.

Appetite can be quickly aroused and quickly quenched. All animals, including man, have appetites. Although appetite has instinctual components and is closely related to physiological functions, it implies even in subhuman animals some kind of learning or appraisal of the stimulus which brings about the craving. For instance, when children have learned to recognize toys or candies, they develop a strong appetite for them. When wishes are equated to appetites, they can be seen easily as biological forces which tend to discharge tension, fulfillment of physiological functions like eating, drinking, and sexual desire.

In a second definition wish is implicitly considered as something much more complicated than a force or an appetite. Like appetite, wish is a pleasant attraction toward something or toward doing something. But unlike appetite it is a *mental representation*. In their psychological dictionary English and English very appropriately refer to this aspect. They define wish as "a desire or longing, without overt attempt to attain; the mental representation of something as desirable."[4] Wish does not require an overt attempt to obtain what is wished.

WISH:

It is a mental representation of something that, once attained, would give pleasure, which means that the representation has a significance and a motivation inherent in it. In my opinion this is how wish should be defined.

At a human level wishing, as a mental representation, is a very important source of motivation. It is more important than appetite, though it may be reinforced by a concomitant appetite. The simplest form of it is mediated by a mental image. For instance, the mother is absent, but the child evokes in his mind the image of her; he thinks about her; he sees her in his mind's eye; he wishes to be with her. The capacity to wish originates in the capacity to have images, which subhuman animals do not have. Even in early stages of human development wishes do not consist only of images, but of many other symbols, especially words, which stand for the objects.

The words "mother," "car," or "sweetheart" may elicit various kinds of mental representations and wishes.[5]

Appetite is a physical condition because it is based on a state of the organism (thirst, hunger, sexual desire), but wish requires mental representations (images, words, etc.), and its power resides in the meanings given to them.

While an animal is motivated only by appetite or immediate biological urges, like hunger, thirst, and sex, the human is motivated by all the wishes which he can conceive with his endless conceptual processes. He may wish to become the president of the United States, to land on the moon, to write the *Divine Comedy*, to conquer diseases, etc. Moreover, by representing the world not as it is, but as he wishes it to be, the human being creates surrogate worlds. He transcends space and time. He becomes aware of eras which he never saw, nor which his predecessors recorded in writing, and he can visualize eras that he will never see. He becomes the spectator of all times and of all existences; he is influenced by millions of ideas; he becomes the arbiter of an infinity of wishes and choices. In his brief life he has to cope with the endlessness of what he can envision as well as with the limitations of what he can achieve.

To avoid possible confusions we must examine another possibility: can man experience not wishes, but appetites, like a subhuman animal?

When an animal reacts to hunger, thirst, sexual desire, it does not choose; it responds. It has no alternative; it has to follow the urge. Although these animal functions are motivated, they are not willed and do not imply conscious selection. Can a man revert to the stage of simple appetite? Only in extremely rare cases, the existence of which are doubted: the cases of so-called irresistible impulses. These cases occur only in conditions of severe pathology, mental illness, or early infancy.

Needless to say, in many circumstances a man follows a pattern of behavior similar to that of an animal. For instance, he eats when he is hungry, drinks when he is thirsty, and satisfies his sexual desires. When he follows these appetites, however, he *chooses* to do so. In other words, his wishes and determinations coincide with his appetites. He wants to satisfy his hunger, thirst, sexual desire, etc. His behavior is not an automatic response to the bodily need; it is a willed action. The wish may follow the bodily need or not. If the wish follows the appetite, it may become very strong. At times, the will must go against the wish and the appetite.

Thus man is in an extraordinary position: by making his wishes coincide with his appetites he has motivations similar to those of animals; but he may follow a path toward much more complicated motivations through a network of conceptual processes. In both cases he experiences wishes; in both cases he must exert his will.

WISHES, NEEDS, AND RIGHTS

Man can entertain an endless number of wishes of various origins and consequences. These wishes involve the satisfaction of bodily needs, or the pursuit of pleasure of any kind, irrespective of other considerations and complications. They may, on the other hand, involve the aim of adjusting to reality by removing a state of disharmony within oneself or in relations with other people.

The concept of wish is often confused with the concept of need: for instance, with the need to be free. This matter requires some clarification. A need implies deprivation of something necessary for the welfare of the organism. For instance, animals need oxygen, food, water, a certain temperature, etc. The need generally evokes an action which aims at reestablishing its equilibrium. For instance, hunger evokes search for food. The need is satisfied when food is obtained and the organism is restored to its normal condition. Need is thus often confused with drive, appetite, and motivation.

At a human level there are needs which do not refer only to

the physical organism. If love, security, peace, freedom, companionship, and other states are absent, the person is in a state of disequilibrium, characterized by anxiety, depression, or at least tension. If the absent conditions are obtained, the psychological welfare is reestablished.

Obviously it is difficult to establish whether needs are really needs or only wishes. Moreover, what is a need for one individual may not be for another: some men may manage even without the love and freedom which seem essential to most men. No conformity is possible on this matter. Generally when there is a preponderant or almost unanimous agreement that the human being requires a particular thing for his physical welfare and for the fulfillment of psychological growth, that requirement is not considered simply a need. In a civilized society it is recognized as an inalienable right, with one proviso: it must not infringe upon the inalienable rights of other people. If the condition of deprivation does not have the properties that I have described, it may be caused not by a need but by a psychotic or neurotic claim, or may just be a wish, not a need. To be a great painter or to own a helicopter are not needs.

The leap between an ascertained need and an inalienable right is a huge one. A need is a physical or psychological state of the individual; an inalienable right is something that others or society recognize as due the individual. If a need is recognized as an inalienable right, then society makes a tacit or manifest agreement not to prevent the prerogative of this right and to facilitate the exercise and fulfillment of it. We must add that although the inalienable right may be considered a legal concept, its psychological connotations transcend legality. A man is hurt not only legally, but also psychologically, when he is deprived of his inalienable rights.

Some wishes, because of their ethical or cultural connotations, may become so strong that they can become needs and therefore claimed as inalienable rights. Different groups and cultures differ on what constitutes a wish, a need, and an inalienable right concerning, for example, such a thing as being free. At times what seems a justifiable wish (to free one's country from the enemy) may actually be a desire to become powerful and dominate others. Man is the only animal which may change a wish into a need; human society is the only organization which may change a need into an inalienable right.

THE BATTLE OF THE WISHES

The various kinds of wishes—to satisfy bodily needs, to gratify oneself personally, to adjust to reality, to expand one's self, to live ethically—coexist in every person. It is not, however, just a matter of coexistence of wishes but of a battle of the wishes, because these wishes are incompatible and the gratification of some of them excludes gratification of others. Even before man is harassed by the difficulty of making choices, he is stirred by the coexistence of his contrasting wishes: he wants to have his cake and eat it too. The battle of two or more wishes gives origin to a conflict. As we shall see in greater detail later, society participates in the production of conflicts, usually, but not always, because it favors the choice which is regarded as more honorably motivated. When society favors a less worthy motivation, the individual may submit to persecution and martyrdom in order to assert his higher aims. When the conflict over different motivations ends with the choice of what is regarded as a higher motivation, people often speak of "redemption" or "salvation." Actually, what seems the highest motivation and the road to salvation at a given historical time may not seem so in a different era. One can thus speak of redemption and salvation only relative to particular ethics.

Until solved, conflicts increase a person's anxiety, insecurity, depression, and guilt feelings. They decrease his efficiency, undermine his self-esteem, block his actions, and sometimes bring about psychiatric disorders. We should not forget, however, that conflicts may also stimulate the emergence of new benefits, new points of view, unexpected syntheses, and unforeseen possibilities of choice.

In concluding this section, let me stress again that ideas as motivational forces (that is, as producers of new wishes and new choices) have been underestimated in psychology, psychiatry, and psychoanalysis. The emphasis has been on the importance of bodily needs, instinctual behavior, and primitive emotions, all of which can exist without the presence of ideas. It seems to me beyond doubt that among the powerful emotional forces which motivate or disturb men are many which are sustained or actually engendered by complicated thoughts. One's concept of himself, his feelings of personal significance, of self-identity, of his role in life, of self-esteem, of responsibility to oneself and others, of ability to give and receive love and affection could not exist without these complex thinking processes. Wishes for love, power, approval, regard, respect, and honor and assertion of one's ideas and rights are crucially important motivations as well.[6]

THE UNCONSCIOUS WISH

If we understand the difficult position of the human being who has to make a choice when he is confronted with many possibilities and implications, we become much more sympathetic toward him when we consider that he is not even aware of a large part of h:s wishes. And those wishes of which he is not aware have a great influence upon his behavior. A commonly quoted statement of Freud is that the unconscious part of man is like the part of the iceberg below sea level; that is, much bigger than the part above water.

The theory of unconscious motivation is almost unanimously considered Freud's major contribution. According to him, many psychological processes, like images and ideas, continue to influence man even when he is not aware of them. They have become unconscious, like many physiological processes of the organism (for instance, those of the heart, stomach, lungs), which exist without the person's being aware of their constant activity. But whereas the processes of the visceral organs were never endowed with consciousness, some ideas and wishes were, but have lost it. They have been *repressed*.

At first Freud thought only the unpleasant events of childhood to be repressed by a special form of amnesia. The memory of these events, however, is not really lost and therefore can be recaptured with special procedures. Later Freud discovered that repression also occurs in the case of wishes which the individual does not want to admit to himself or others. He is ashamed of these wishes, either because they represent, directly or indirectly, immature, infantile strivings, or because he knows that society would condemn them. Psychoanalysts consider a wish to be unconscious in at least two cases. In the first, the person has carried out an act which seems to have been wanted, and yet the person claims that he was not aware of the act itself or does not know why he did it. In the second case, the person gives a reason for his behavior, but such reason is unconvincing; he *rationalizes*.

My strong conviction, however, is that what the human being

denies does not concern only his most primitive wishes and infantile strivings. Much more is excluded from consciousness through repression or distortion. Moreover, as we shall see later in this book, society collaborates with the individual in repressing many thoughts and feelings. Both the individual and society as a whole repress many thoughts which are unpleasant because they threaten the image of the individual himself or of society. These repressed thoughts involve the images of people or institutions that the individual (or society) loves or hates or has learned to revere or despise. They concern (the individual's or society's) likes or dislikes, the individual's interpersonal relations, his philosophy of life, vision of the world, family or group allegiances, etc.

Emotions which an individual is not able to rationally justify—such as some specific loves, enmities, prejudices, or a need for hostility, approval, self-effacement, cowardice, vindictiveness, power, or glory—tend also to be repressed, minimized, distorted, or rationalized. At times the failure to gratify a primitive wish gives rise to a group of notions which are more traumatic than the original deprivation, and therefore are more likely to be repressed. For instance, sexual deprivation may be unpleasant, but the image that the sexually deprived person may form of himself as a sexual partner can be much more devastating. Am I sexually adequate? Am I sexually desirable? Would anyone have a sexual feeling for me?

Not only does society repress many ideas and feelings, but it requires the individual to repress or suppress additional ideas and feelings. Man often wants to live in accordance with the highest levels of motivation which he attributes to society. He has to battle among the unconscious wishes, those which are conscious, the dictates of society, and the personal urges. The following example is typical.

A married man in his middle thirties is on the verge of divorce. Hostility and lack of tenderness characterize his marriage. Nevertheless, as he comes home from work one evening, he finds himself acting warmly and considerately toward his wife. He does not understand why. Shortly afterwards, he becomes aware that his behavior possibly has a motivation which may embarrass him: he feels sexual desire for his wife. Only if he prepared the ground could he have sexual relations. He concludes then that his desire, which he had been unaware of up to that moment, had caused him to change his attitude toward her.

If we were to accept this simple explanation we would say that a state of his organism which he had not at first recognized caused him to be loving toward his wife. Strengthening this hypothesis is the fact that this man recently has had no sexual desire for his wife and has abstained from sexual relations. Since he possesses a certain degree of sophistication, he tends at first to believe that the abstinence alone has produced a tension strong enough in him to make him change his attitude toward his wife without realization on his part. Quite correctly, he does not dismiss this possibility as too superficial; but soon he becomes aware of a second motivation, for he experiencecs what up to then has been an unconscious wish for a reconciliation with his wife. This wish was in its turn the outcome of many other psychological processes: a feeling of guilt toward his wife, love and a feeling of responsibility for the children, fear of loneliness, awareness that his friends, relatives, and society at large would welcome a reconciliation, etc. At any rate, the wish for a reconciliation which he denied to himself makes this man become conscious of erotic attraction toward his wife. The wish for a reconciliation is a much more elaborate motive than the mere sexual desire; nevertheless, for a long while it has remained unconscious.

That a wish can be unconscious, even when the accompanying ideas are at least partially conscious, is common experience. Let us consider a simple example in which Smith and Jones have a political discussion. Let us say that Smith is a Democrat and Jones a Republican. In most instances it will be possible to recognize that Smith's arguments are directed by an underlying wish to show that the Democratic party is right. Similarly, Jones's thoughts reflect the underlying wish to demonstrate that the Republican party is right.

Now, it may happen that Smith and Jones are conscious of what they are doing; however, most of us have witnessed honest speakers who sincerely believed that they were following reason alone and not their emotions. They experienced emotion only at the end of the debate, over winning or losing; but not before. I have taken this example from politics, but the same observations could be made about honest debaters in other fields, including science.

We must therefore take a position much more inclusive than Freud's and say that many wishes, and not only the primitive ones, can be or become unconscious. But if it is correct that

our actions and behavior are generally determined by unconscious wishes, then we are in a serious predicament. We
are like men shouting in the dark or like blind men moving in
a world they don't see. We are moved and controlled by wishes
of whose existence we do not even know. This conclusion would
please those scientists who have never relished the idea that
man can will his actions. In a world where everything is determined by previous causes, man's ability to choose and will
seems an absurdity, an impossible exception, something inconceivable in a mathematically precise physical world. If in
psychology we substitute "wish" for "will," we come close to
a state of affairs that even rigid determinists would accept.
This is actually part of the great ambition on the part of Freud
and some psychologists and psychiatrists to make psychology
as rigorous as other sciences. The problem can be summarized
in this way: wishes are determined by causes of which we are
not even aware, and wishes determine our behavior. Thus we
do not live; we are "lived" by our unconscious wishes and
purposes.

This position of Freud, which, as we shall see shortly, con-
tradicts another basic one that he took, was not motivated only
by his desire to give psychology and psychiatry the respectability of other sciences, but also by his determination to combat the prevalent nineteenth-century ideology that praised only
will and will power. One's will was supposed to be the captain
of one's ship. Rollo May [7] has well illustrated that "will power"
and "free will" have been fought by psychoanalysis as a reaction to this kind of ideology. May writes that "will was used
to deny wish . . . Freud saw will as an implement in the service
of repression, no longer a positive moving force."

In the early psychoanalytic era, in which one of the main
concerns was to fight Victorianism, will came to be seen as the
agent of repression, not as the agent of liberation. Certainly it
was to the good that repression was fought; but was this
total denial of the will necessary? The result was that almost
all of twentieth-century psychology, psychiatry, and psychoanalysis joined arms to fight the concept of will. Papers or
chapters on will were soon eliminated from scientific meetings
or textbooks, or received very little attention. Any study of will
or volition—when differentiated from motivation—fell into disrepute and was considered unscientific, to be relegated to the
novelist, the theologian, and perhaps to the philosopher.

Will is now again the object of interest—witness the books by Farber [8] and May [9]; but the change is slow. Is this neglect of will justifiable? Did Freud really mean to put will in disrepute?

Like many other great thinkers, Freud contradicted himself on many issues, including the question of will. More than any other predecessor or contemporary he revealed the role of the unconscious wish as a determinant of human behavior. But this great contribution does not imply that will has no role to play at all. Let us remember another one of Freud's famous statements: "Where id was, ego must be." The id is the agency of the psyche where most of the unconscious wishes are located. As a result of psychoanalysis, Freud thought that the unconscious wishes must become part of the ego; that is, become conscious. But what is the purpose of their becoming conscious? To make the id part of the ego does not mean to unleash the unconscious wishes, to give them free reign or unrestricted access to conscious behavior, although this is the way in which some people prefer to interpret Freud's statement. Freud meant that once the unconscious wishes become conscious they will be regulated by the functions of the ego. The individual will be in a better position to accept them or reject them. In other words, psychoanalysis, as conceived by Freud, is no liberation of the id—in the sense of unleashing primitive unconscious wishes—but is a liberation of the ego from the unwanted, unconsciously determined, oppression exerted by the id. Thus, *psychoanalysis has the function not of restricting, but of enlarging the sphere of influence of the will.*

Unfortunately, Freud sometimes has not been very clear on this point. It is true that when unconscious wishes become conscious they can be fulfilled. It is also true that some wishes which were repressed because the individual was unjustifiably afraid of them are fulfilled with great relief, once they become conscious. But many other kinds of wish will be amenable to rejection or control.

Wishes, then, conscious and unconscious, certainly influence our decisions; but there is a huge difference between influencing and determining in an inflexible, ineluctable way. It is one of the major functions of consciousness to permit man to decide and to will. The greater the realm of consciousness, the greater the realm of choice and the kingdom of the will. The greater the area of unconsciousness, the smaller the area in which man can exert his will.

THE MEANING AND SCOPE OF REPRESSION

Ideas and wishes are conscious before they are repressed. Evolution has endowed man not only with consciousness but also with conceptual functions which make him superior to any other animal. But the potentially infinite expansion of the conceptual functions and their emotional accompaniment constitutes too great a burden. Thus evolution has also endowed man with the capacity to liberate himself from part of this burden, by repressing it from consciousness.

Freud believed that the child represses infantile wishes, since if he tries to put them into practice he will incur the punishment of his parents, of whom he is afraid. Later on, when he develops a superego or conscience, he feels guilty if he allows himself to experience wishes which he cannot control. Thus he represses them. As I have illustrated in other writings [10] and already mentioned in this chapter, not only infantile strivings but a great part of one's inner life is thereby eliminated from consciousness. Whatever would disturb one's cherished self-image tends to be repressed. Whatever might make the individual appear to himself unworthy, guilty, inadequate, sadistic, inconsistent with his ideas or ideals, escapist, or not living up to one's ideals tends to be removed from consciousness. Indeed, some of these evaluations of the self remain conscious; but even so, what is eliminated from consciousness is much more than the individual realizes.

In a succinct way we could say that repression is a method, although not a successful one, of escaping fear, injury to one's self-image, and guilt. The aim of repression is thus preservation, not only in the sense of physical survival, but also in the sense of preserving an acceptable self and a moral self. The moral issue is important. If the individual represses and becomes unaware of certain things, he may not feel guilty. But once awareness returns, guilt feelings return. The more man represses, the more he loses his uniquely human prerogative of willing and being responsible, and the more he returns to the amorality of the nonhuman universe.

To make things even more complicated is the fact that not only does the individual repress, but society does, too. Thus the individual has a double burden to repress: his own and that of society. How does society repress? By teaching the individual not to pay attention to many things (selective inattention); by disguising the real values of certain things; by giving an appearance of legality and legitimacy to unfair practices; by transmitting ideas and ideals as absolute truths without any challenge or search for the evidence on which they are supposed to be based. The defenses against objectionable wishes which Freud described in the individual (for instance, repression; reaction-formation, or doing the opposite of what one intended to do; isolation, or removing the feeling from unpleasant actions by making them compulsive, in an almost legalistic manner; or by rationalization) can be found in society, too.

Freud was very skillful in uncovering the ways by which the individual represses in order to escape the punishment of society, but he never became concerned with the other side of the coin: the repression that society itself carries out and transmits to the individual.

The analyst is the best person to help the individual resolve his personal repression. When it comes to societal repression, the action of liberation is generally the work of innovators, great thinkers, revolutionaries, sociologists, etc. So far, psychiatrists, psychoanalysts, and psychologists who have worked in this field have been a small minority.

If in the mechanism of repression we include also removing from the focus of consciousness whatever the individual and society do not want to acknowledge as existing, we come to see an ethical problem involving man and society whose significance far transcends the original Freudian conception.

FREE WILL AND DETERMINISM

At this point I wish to reopen the problem of free will versus determinism, from the point of view of psychoanalysis and others. The position of the Freudian psychoanalytic school seems to be that the psyche is ruled only by strict determinism: in other words, psychological life, like everything else in nature, is determined by previous causes, and is not related to will. The position of Robert Knight, that dynamic psychology as a science must be deterministic, is often mentioned as the official position. In 1956 Knight wrote: "Whatever human actions or decisions seem to indicate the operation of free will, or a freedom of choice, can be shown, on closer inspection and analysis, to be based on unconscious determinism. The causal factors were there and operative, but were simply not in the conscious awareness of the individual." [11] Knight concedes that the psychologically mature person has a "sense of inner freedom" and states that psychotherapy "operates deterministically to achieve for the patient this subjective sense of freedom." Thus Knight implies that this subjective sense of freedom in normal man is an illusion.

Rollo May very appropriately wrote that if psychoanalysts would accept these concepts they "would find themselves in the curious, anomalous position of believing that the patient must have an illusion of freedom in order to change, and they therefore must cultivate this illusion, or at least do obeisance to it." [12] May adds, referring especially to Knight, "Some analysts indeed admit openly that they are engaged in the cultivation of an illusion, and undertake to rationalize this in their theory. Consider what this means. We are told that an *illusion* is most significant in effecting personality change; that truth is not fundamentally (or is only theoretically) relevant to actions, but *illusion* is. Thus, we are to strive not for truth but for an illusion." May rightly expresses his indignation at such a point of view. In the name of would-be science we are asked to give up our belief in free will. We are asked to renounce the responsibility for our actions that tradition, religion, law, and our own subjective feeling indicate we must assume. This indeed would be a Copernican revolution. But Copernican revolutions do occur and this may be one—our hypothetical adversary would say. I believe May is right in his indignation, but unfortunately he is not able to demonstrate that free will exists. No one can with a scientifically acceptable procedure; thus we are left to believe or not to believe the assertion of Rollo May and others who share this opinion. There are other thinkers from various fields who believe that even the most worthy characteristics of man— his moral and aesthetic qualities—are apparent sporadic anomalies of the cosmos which further progress will ultimately explain in consonance with the laws of inanimate matter.[13]

I believe that the illusion to which Knight and others refer is not freedom, but "complete freedom." We never have complete freedom, and it is illusory to think so. The issue is not betweeen determinism and free choice, but between *relative determinism and relative free choice*. The extent of this relative determinism and free choice depends on health or disease, intelligence, amount of knowledge, state of the organism, environmental opportunities, social factors, emotional conditions, and, importantly, the state of *consciousness or unconsciousness* of many of our ideas and attitudes. It is one of the aims of man to increase his capacity for choice and to decrease determinism in every possible way, to move away from physical necessity and toward free will. It is one of the aims of civilized man to fight all restrictions of free will, no matter from what directions they come. I believe that the greatness of psychoanalysis resides mainly in having recognized the restrictions to free will imposed by repression and in having developed methods to remove these restrictions. In this respect psychoanalysis assumes a major role in ethics. It is the science which reaffirms the prerogative of man to have a certain amount of free will.

We must recognize, however, that total freedom is not available to man. In accepting this limitation man acknowledges his kinship with the rest of the animal kingdom. And even partial freedom is not something he was born with; it is a striving, a purpose, something to be attained. Being born free is a legal concept which, although valid in daily life, has philosophical limitations. Striving for freedom is an unceasing attempt to overcome the conditions of physicochemistry, biology, psychology, and society that affect human life. To the extent that man succeeds in transcending these conditions he becomes self-caused. It would be unrealistic to forget, however, that this self-causation is only a thin margin of a totality in which the majority is ruled deterministically. To borrow again Freud's simile, the thin margin is that part of the iceberg which is above water. But this thin margin is important enough to change the world.

At this point it is pertinent to mention a fact which may appear coincidental and inconsequential, and yet one which cannot help but make a deep impression on a psychiatrist. Not only a host of great thinkers like Helmholtz, Darwin, and Marx, or prominent psychologists like Skinner and Hebb, deny the influence of one's will on one's life; but so also do many schizophrenics, some of whom have been confined for many years in back wards of state hospitals. Frankl calls this phenomenon *Passivierung* in German. I do not want the reader to misunderstand me. In reporting this similarity, I do not suggest that a deterministic conception of life is a schizophrenic delusion. On the contrary, I wish to add a dimension to the argument. Often people with totally different perspectives and backgrounds end up with the same conclusion. This phenomenon cannot be dismissed as coincidental but has to be understood.

Not all, but many schizophrenics believe that they do not live or will. They are lived, they are caught in a network of situations where other people, other facts, other events determine their life. They have no part whatsoever in determining the world but are reduced to the state of inanimate objects. If that is all their life is about, they either give up entirely or become even more passive. Contrary to the deterministic thinkers, however, these patients do not believe life is ineluctably that way. They believe that other people—as a matter of fact, any one other than they themselves—do have a will and determine the world. Such function is denied only to them, and therefore they cannot accept this deprivation. Inherent in their mental condition is this lifelong protest. For particular reasons having to do with their early family environment and other situations, these patients were left with a margin of freedom even smaller, as a matter of fact much smaller, than that of the average man. The normal man intuitively believes that his little margin of freedom can grow, and he regards that margin as the symbol of his life, or of that part of life which counts most, because it is caused by himself. The schizophrenic, on the contrary, not necessarily through his intellect but in a general experiential way, is aware only of that part of life which is ruled deterministically and is more similar to a vegetative existence.

For us, in this chapter, the schizophrenic's protest is more important than the error he makes in thinking his life has to be that way. The fact that he protests is indicative that he senses that his error is an error, that his life was not meant to be totally determined. As we shall see in Chapter 10, he reclaims his will.

FREE WILL IN THE MESOCOSMOS

Readers who are not interested in problems of physics or theology in the context of free will may skip the rest of this chapter and move directly to Chapter 4. There are, however, some important issues that deserve consideration.

We have seen that some thinkers object to free will on the ground that it is something against the order of nature, for there is nothing suggestive of free will outside of man. Why should we believe in an exception? But emerging innovations do occur in biological evolution, and free will may be one of them. As a matter of fact, free will could not have emerged as an innovation in the cosmos if it had not been preceded by other innovations. Let us enumerate the most important: (1) the emergence of life in the previously inorganic world; (2) the capacity for subjective experience or feeling in animal life; (3) the capacity for symbolism in man (language, thoughts, ideas), which permits the representation of choices.

Many thinkers have also tried to establish whether free will is the only phenomenon which is not subject to cause and effect. An instance of another possibility of this kind is represented by the principle of uncertainty or indeterminancy, formulated by Heisenberg. According to this principle it is impossible to determine simultaneously both the position and velocity of an electron. In other words, strict causality has to be abandoned in reference to individual subatomic occurrences. This principle applies, however, only to the extremely small particles of nature which form what Capek [14] calls this microcosmos. When we reach particles of dimensions which are visible at least with our microscopes, we enter what Capek calls the mesocosmos, to which man, too, belongs.

The fact that the microcosmos (the world of electrons) is not ruled by determinism shows that indeterminism *can* exist. Determinism enters as an innovation in the mesocosm. The mesocosm is the world of the Euclidian-Newtonian-Kantian tradition: it does not include the macrocosm of Einstein, or the microcosm of Heisenberg.

Reichenbach [15] and Capek [16] made it clear that modern physics does not deny the validity of the Euclidian-Newtonian-Kantian world. It only restricts it to the mesocosm, a world of middle dimensions. For the microcosm (a world of subatomic dimensions) or the macrocosm (a world larger than solar systems) the Einsteinian-Heisenbergian physics applies. Life exists in the mesocosm. In order to originate and evolve, it had to incorporate mesocosmic laws, including determinism. Without such incorporation, life could not exist. Determinism reigns supreme in that era of hard-to-imagine proportions, which extends from the beginning of the mesocosm to the arrival of the human cerebral cortex and consequent free will.

The simplest (the subatomic particles) and the highest (some parts of the human cortex), respectively, open and close this huge era which unfolded over billions and billions of years. The highest product of creation, the human cortex, again permits independence from causality as it existed at a subatomic level. The freedom of man, however, as made possible by his cortex, is different from the so-called freedom of the subatomic particles. It is integrated with the essence of man. Although it produces an interruption in the deterministic chain of causes and effects, it immediately rejoins determinism, thereby reestablishing the continuity, for the will of man becomes a *cause* of action. In philosophical language, teleological causality is added to deterministic causality, but is still causality. It is a causality compatible with free will. Whether subatomic "freedom" becomes incorporated in some particles of neurons and changes ideas into free actions, and thus reintegrates itself into the essence of man, is for future research to establish.

BACK TO JONAH

The existence of free will has been put in doubt not only by scientists, but, strangely enough, even by some theologians. In simple terms the problem is this: according to the Judaeo-Christian tradition God is omniscient. He knows what man will do, how man will choose. If He knows what man will do, then man is not free; he will act in a way which corresponds to what God already knows. Free will thus does not exist since it is incompatible with the fact of God's knowledge of the events which have not yet occurred. But if free will does not exist, salvation does not depend on the action of man, but on divine grace. God has determined in advance who will and who will not be saved.

Paul of Tarsus, in the Epistle to the Romans, stated that grace is a gift from God to man. Augustine made the concept of grace one of the cardinal points of his doctrine. Later the Protestant Reformation also gave to grace an important place. In *De Servo Arbitrio* (1525) Martin Luther supported that part of Augustine which seems to imply that man is not free. According to him, God's omniscience and predestination imply that nothing occurs that God does not will: this fact removes from man the possibility of free will. Only divine grace, not his own actions, will save man. Anselm (1109) had tried to find a solution by stating that God's predestination takes into account human will and does not control it. He grants grace to those of whose good will He knows of beforehand. This is a play on words. How can He know the good will, if the will is free?

The idea of grace can be connected with the Greek idea that fate is outside of morality. In the Greek tragedies of Aeschylus and Sophocles the hero is guilty of a crime he committed independent of his will, like King Oedipus. Oedipus feels guilty, although he was not aware of doing anything wrong at the time he committed the crimes. Because he is guilty, he has to accept his fate; that is, the punishment of his actions.

The Book of Jonah, to which we have referred several times, indicates that free will exists in man. From a moral point of view, the human being is not at the mercy of a blind fatalism.

God told Jonah to announce to the city of Nineveh that the city would be destroyed because the inhabitants had sinned. We know, however, that the city was not destroyed, and this unexpected outcome made Jonah angry. Must we believe that the biblical text indicates that God lied? Obviously not. There is another possible interpretation. Even God did not know that the people of Nineveh, from the best to the least important of them, would repent. The people of Nineveh had been terrible sinners, and the probability was great that they would not listen to Jonah's message and would continue to sin. But they did not. The improbable action, unknown even to God, occurred, and they repented. God thus changed his plan and the city was saved.

Similar myths were not possible in classical Greek mythology. The Greek oracle is always right, always able to foresee Fate, for Fate is outside of the will of God, of man, and of any moral consideration.

Jonah can be interpreted as implying that if man has free will even God cannot be omniscient. When God created the mesocosm with a deterministic structure, he could foresee; but when, with the creation of man, he allowed free will to emerge, he gave up a part of his omniscience.

But what about the microcosm which is not ruled by rigid determinism? Does indeterminacy mean that God has no knowledge of what is liable to occur there? Not at all. If my interpretation is correct, people who adopt a theological frame of reference can believe that God knows what is going to happen in the microcosm, obviously because God is able to understand a nondeterministic universe. But God cannot be absolutely sure of what man is going to do without depriving man of free choice.

CHAPTER 4

Sex
and Aggression

WHY NOT?

WHEN WE BECOME AWARE OF OUR WISHES, WHAT ARE WE TO DO
with them? Freud believed that by becoming aware of his wishes
the individual is in a better position to control the objectionable
ones and to behave as society demands. Had it been easy for
man to control the objectionable wishes, he would not have
needed the mechanisms of repression and suppression. But he
needs these mechanisms, and because of them, according to
Freud, he becomes neurotic.

Let us pose another apparently naive question. Why shouldn't
we satisfy our wishes, even if they seem objectionable? Why
not enjoy life and avoid neurosis? It does not matter what will
happen later. Let's have pleasure now. Why wait?

Many people have described the beauty of this abandon. No
consideration is permitted to deny or adulterate the positive,
genuine reality of the experience, so the "why not" receives no
answer. The Dionysian flavor of the poet and the gusto of the

bon vivant join together in the celebration of an intense "here and now." Forget being called impulsive, immature, or childish, or even a psychopath! Savor the flavor of life!

To my knowledge there are no multitudes of people who follow this pattern as their usual way of life. Some individuals, however, especially adolescents and young adults, become aware that the group of which they are part encourages satisfying the wish, and they go along. In addition, there are some people who decide, after careful deliberation, to gratify their wishes. Their choice is not impulsive or capricious, but has required thought and reaching out for new positions. This last group of people do not think they should be confused with the immature; as a matter of fact, they consider themselves more mature than those who, in compliance with tradition, control their wishes. Like the abovementioned persons they make their will coincide with their wishes. They believe that satisfaction of the wish is not only desirable but also very mature. A life which has achieved concord between the wish and the will is considered by them as one of the best possible, no matter what the wish was.

As we shall see later in this chapter, theoretical leaders like Wilhelm Reich and Herbert Marcuse provide in some respects the ideology necessary for this type of life. Obviously we should not attribute to these thinkers, or even to the group of people who accept this type of life after deliberation, the responsibility for the fact that many immature, impulsive, and even psychopathic persons join and largely increase their ranks. Nevertheless, a basic question presents itself in reference to all these groups: is inhibition of wishes or inhibition in general a useful or a harmful aspect of life; is it a sign of maturity or immaturity, especially in reference to fundamental biological urges, like sex and aggression?

Some who advocate disinhibition find support even in the works of Freud, which amply illustrated how much sexuality has been repressed. But a conceptual error is made here. Repression and inhibition are two different phenomena. Repression makes us unconscious of our wishes so that we cannot decide whether to inhibit them or not. Inhibition is a mechanism of control found at all levels of neurophysiology. It is particularly important to understand this difference for the group of young people of the "new culture," whom we shall describe in later chapters and call "the Newly Committed."

INHIBITION

Since the early part of the nineteenth century, physiologists have been aware of the fact that some events occurring in the cells of the nervous system were checked or diminished in intensity by others.[1] In other words, the nervous system is not just an apparatus which is excited by the environment and transmits the excitement in various ways to parts of the body or to the whole organism. The nervous system has also the important function of checking excessive stimulation and excessive response. Without some mechanism of control, generally called "inhibition," all excitation would flow directly into motor activity. Inhibition regulates the motor activity, although the stimulus continues to be present. As Morgan wrote, "The arrest of motion creates the opportunity for the mind to occupy itself more and more completely with the central processes, perception and emotion, and also, in human beings conceptual thoughts and emotions." [2] What was observed at first in reference to simple motor phenomena was later applied to complicated behavior and to all the functions of the psyche.

In their psychological dictionary English and English define inhibition as "a mental condition in which the range and amount of behavior is curtailed, beginning or continuing a course of action is difficult, and there is a peculiar hesitancy as if restrained by external agency." [3] However, there need be no external restraint.

Stopping or retarding the response permits the organism to focus attention on several possibilities, to become aware of new levels of sensitivity and greater range of nuances. Diamond, Balvin, and Diamond, who have written one of the most scholarly books on inhibition, believe that as the capacity for inhibition increases, organisms "could acquire new means of responding to the same situation with different elements of their behavioral repertoire, and different combinations of these elements." [4]

Diamond, Balvin, and Diamond accurately describe the neurological and psychological mechanisms which repress lower functions and permit the operation of higher ones. The authors find throughout the whole nervous system and psyche that inhibitory mechanisms differentiate psychological unities and prevent potentially self-destructive excess. Thus Freud was in the line of a good neurological tradition, that has continued up to

political or sociological. Man would grow free, would not need to become submissive, and would not build his own restrictive character armor.

If Reich appears an extremist in the area of unrepressed sexuality, Herbert Marcuse, in *Eros and Civilization*,[7] is so only to a slightly lesser degree. Marcuse is one of the great thinkers of our era, and his ideas are particularly relevant. In this chapter, however, we shall consider him only in relation to some important, although questionable, positions that he has assumed concerning sexuality.

Marcuse believes that Freud's greatest merit consists of having emphasized the biological-sexual component of the psyche. At a time (the 1950s) when the emerging American neo-Freudians were challenging some of the tenets of Freud, and especially his stress on sex and libido theory, Marcuse reaffirmed the importance of sexuality in psychoanalytic theory. Like Reich, Marcuse feels that Freud, although deserving credit for discovering the role of sexuality in human events, did not do enough to liberate it from the cultural forces which repress it. Marcuse feels that Freud is correct in his formulation of "the reality principle," according to which some activities of the id have to be repressed. He feels, however, that society has become too repressive. The so-called *performance principle*, which society has adopted, requires a *surplus repression*; in other words, it suppresses sexuality more than is necessary.

Marcuse gives a political and sociological explanation for this repression. Firstly, sexuality is reduced to genitality; that is, it becomes focused on the genital organs while the rest of the body is gradually desexualized. When this desexualization is accomplished, the body is used only for work; it becomes an *instrument of labor*. Marcuse wants the whole body to be resexualized. According to him, the human being desires a state of "polymorphous perversity." So-called sexual aberrations may be partially interpreted as protests against reduction of sex to the genital organs. Marcuse believes that if people had been allowed to indulge more in sexuality, they would have been less efficient as instruments of labor. Here, according to him, lies the origin of the Establishment's antagonism toward sexuality. Even the anthropological hypotheses expressed by Freud in *Totem and Taboo* have undergone a revision by Marcuse. The sons who, according to Freud, in prehistoric times killed the father, were not just the sexual rivals of father. They were proletarians exploited by a capitalist father who wanted from his children too little sex and too much work. According to Marcuse, it is now not the family but society which is antagonistic to sex. But now that modern industry permits a reduction of the working day, and now that the necessities can be available to all citizens, there is more time and energy for sexual pleasure.

Many young people have found inspiration and support in the writings of Reich, Marcuse, and other writers with similar views in their special interpretation of Freud. These people view psychoanalysis as conducive to a philosophy of life which permits unrestricted sexuality and uninhibited sensuality. Hedonism finally acquires respectability. What Aristippus and Epicurus were not able to do, Freud, Reich, and Marcuse would have accomplished: the unification of will with the primitive wish —and not an incomplete immature will, similar to the impulse-response mechanism of the animal, but a more complicated mechanism by means of which "advanced" human beings remove the distance between stimulus and pleasant response.

In Reich and Marcuse, under the presumed aegis of Marx and Freud, we witness an attempt to analyze society's transformation of the human body from an instrument of pleasure to an instrument of work. We now understand the words that during the revolt of May 1968 the French students wrote on the walls of the Sorbonne: "The more I make love, the more I want to revolt; the more I revolt, the more I want to make love."

In this ferment of ideas, we have to distinguish the correct positions from the errors. Freud, Reich, and Marcuse are indeed right in affirming that sexuality has been drastically repressed. The Victorian era is only the culmination of a trend which has existed since prehistory. Marcuse is also right in formulating "the performance principle" and asserting that there is a surplus of sexual repression. He accepts that sexuality should be repressed, but by no means to the degree that it has been. Marcuse is, however, incorrect on many other counts. It is not true that sexuality has been removed from the rest of the body and confined to the sexual organs. In man, more than in any other animal, sex involves the whole body, although for anatomical physiological necessities, the genitals remain the culminating organs in the sexual encounter. The kiss, the caress, the embrace, the touch, etc., retain and claim their role in the act of love.

It is also not true that the body has been desexualized in order to make it an instrument of labor. The restriction imposed on sexuality had a different origin. Fear of incest was one of the strongest causes of sexual restrictions. Why was incest so frightening and so strongly condemned? It is doubtful that it was forbidden, as some authors believe, because generations of men had witnessed the decay of the race, following an accumulation of inferior genes in members of the same family. It seems more probable that incest and related forms of tribal sexuality were forbidden because they produced a great deal of rivalry, fights, and bloodshed in primitive societies. In those times all members of the group needed to cooperate to the utmost and work together against common dangers: enemies, famine, weather, etc. No internal strife could be permitted.[8]

Unlike what happens in other animal species, sexual craving is almost constant in young human beings and demands prompt gratification unless restricted. But immediate gratification leads to rivalry for the favors of the best sexual partners and to revenge in cases of frustration. Presumably primitive tribal societies had to devise and enforce strong rules to prevent these difficulties. Even today a large number of crimes are committed in relation to sex. As Freud has described in *Totem and Taboo*, the inhibition of sexuality which civilization requires is probably a device to curb the violence which sexual desires caused in prehistoric times. We still abide by laws which were instituted in primitive times. Our moral codes in relation to sexuality were to a large extent established before man could write. And yet most facets of human society have changed drastically since then.

It is true that sexual crimes are committed today, too, as a result of sexual suppression. We must determine, however, whether more crime or less would be committed as a result of complete sexual freedom. Today, as in primitive times, sexual freedom would lead to violence unless the individual man agreed to share sexually the woman he loves with other men. He has never been willing to do so, and at least for two reasons. In most cultures, men do not want to support or have the responsibility for children they have not fathered. Although the invention of "the pill" and other contraceptive devices has made this easy to avoid, there is still another reason for not sharing the loved woman. The human being, through the expansion of his symbolic processes, has united sex and love. He believes that although he may share sexually other women, the one he loves is only for himself. He must share every intense experience of the person he loves, or else the unity of love is fractured. Perhaps this way of feeling seems unjustified to some people; nevertheless, it is very common. The sharing of the loved woman would require first a transformation of a psychological attitude and feeling which has existed for thousands of years. Women in most "advanced" communities adopted a similar attitude. Although a few people today, living in small communes, are able to share sexually the loved person, the majority of men and women are unable to do so, and as long as they feel this way, some kind of sexual repression is necessary.

Although a tremendous amount of sexuality would to some extent decrease the physical energy of human beings available for other activities, such an antithesis as expressed in Marcuse's words "less sex, more labor" is not the rule. Unless we consider only extreme cases, which indeed require medical attention, more sexuality does not diminish the capacity to work. The antithesis is fictitious, and actually the result of a desire to repress sexuality. It is identical to the exaggerated fear of the harm produced by masturbation. Similarly, operatic singers are traditionally warned not to have intercourse before their singing engagements; yet I have been told by many singers that they have been able to work well after sex. When the point of harmful exaggeration is reached, the sexual appetite is extinguished or greatly diminished. It is true, however, that excessive sexual activity may be harmful at advanced age, but people who have passed their middle years do not in fact perform the bulk of physical labor.

Marcuse and Reich give the impression of believing that the desire for sex is inexhaustible. The more you have, the more you want, just as the more money the miser has, the more he tries to get. But sex and capitalism cannot be equated. Theoretically at least there is no end to the amount of money a person can have, but there is an end to the amount of sex. Even with an abundant sexual life, there is time, energy, and interest left for other activities. The human body does not have only two possibilities: to be an instrument of sex or of labor. There is room for other pleasure and activities—aesthetic, ethical, playful, philosophical, creative, exploratory, etc.

Both Marcuse and Reich built on the part of the Freudian theoretical framework which is the weakest and which had started to be rejected even within the orthodox Freudian circle. The concepts of libido, pansexuality, and sexual sublimation have increasingly lost credit. Almost every psychiatrist today uses such Freudian concepts as the importance of childhood, the psychodynamic development of life, the symbolic aspects of behavior and mental processes including dreams, the existence of an inner psychological reality as important as the external, the unconscious state of much of our mental processes, and a special relation with the analyst called transference. The list of discoveries and theoretical formulations is so impressive that just one of its items would have been enough to immortalize Freud. This does not need to be enlarged. Marcuse and Reich, instead, not only concentrate on the libido theory, but make it the center of their argument. They speak of libido and pansexuality as if they were proved scientific facts and not hypotheses. Their version of Freudianism is an ideological position disguised as a scientific truth.

The libido theory is based on the proposition that psychological phenomena, including neurotic and psychotic disorders, should be interpreted in terms of the quantity of a type of energy called libido, which was for a long time identified by the Freudian school with sexual tension. Recently this energy has been viewed less as exclusively sexual and more as a psychic energy used in all mental functions. Moreover, there is no evidence that any such energy exists.[9]

In their ideologies, Reich and Marcuse purport to liberate the libido; that is, according to their conception to liberate the id. The id, which, in the Freudian system may be seen as Satan inducing man to fall, is instead seen by Reich and Marcuse as the agent of salvation. Not only must we not resist what in the Judaeo-Christian tradition was considered satanic temptation, we must follow it as the means to the good life. If some say today that God is dead but Satan is very much alive, the Reichian-Marcusians' response might be that Satan, too, is dead because the old Satan is not the prince of darkness at all. He is the liberator of man.

Is he really? Is disinhibition of the instincts equal to liberation? We have seen that Reich tried not only to liberate the id, but also to attack the ego, the would-be tyrannical jailer of what is best in man.

Reich and Marcuse in fact continue that trend of the Freudian school which sees man as a fundamentally hypothalamic organism. The hypothalamus is a small part of the brain which controls the basic vital functions of the body. It is there that the two functions of man that Freudian psychoanalysis has stressed—sex and rage—are mediated. All the structures above the hypothalamus, and especially the neocortex, are seen predominantly as working to restrict or control the hypothalamus and related organs.

But the structures of the nervous system above the hypothalamus do more, much more, than restrict hypothalamic function. Whatever is above the hypothalamus meets, assimilates, transforms, expands what comes from the external interpersonal world as well as from within or below the hypothalamus. The integration of all these interpersonal and intrapersonal factors opens up a new universe, the universe of symbols and concepts. Strictly from the point of view of survival, symbolic and conceptual functions are not as important as hypothalamic regulation; but from the point of view of human psychology, they are much more important.

The functions of the human psyche (intellection, volition, aesthesis) would not be possible without the part of the nervous system which is above the hypothalamus. But, and here lies the crux of the problem, in order to function, the higher parts of the nervous system have to inhibit the lower.

In conclusion, inhibition of sexuality and, as we shall see later, of aggression is in accordance with the developmental structure of the nervous system and of the psyche in general. As neurology teaches, however, it is true that inhibition may become excessive and has to be counterbalanced by other mechanisms which inhibit inhibition. Neurology and neurophysiology are replete with examples, which will not be repeated here. In our specific case, we must fight excessive inhibition of sexuality, not by disinhibiting the sexual drive, which would be a return to a hypothalamic life, but by limiting the inhibition. The result will be a partial disinhibition, which we shall discuss in the next section.

THE PARTIAL DISINHIBITION OF SEXUALITY

Although Wilhelm Reich and Herbert Marcuse seem extremists, even they do not sponsor a totally unrestricted sexual life. And of course my position about limiting sexual inhibitions is more modest than their disinhibiting attitudes. For example, my point of view is that the traditional attitude toward premarital sexuality should be altered. There is really no good reason to forbid premarital sexuality in our times. The fear of unwanted pregnancy has been removed by modern contraceptive devices. Obviously I do not advocate that everybody be induced to indulge in premarital sexuality. If some people value virginity or consider it a prerequisite for marriage, they should be encouraged to follow their private principles. Let us make them realize, however, that these principles, or their opposite, are private; they have no claim to society's approval or disapproval.

Sexual faithfulness is still the preferable form of sexual behavior within the marriage. When a person marries another, he commits himself to give up some ways of living for the sake of acquiring others. Love requires commitment.

In human beings, just as aggression becomes associated with symbolic processes which may lead to hate, sexuality becomes associated with symbolic processes which may lead to love. Civilization and the maturation of the human being tend to associate sex more and more with love. When the human being has reached the level of mature love, he should include sex in it. But why? Many opponents could object that this union is artificial, sponsored again by archaic codes. Why can't a man love his wife and have relations with other women? He could indeed, but to the extent that he does that, his love is not liable to grow: it either remains stagnant or is already declining. If a man succumbs to the seductive influence of another woman, he does not necessarily cease to love his wife; but certainly his love is undergoing an injury which may not be healed. Any strong experience, such as mature sexuality, reaches the heights, or what Maslow called a peak experience [10] only if it is shared with the person one loves. To know that the loved one had attempted to have a peak experience with somebody else is difficult to endure. Love, like freedom, is something which has to be safeguarded, not taken for granted; it requires a sustained effort, a commitment.

Certainly the spouse may have many deep experiences (moral, aesthetic, working, etc.) with other people; but the act of love, which in its consummation and attainment requires the achievement of a unity through two people, is better fulfilled by people who are committed to each other.

In Chapter 12 we shall see how the human being is ultimately destined to be alone in the universe. This aloneness is due to the fact that one's feelings ultimately remain a private affair. Pain and joy can be expressed, evoked, and communicated, but they remain inside of the individual. But the act of complete love—that is, sex plus love—implies participation in a peak experience in an ensemble for two, and is the only feeling which almost transcends the oneness of one's life and almost overcomes one's inherent solitude. Let us not spoil the beauty and meaning of "two."

Certainly sex has a most important biological function (reproduction), but its meaning remains tied to biology unless it becomes connected with other levels of human existence. Sex without love remains sex, with its beauty and its limitations. Romantic love without sex does not remain love. It may decline into a form of pale platonism, not renewable by any vital force.

Marital faithfulness is not advocated here on legal grounds. A better term for it would be love faithfulness, something which love requires. It is questionable whether a marriage which is without love and for some important reasons cannot be dissolved is morally entitled to faithfulness.

AGGRESSION

In the Freudian theoretical system aggression is attributed originally to the id. It derives from an instinct *thanatos* (from the Greek word for death), which aims at the return of the organism to an inorganic state. Although Freud thought that thanatos, like sex, has an energetic function, he did not name the energy of this instinct; other analysts did. Federn named it *mortido* and Weiss *destrudo*. *Mortido* and *destrudo* both refer to destructive power. Thanatos would be the biological equivalent of entropy, the tendency which (according to the second law of thermodynamics) leads to a progressive decay of whatever exists in the universe.

Many students of biology have recently pointed out that aggression has an important constructive role in the animal kingdom; thus aggression has to be considered as a manifestation of the instinct of self-preservation rather than a destructive tendency.

Konrad Lorenz in *Aggression*,[11] Robert Ardrey in *The Territorial Imperative*,[12] and the British psychoanalyst Anthony Storr in *Human Aggression*[13] have in various ways demonstrated that aggression is for many animals a vital necessity in the wild. Many species would not survive if this instinct did not enable them to chase enemies, to consume food, and to procreate. These authors remind us that the origin of human aggression lies in animal aggression. In man, as in other animals, aggression is used to space out population, to implement sexual selection, and to protect the young.

As I wrote in a previous book,[14] aggressive behavior in man is accompanied by at least one of three emotions: rage, anger, or hate. Rage, which man has in common with lower animals, impels the individual toward an immediate motor discharge which aims at destroying or impairing whatever has provoked this emotion. The motor behavior is directed against the danger, the prey, the rival. Anger and hate are purely human. Anger, although not causing an immediate motor discharge, is still impelling and manifests itself in gestures, sounds, or words. Hate lasts longer; it has the tendency to become a chronic state which is sustained by special thoughts. Although hate, too, eventually aims at some motor actions, a feedback mechanism is established between the sustaining thoughts and this emotion. In other words, hate stimulates hateful thoughts and hateful thoughts recharge the emotion. Hate leads to calculated action and, at times, to premeditated crime.

At first it would seem that hate possesses only a negative quality, but in some conditions it actually has positive survival value. In primitive societies men learned that other human beings could be harmful if they were enemies of the tribe. When the enemies were present, the tribe confronted them with aggressive behavior engendered by rage and anger. A negative feeling toward them had to be sustained even when they were absent, so that the tribe could maintain vigilance and a destructive propensity necessary for future defense. Hate thus enables people to cope with the enemy by long-delayed actions. At a human level, aggression may lead to more complicated emotions which are derivative of those mentioned: for instance, it may become vindictiveness or domination.

There are basic differences between the two major types of behavior originating at lower levels of the psyche. Sexuality remains associated with erotic pleasure, procreation, and may be connected with love. The individual may increase his or her sexual or genital and romantic activities, but only to a certain degree because of the limitations imposed by the biological constitution. Ethologists and animal psychologists teach us that aggression, too, is limited in subhuman animals. Killing is not the usual aim of aggression when directed toward members of the same species. Almost always the aim is to scare and chase away rivals. But in the human being the aggressive tendencies, sustained by anger and hate, are potentially endless. These emotions become connected with a very complicated process of symbolic and conceptual processes which may lead to disastrous consequences. What started as a defense and a protection of young may end up with massacres. Hate may be artificially kept alive and nourished by well-organized hostile propaganda for the purpose of facilitating the destruction of adversaries and the acquisition of power. Furthermore, the complexities of living together at a human level engender hate not only toward recognized enemies, but often toward people who live in our immediate environment and even members of our own family. Finally, hate may unchain hostile behavior toward anyone whom we, for one reason or another, do not happen to like. Although we are entitled to dislike some person for one reason or another, very seldom are we justified in hating.

Unlike disinhibited sexuality, disinhibited aggression may thus lead to multiple murder, massacre, persecution, genocide, and even destruction of the whole world with atomic weapons. And, as has been remarked, aggression at times becomes vindictiveness. Under the pretext of avenging an injury or of acting for an ideal of justice, extreme or bizarre forms of retaliation are perpetrated. How aggression becomes connected with power seeking and terrorism, we shall discuss in subsequent chapters.

Here it is fitting to stress again that these aggressive tendencies variously called id behavior, primitive impulses, instinctual drives, hypothalamic urges, etc., cannot be accepted indiscriminately and allowed free expression. This statement is so obvious that it seems almost unbelievable that it has to be repeated. And yet the almost romantic fascination that violence exerts over some people today requires that this point be reiterated.

The normal man adopts a divergent attitude toward the two major forms of instinctual life. Recently he has learned that sexuality is not so dangerous as people used to think. He realizes that its danger largely resided in the fact that it could not be expressed without violating codes of behavior established in prehistoric times. The opposite is true for aggression. The increase in population and in the means by which power can be accumulated and violence and oppression exercised make aggression much worse than ever before, and diverted from the original phylogenetic aims. The aggressive behavior of animals toward members of the same species is no paradigm for human aggression, but only a pale precursor of it.

Individual aggression by psychopaths, criminals, or people deranged in various ways, though very regrettable and to be prevented, is not one of the great dangers in human society. More dangerous is the aggression exercised by people who feel inferior and try to compensate for their feelings of inferiority by becoming aggressive. The most dangerous form of aggression, however, is the one which finds support in the intellect or traditions of society. As we shall see in subsequent chapters, when the intellect, in the form of writings, propaganda, traditions, and especially political institutions, instead of inhibiting instinctual life promotes it, man and society undergo a state of primitivization.

CHAPTER 5

The
Endocratic
Power

JONAH AGAIN AND VICTOR HUGO

AFTER HIS REPENTANCE, RELUCTANTLY JONAH WENT TO NINEVEH
and announced to the inhabitants that God had decided to
destroy the sinful city. But the people listened to Jonah, repented, and God repented, too. He accepted their prayers
and Nineveh was saved.

Jonah was full of indignation, as God had made a liar of him.
Jonah had, in fact, suspected that God would be merciful and
would change His mind. But how can God change His mind?
He is supposed to know the future and had already established
that Nineveh should perish. As a matter of fact He had requested Jonah to announce that to the city. The word of God
is supposed to be absolute and immutable, a binding law
which cannot be broken. How can God Himself not fulfill the
word of God?

In Chapter 3 we saw that Jonah wanted God to be paternal
and not maternal, to be omniscient to the extent of knowing

that statistical improbabilities, like Nineveh's repentance, would not occur, and rigid to the point of denying the choice of redemption to the citizens of the sinful city.

We have to stress another point. Jonah wanted to be the representative of the law of God, of the supreme command; he did not want to be an agent of salvation. When he escaped to Tarshish and refused to go to preach to Nineveh, he felt strong enough to disrespect the order. He rebelled because it was risky to bring a prophecy of destruction. The inhabitants may repent, God may listen to their prayers, and Nineveh may be saved. He did not want to be a Hebrew prophet, but a Greek oracle revealing fate, unchangeable by morality or will.

After his repentance Jonah went to Nineveh, but again as a messenger of an unbreakable law, or an inviolable decree. But in an act of love God accepted the community of Nineveh back into his heart. Jonah was disturbed, not because Nineveh was an enemy city of the Jews, but because the Jewish God had not maintained His word. Instead of rejoicing he was deeply perturbed and melancholy. What he believed in proved not to be so, and life seemed no longer worth living. He asked God to let him die.

After his repentance, Jonah had believed that his ultimate loyalty was to God. This, which at first seems a good attitude, was actually the cause of his trouble, as it is for many of us. Our ultimate loyalty should not be to an idea, an ideal, a word, or even the word of God. The story of Jonah proves that God Himself is not loyal to His word. Our *ultimate* loyalty and concern must be toward our fellow men, who need compassion and help. What could God consider more important? Love has to be taken into account, too. God loved the Ninevites, although they were sinners. They had been the object of His care; they had grown to be over 120,000 people. In the act of love God included the animals that lived in Nineveh, for they too were spared destruction.

When Jonah was concerned about the fate of a dying gourd which had protected his head from the sun, God told him, "You pity the plant for which you did not labor, nor did you make it grow, which came into being in a night, and perished in a night. And should not I pity Nineveh, that great city. . ." Here again, Jonah's concern with himself, his passivity, and his involvement in what he had not labored for are stressed. But Jonah did not die. Although the book, in its eloquent brevity, tells nothing of the subsequent life of Jonah, it is understood that he saw God's light and was able to overcome the inner power which had chained him to a formal sense of duty rather than to goodness and mercy.

It is not always so. Persons committed to law and abstract principles rather than to goodness itself often prefer to die than to break the law. Such persons have been vividly portrayed in literature. I want to mention one of them, Javert, a principal character in Victor Hugo's *Les Misérables* (1862). This remarkable book has fascinated many generations in spite of its aesthetic weaknesses. From the complicated development and the many digressions of the book two persons emerge in the contrasting meaning they give to their lives: Jean Valjean, the hero, and Javert, the antihero.

Valjean, imprisoned for having stolen a loaf of bread, remains in jail for twenty years because every time he attempts to escape, more years are added to his original sentence. Finally he succeeds in escaping. Made angry and callous by the long and cruel imprisonment, he is destined to become a hardened criminal, but something unpredictable diverts the course of life. Chance directs him to the home of a clergyman, Monsignor Myriel, a saintly person. Brief is the crossing of their paths, but significant enough to change the path of Valjean's life. The monsignor offers his hospitality to the unexpected and terrifying guest, who needs food and repose. During the night, while the clergyman sleeps, Valjean steals the two beautiful silver candelabra which had been used to light the dinner table, and runs away. He is caught by policemen, who recognize the candelabra as belonging to the clergyman. They arrest him and bring him into the presence of Monsignor Myriel for a confrontation. Here again the unexpected occurs. Myriel tells the police that he has given the candelabra to his guest, who is not a thief but a person who has received a gift. What a momentous gift! Those candelabra will indeed lighten Jean Valjean's whole life. They show him that goodness exists in the world and that he, too, can actualize it. From that moment on his life is characterized by one good deed after another. He helps "les misérables," the poor people whom he meets in life. He is eventually so well liked that, under an assumed name, he becomes the mayor of the town where he lives. He does well. He has forgiven the world that has mistreated him, and he is forgiven by God. According to the law, however, Jean Valjean is still an escaped convict.

Javert personifies the formal, rigid law, which admits no exception. As chief of police for many years he tries to discover the ex-convict. Finally he finds him when Valjean gives himself up in order that another person not be mistaken for him and sent to jail instead of him. Valjean breaks the law again by escaping a second time, and Javert again tries to find him. Javert operates a system of investigation, surveillance, and persecution with the aim of returning Valjean to prison, where he thinks he belongs and as the law requires. But Valjean is not found. It also happens that, during the French political insurrection of 1832, Valjean could kill Javert, who is fighting on the opposite side. Valjean could get rid once and for all of his persecutor, but instead he helps Javert save his life. But Javert cannot accept this gift as Valjean once accepted Myriel's gift. Can goodness be stronger than the law? Would Javert be willing to arrest Jean Valjean again if the opportunity arose? Admitting that goodness is superior to his duty and to the law is something Javert cannot tolerate. It shakes the pillars on which he has sustained his existence. He prefers to kill himself by drowning in the Seine. Unlike Jonah, and unlike Valjean, Javert is untouched by the light of God, the light of goodness, the unexpected gift. His will is imprisoned by the chains of an inner power.

What is the origin of this power which gives orders from inside, and which (from the Greek words *endon* and *kratein*, to rule from within) I have called "endocracy"? In order to understand its nature we have to retrace the early stages of development of the child.

BASIC TRUST

In Chapter 3 we stressed the role of the individual in fulfilling or inhibiting his wishes. We have to examine more accurately now how his whole history of interpersonal relations influences that role.

Early in life, an attitude of trust develops between the child and the people who take care of him. The child soon comes to feel that all things in life result because of others. It is up to mother to keep him on her lap, to fondle him, to feed him. But there is also the feeling that people *will do* these wonderful things. In other words, the child expects the wonderful things to happen; he trusts adults. Later, the child expects the important adults in his life to expect something from him; the child *trusts* that the adults will trust him. In other words, there is a reciprocal trust that things are going to be well, that the child will be capable of growing up to be a healthy and mature man. The child perceives his mother's faith and accepts it. He finally assimilates the trust of the important adults and he trusts himself. Thus, things will no longer depend exclusively on others, but also on himself.

A feeling of favorable expectancy originates which at first is limited to the immediate future, but soon extends into a feeling of favorable anticipation of a more distant future. A basic optimism, founded on basic trust, is originated. If the adult is perceived as bigger and superior, he is also perceived as a benevolent doer. This atmosphere of trust and security makes the child ready to accept without reservation the world the adults gradually present to him. He accepts their attitudes, their feelings, their ways, their language, their ideas. And the self grows, nourished by what is psychologically given and assimilated.

The philosopher Martin Buber defines trust as "a contact of the entire being with the one in whom one trusts." [1] In Buber's terminology, it is this trust which permits the I-Thou relationship to exist.[2] Psychologically, this means that without the Thou (first the mother and then the important others) there would be no I, no development of the self. The man who has studied and revealed the importance of this feeling of basic trust in the development of the child more than anybody else is Erik Erikson,[3] whose lead many psychologists and psychiatrists have followed.

If basic trust existed in a complete form, no hostile force coming from the human environment would be experienced. A feeling of solidarity and communion would exist among people which would promote the growth and flourishing of the personality, and on account of which the joyful fleeting moment would leave a wake of trust in the future. The good mother is the representative of this world of trust.

Unfortunately our world is not full of trust. Even when the individual is exposed to good motherhood, the complexities of human existence make him gradually aware that he must mistrust. From early childhood onward he experiences in varying degrees some people as unfriendly or even hostile. At times this experience is very mild and may promote constructive vigilance; but most of the time it is better defined as fear. Again the fear may be mild, as it is in most cases, or very pronounced. The child must learn to deal with an unfriendly external power with which he must coexist. He may learn to yield to this power; that is, to become a compliant, subservient, pleasing personality. Karen Horney [4] called this type of personality "moving toward people," but today we may call it an "Uncle Tom" type of personality.

The child may learn instead to fight back, in his turn to intimidate others, to move against people. From childhood onward he may feel that he has more chance to preserve his own integrity by fighting and arguing than by pleasing, obliging, and submitting. The child may learn to deal with the hostile power by removing himself from it, either by physical distance or by emotional detachment. He may become an aloof, withdrawn person.

These patterns of response, which come to constitute important parts of the personality, actually grow out of fear for the other, when the other is seen as a person possessing varying degrees of enmity. When the resulting way of living is not too affected, the individual may still be considered normal or mildly neurotic. When he exaggerates these tendencies, he may actually develop a paranoid attitude toward the world, which he sees as a conspiracy of many inimical powers or as a single huge, omnipresent, all-engulfing threat. These last possibilities will be discussed in Chapter 10. Here it is important to indicate that these feelings of trust and mistrust are necessary for the development of other feelings and mechanisms related to the ability to choose. One of the first and most important is the feeling that one *must*.

MUST

Although one may choose in accordance with his wishes or judgment, he often acts in a certain way because he feels that he *must*. This feeling is at times in agreement, at times in contrast, with one's wishes or reason. The feeling of "must" may be experienced as an irresistible force, similar to the compulsion of the obsessive-compulsive person. Most people, however, do not follow the "must" because of compulsion but because they *choose* to do their duty: "I must do this because it is my duty to do so." For many people one's duty prevails over every other consideration.

It is natural to ask why the urge to be dutiful exists. What is its origin, pertinence, merit, and fault? At first glance, at least, it seems an irrational mechanism of the psyche. In fact this feeling of "must" is not necessarily associated with reason. Antigone was willing to give up her life to follow her conviction that she must give appropriate burial to her dead brother Polyneices.

With the concept of superego Freudian psychoanalysis has enabled us to begin to understand this complex problem, but we must stress that this understanding is only beginning. The child learns to obey mother and father; the parental command is introjected and is transformed into a sense of duty. Mother and, later, father say, "You must do this; you must not do that." But what kind of orders do mother and father give? At first they are orders which will prevent the child from hurting himself or others; later they are orders which will benefit the child or others.

Why must mother and father command? In this question lies the crux of the problem, not sufficiently emphasized in previous studies. At a very early age the child must follow orders at a level of complexity that he cannot understand. How can a year-old child understand that he should not break a glass, that he should not eat two big ice cream cones? Soon he will learn the rationality of these orders, but by that time he will have to cope with other orders that he cannot understand and which he is nevertheless required to follow.

At a human level life is very complicated, even for a small child. He must do many things which are unpleasant and he does not know why. He must defecate in the proper place, he must wash himself, he must go to bed, he must eat no more than a certain quantity of food that he likes, he must eat another food which he does not like, he must go to school, he must leave mother, etc.

A few years ago my office was located one floor below that of a pediatrician. One day a week the pediatrician would give immunizing injections to infants and young children. That day the doctor's office sounded like a slaughterhouse. Constant crying and noise echoed from his office. I knew the pediatrician: a tender, sympathetic human being who treated the children with the greatest care. But how could the children like the shot or understand the necessity of the injection? In my office, my psychiatric patients who heard the noises and the crying occasionally had the impression that the children upstairs were badly treated and lamented, quite often, in depressing fantasies about the human predicament.

The parental order is a substitution for the understanding which the immature child lacks. A gap between the required action and the understanding of it is unavoidable. This is what I call the *comprehension-action gap*.

Presumably this gap existed also in the small groups of members of races immediately preceding the human, as an intermediary stage between imitation and understood command (see Chapter 2). Possibly the leaders of the hominids grasped the value of certain actions, but in order to transmit the ideas to the members of the clan they resorted more to the gesture of the arm, and to the imperativeness of the gesture, than to the ability to understand and use language.

In comparison to the command given in the most primitive groups of humans or prehumans, the command given to the child tends to lose somewhat, but not completely, the benevolent and cooperative quality that we described in Chapter 2. It is no longer a message between adults but a message between a superior adult and an inferior child.

In ordinary life, how does mother enforce an unpleasant order? At first we may interpret the relation purely in a behavioristic frame of reference and say that mother enforces her order by punishment or reward. The process seems similar to the conditioning mechanism used experimentally with animals. The experimenter reinforces a habit of an animal by rewarding it with food, or weakens the habit of the animal by punishing, let us say, with an electric shock. The parent would seem to do the same with an act of love or anger. Receiving approval, affection, or love makes the child behave in a certain way, and receiving anger and punishment makes him avoid behaving in that way. The child cannot see that the forbidden acts are harmful and the recommended acts are beneficial. He has not enough experience from life and cannot predict the distant effects of his actions; but he learns very quickly to recognize and evaluate the effects of present or impending punishment and reward.

The comparison with animal conditioning ends here, for there are other circumstances, connected with the symbolic functions, which enter in the human situation.[5] Conditioning —punishment and reward—although very important, would not be sufficient to influence the child to accept and to obey if he had not developed that feeling of basic trust which we discussed at the beginning of this chapter. The attitude of trust makes the child receptive to everything which comes from people he trusts, receptive even to the command and to the punishment.

How this feeling of trust actually influences the child to accept what may prove harmful to him will be examined later in this chapter. But we must now reconsider punishment and reward before considering other important questions. First of all, punishment and reward are *neutralization* of the child's act. The punishment received, let us say, after eating the second ice cream cone, neutralizes the pleasure experienced in eating it; in a certain way it attempts to eliminate the trace of the pleasant memory of the ice cream. The reward, on the contrary, is a compensation for the sustained deprivation of the second ice cream. Mother offers a different pleasantness: approval, keeping the child on her lap, hugging him, etc.

In the second place, punishment and reward are symbolic or *anticipatory* of the consequences of the child's act. Thus, the punishment that the mother inflicts on the child who has eaten the second ice cream is symbolic of the bad effect eating excessive ice cream will cause. The immediate punishment takes the place of the painful condition which the bad act, if allowed to be repeated, would eventually cause. Conversely, the reward (as approval, tenderness, or love on the part of the mother) is symbolic of the state of welfare and happiness which characterizes a life resulting from doing the right thing.

The importance of the future is implicit in the act of command. One of the functions of the command is to anticipate the value of the act from the distant or near future. When parents are replaced by teachers or other social authorities, the future is still inherent in the command. A sort of retribution is expected for the present act. According to several religions, if you do not behave well in life, and especially if you do not repent or escape earthly punishment, you will be punished in hell. If you always did the right thing and were not rewarded duly on earth, you will be rewarded in paradise. Since relatively few people are visibly rewarded for their good deeds, many people rely on paradise.

Another important point has to be considered. If the person expects either punishment or reward in the future, he prepares himself psychologically for this event. The individual who knows he has done something wrong generally feels he deserves to be punished. It is then in the natural course of events to be punished. Indeed, unless he is punished, the psychological equilibrium will not be restored. The bad deed has produced a rupture, a gap, a state of tension or disequilibrium (remotely reminiscent of the state of a conditioned dog which is prevented from responding to the conditioning stimulus). Punishment will reestablish the equilibrium and therefore may even be welcome. If punishment is considered the natural way to restore the individual's psychic well-being, a feeling of guilt will ensue until punishment is received. This is the beginning of the feeling of guilt, but, let us remember, only the beginning. Later we shall discuss more complicated characteristics of guilt. At this point I wish to stress that guilt may be a very strong emotion, even stronger than anxiety, depression, and anger.

The situation is very different when the individual feels he has done the right thing and expects a reward. Very few have reached the high degree of morality where the reward for doing good is in the doing itself. Expectation of a reward, moreover, is a very weak emotion in comparison to the expectation of punishment. This topic is very complicated and requires an ample discussion. I shall summarize here some concepts which explain the weakness of this emotion: (1) Even when he has done good deeds, one may never be satisfied. He thinks he could have done better. Because of his conceptual processes he can always visualize situations better than the present. (2) Man has learned from experience that reward is more uncertain than punishment, and thus not to be relied on. (3) Because of its survival value, biological evolution has favored a stronger emotional reaction to threat and fear (and consequently to fear of punishment) than to hope and security.

THE ORIGIN OF OUGHTNESS

This feeling of "must" and "command" cannot be entirely reduced to conditioning, or even to conditioning plus the symbolic value of reward and punishment. Although these phenomena explain many things, they do not explain the transformation of something external into something internal. The external command becomes a "duty," a "must." Something objective, like the external command, becomes subjective, is appropriated by the individual as a subjective experience, acquires a subjective reality, and becomes part of the individual himself. As I have indicated elsewhere,[6] this subjectivization is not adequately accounted for by psychological or psychiatric authors who exclusively or almost exclusively stress the role of the environment. This subjectivization is a phenomenon as difficult to understand as the whole mind-body problem. The intensity of a subjective phenomenon does not correspond to the external objective event or stimulus to which it is related. It depends on the mechanisms triggered in its formation and on the other psychological processes with which it is related.

The atmosphere of basic trust is a prerequisite for transforming an external command into an inner one. We must now analyze other concepts which, like basic trust, we cannot explain with scientific exactitude. I must also advance new concepts.

The person, parent, adult, or leader who gives the command has a quality which I call the *imperative attitude*. This imperative attitude is experienced in its totality as a benevolent force, although it has attributes which may not seem entirely positive. These attributes are the properties of magnetizing, electrifying, hypnotizing, charming, seducing, fascinating, intruding, possessing, capturing, enchanting, etc. "Imperative attitude" cannot be replaced by any of these terms because it contains an element of the meanings of each of these terms.

The person, generally the child, who responds to this imperative attitude experiences a tendency to obey, what philosophers call a sense of "oughtness." You ought to do what the commanding person wants you to do, and you must do it, no longer because he wants you to do it, but because you must want to do it; you must. An external power no longer obligates you; now it is an inner power, what I call *endocratic power*, a sense of "I ought to." If you do not do what you must do, you will no longer incur only external punishment but will also *feel guilt*.

The sense of "oughtness" is partially experienced unconsciously, and in a certain way constitutes the Freudian superego; but to a large extent it is also experienced consciously and manifests itself as a sense of duty.[7] The imperative attitude engenders endocracy or internal command in the individual. How the external factor brings about an inner condition is difficult to explain biologically.

We have already discussed some of these phenomena in Chapter 2, in relation to development of language and primitive society. Imperative attitude and endocracy were also important in removing the sense of guilt which occurred in primitive man when he followed his own spontaneity and originality.

I must stress that with the term imperative I do not mean

only the act of commanding. I mean influencing a person in such a way that he will command himself to obey. The person, at least initially, responds to external power, but only by means of his inner self. If he obeyed only because afraid of the ex-ternal power, the psychological mechanism would be simpler. But under endocracy the person responds to an inner force, not an external one. An external force, however, can always reinforce the internal force with the methods of reward and punishment.

The fact that feelings of duty, morality, or oughtness require psychological mechanisms has nothing to do with their being valid or not. They have to be evaluated on their own merits. The primitive origin or mechanism of a feeling or a thought is not a sufficient reason for rejecting it. Not only morality, but also art and science originated from and are carried out through primitive mechanisms which in themselves would seem obsolete, rudimentary, or invalid. On the other hand, when these feelings of oughtness are based only on primitive mechanisms, they require some critical reevaluation.

If we try now to reexamine the problem posed by Hume mentioned in Chapter 2, the change from a descriptive to a prescriptive attitude or from "is" to "ought," we may still be perplexed about the metaphysical essence of duty and the validity of the "ought." We do, however, understand the psychological origin of the problem.

What starts at the interpersonal level is extended to impersonal institutions. Law, religion, society, school, and culture not only teach and describe, they prescribe. In the general attitude of basic trust that the individual has toward these institutions, he accepts their prescriptions. The imperative quality is now possessed by the institution and reinforced by the mechanisms of reward and punishment, actual or symbolic.

Organized society since ancient times has tried to connect the feeling of oughtness to a principle of action. Young children and primitive men may not understand the principle and therefore are confronted with a comprehension-action gap. The older the individual is and the more civilized society is, the more the gap should be filled and the principle understood. Such principles as "Do not kill," "Do not steal," "Tell the truth," "Help the needy," make sense. Often, however, the oughtness or endocracy becomes more important than the principle of action. The person feels compelled to obey the inner dictate independently of its content. The principle of action may eventually be recognized as undesirable, and yet the endocratic mechanism connected with it remains powerful and difficult to resist. It is a mechanism which follows oughtness and not necessarily goodness.

Even the two systems which regulate our social and moral life (religion and the state) often become more concerned with oughtness than with the value of the principles. At times the oughtness becomes so pronounced and overpowering that it is considered the voice of our conscience, or the voice of God, the principle which must be respected at any cost, even if we do not understand it. Some of Kant's teachings, rightly or wrongly, have been interpreted as suggesting this inflexible attitude.

Oughtness is pronounced in religion because, after all, the order is supposed to come from God; and how can God be wrong? We have seen that until his final illumination, this was Jonah's position. Oughtness is not limited to actions, but is extended to ideas, in the sense that you *must* believe them when they come from God. For instance, you *must* believe that the sun moves around the earth, even when Galileo has demonstrated that Copernicus was right in believing the opposite. The law is also supposed to be superior to the particular circumstances it deals with, and cannot be broken. This was Javert's position, as portrayed by Victor Hugo.

SOCIETY'S EXPLOITATION OF ENDOCRACY

Endocracy, which has a very useful role at some stages in the development of the individual and the human race, and which, when accompanied by good principles of action, may lead man to the peaks of life, may actually be exploited by malevolent social forces.

In subsequent chapters we shall describe how malevolent forces tyrannize and enslave men by resorting to external threats and the application of stern forms of punishment and cruelty. Although we may refer to external threats in this chapter too, the focus is on the inner effect or endocracy, which may result both from an external threat or from the application of a sense of oughtness to unjust principles of action. An effective endocracy will make a slave feel that it is just and right for him to be a slave: he should accept being a slave, enjoy being a slave, and feel like a slave.

External power and endocracy concur in restricting the will of men. Tyranny resorts to both: on one side external terror;

on the other side, imparting a feeling of oughtness, associated with inhuman principles of action. A typical example of this double attack is to be found in Nazi Germany. Fiction writers like Orwell, Huxley, and Koestler have done an excellent job in depicting these methods. They have actually not exceeded by far the real events of our century. Others have written scientifically about the techniques of persuasion, from propaganda to brainwashing.

Some people have tended to equate the totalitarian method, which instills a sense of oughtness for a false principle of action, with the propaganda made in capitalistic countries, which persuades a potential consumer to buy certain products. As we shall see in Chapter 6, commercial advertising has many negative qualities, especially when it acts as a "hidden persuader." We must be careful, though, not to confuse the two issues, as some contemporary writers do. These advertising techniques affect one's ego, not superego. In other words, they affect the habits of life, but not necessarily the basic moral principles. Like many other practices prevailing in our contemporary society they lead not to crippling endocracy, but to another unfortunate outcome, described in Chapter 7, which I call deformation of the self or of the ego.[8]

It is the totalitarian state that especially uses endocracy to change basic moral principles to its own advantage. Those readers too young to have witnessed what took place in the world in the fourth and fifth decades of this century should not consider this matter as having merely historical interest. Not only are these terrible events liable to occur again if we do not prevent them; not only do they still take place in some nations; but in every country, including our own, we may recognize signs of them which have to be opposed. Everybody should become familiar with these methods in order to help his own society.

A principle of action often instilled in totalitarian states is that you owe everything to the state: your life, your property, your work. What is good for you should be considered subordinate to what is good for the state. But what is good for the state, you, the simple citizen, cannot understand most of the time. Only the Fuehrer, the Duce, the Party, the chief of your country, understands. They are vigilant and protect you, as mother did when you were asleep in your crib. A situation is created similar to that between the parent who commands and the child who does not understand. The comprehension-action gap is restored with the techniques which go with it. The system of reward and punishment is used to reinforce endocracy. The most important characteristic, however, is the imperative attitude of the leader or of the institution, which evokes endocratic power. In typical instances, the leader has charismatic qualities that will make you do what he wants you to do. He will be completely successful if he makes you believe that you follow him not because he wants you to, but because you choose to do so. You are an adult now. There is no longer any comprehension-action gap. You do not accept him blindly. Because of your own intelligence you know he is right. You are now enlightened and you know his superior purpose, his sublime truth.

It does not matter whether this "truth" is actually a lie. Hitler said that the bigger the lie, the more it is believed. In a system which exploited endocracy as he did, he was probably right. The dictator, of course, not only does not offer new truths, but he exploits the prejudices and the popular fallacies which have long traditions. He summons and uses them to increase your endocracy. He edits historical events to make more plausible the principles of action that he wants you to adopt. He does not literally hypnotize you, but often succeeds in making you believe what he wants you to believe. If he controls your ideas he will soon control your actions, because every action is preceded by an idea. He will have completed his job when you obey him not to avoid punishment, but in order to avoid your own guilt feeling; when your almost total blindness will appear to you the greatest possible clarity and wisdom, and the cruel duty imposed on you as the noblest dictate of your conscience, the greatest deed. In front of such greatness, how can you, Mr. Nobody, resist?

PERSONAL MEMORIES

The Nazis and the Stalinists have committed crimes many times more horrendous than the Italian Fascists, but my experiences with the latter permit me to write about them with personal involvement.

When Mussolini came to power in 1922, I was eight years old and attending the fourth grade. To us children he was soon portrayed as the savior of Italy. France, Great Britain, and the United States had abandoned Italy, their poor ally in the First World War. They had not compensated her for the sacrifices made during the long, costly, and bloody war; and now our beloved country was in the process of falling prey to that atheistic chaos, bolshevism. But fortunately Mussolini, the Duce, was there, the man who would lead Italy. Lead it where? In the beginning it was not openly stated, but soon it became apparent: to the greatness of Rome. Rome's greatness was our omnipresent goal. The Romans, after all, were the ancestors of the Italians. This historical fact proved that the Italians had all the potential for becoming great like the Roman conquerors. Once this legacy was accepted, extreme patriotism, discipline, sacrifice for the fatherland, law and order above all, war mentality, and imperialism became principles of action.

A better understanding of history could have easily demonstrated that modern Italy had little in common with ancient Rome. The spirit of ancient Rome had become alien to the peace-loving and undisciplined Italians. Since the Renaissance, Florence, not Rome, had been the spiritual capital of Italy. No longer Latin, but Tuscan, the melodious and gentle idiom of Florence, was spoken in Italy. The city of flowers and love of art had replaced the belligerent ways of the *caput mundi*. The Roman ideal, however, remained in the psyche of a minority of Italians as an archaic complex which could be resurrected.

"Duce, Duce, Duce," shouted the regimented crowd, implying, "Lead us to Roman glory." Slogans and mottos were painted and printed a thousand times on walls, posters, newspapers, to become imprinted in the minds of all Italians. The trinomial motto of the French Revolution, "Fraternité, liberté, égalité" (brotherhood, freedom, equality), was supposed to be supplanted by the triple affirmation of the so-called Fascist revolution: "Authority-Order-Justice." In the Fascist context, authority meant the authority of the Duce, who always knew the truth; order meant the law imposed by the Fascist government; justice meant only what the government considered justice.

Another important motto, also repeated thousands of times, was "credere, obbedire, combattere," which meant that the good citizen must do three things: he must believe, obey, and fight. To believe meant to believe in the principles of action of Fascism, which became dogma and virtue, no matter how iniquitous and outrageous they were. To obey meant to follow the orders of Fascism, no matter how incomprehensible they were to you. The most important of these imperatives was to fight, meaning, of course, to fight the enemies of Fascism. After all, another dictum of the Duce proclaimed, "Molti nemici, molto onore"

—"Many enemies, much honor." It was no longer desirable to make friends but to hate and to have enemies and to be ready to fight them. War was man's supreme, most sublime activity. "Military science" was a subject that all students had to study. Even medical students, like myself, during medical school had to take a course in military science.

Here are some of Mussolini's thoughts, often mentioned to us during our school years:

> A doctrine which is founded upon [the] harmful postulate of peace is hostile to Fascism . . .
> Fascism . . . affirms the immutable, beneficial, and fruitful inequality of mankind.
> Fascism . . . believes neither in the possibility nor the utility of perpetual peace. It thus repudiates the doctrine of pacifism.
> . . . War alone brings up to its highest tension all human energy and puts the stamp of nobility upon the peoples who have the courage to meet it.[9]
>
> (MUSSOLINI, 1922)

We know that these were not just rhetorical ideas in Mussolini's head in 1922. He soon put them into action. He participated in the Spanish Civil War on the side of Franco; he waged war against Ethiopia, in a purely imperialistic adventure; he invaded a little ally, Albania; he fought against Greece and finally against Yugoslavia, France, England, the United States, and Russia.

Mussolini's ideas seem obviously absurd to us today, but not to the child and adolescent who learned in school to revere them as sacred ideals. At the beginning of this chapter we saw that an atmosphere of basic trust prevails in the socialization and education of the young. The young trust the adults and are prone to accept their world and their ways. It makes sense to trust the leader, who represents your fatherland, the country which gave birth to you, and which gives you sustenance. There is something wrong with you if you mistrust. In adolescence there is also a search for the absolute, a mystical power which gives you immediate knowledge of the truth. Some adolescents today try to reach the universal and absolute through drugs; in the 1920s and '30s it was through blind acceptance or veneration of a hero. In that atmosphere there was an illusion that what you incorporated or introjected was within the realm of your full understanding. But even if you did not fully understand and reached only an approximation, that approximation made you sense the ultimate concern and need of your whole people, your whole country. Finally the leader became the real hero, a man chosen by destiny at the right time in the right place.

And this is the hardest thing for me to tell my readers. Mussolini became the hero . . . for me, too, when I was ten to thirteen years old. The evil effects of indoctrination convinced me that Mussolini was another Julius Caesar, a Scipio, and greater than Garibaldi. I am Jewish, and, contrary to his later position, il Duce at that time professed friendship for the Jews. My high school teacher Pellegrinetti, nicknamed Cecco, was in awe of il Duce and contributed to my feeling. Pellegrinetti was a poor soul, a vegetarian, a man so submissive that he was not able to maintain discipline in the class. The students often played tricks on him and made fun of his ways. Because of his weakness Pellegrinetti was not effective as a teacher, except with a few pupils like myself who preferred independence and individuality to methodical routine. Pellegrinetti instilled in me a love for literature, especially for Dante and Shakespeare. I liked the weak old man.

And yet this man, who did not eat meat because it required killing animals, was a fervent Fascist, an admirer of Fascist discipline and especially of il Duce, a person completely unlike himself. Pellegrinetti used to write poems in Latin and Italian celebrating the glory of the great dictator. He often would declaim them to the class. Only when he would recite these poems would the class lose its habitual somnolence or distractibility. All the necessary incentives were there, and I too became an admirer of the dictator, but never to the extreme degree to which some of my peers did. For instance, I could never accept another Fascist slogan, "Il Duce ha sempre ragione"— "The Duce is always right." I had learned in the Bible that even Moses had erred, and Jews were not to believe in the infallibility of any man. I felt that that slogan was for mass consumption. In spite of these excesses, for which I found excuses, I became an admirer of Mussolini, and, alas!, I myself wrote a poem celebrating the great dictator.

Naturally I showed the poem to Pellegrinetti, who was enthusiastic. He asked me to read it to the whole class, and I was very much applauded and envied by "the less gifted" students. I went further than that. Together with other poems on biblical themes, I read the poem about Mussolini to the club of the Jewish congregation of Pisa, to which my family belonged. Now we have to remember that we are in the year 1927, long before Mussolini made his alliance with Hitler. At that time Mussolini professed feelings of friendship for the Jews and for the Zionist cause. We Italian Jews were so few that even Jews living elsewhere in the world hardly knew that we existed. At that time many Italian Jews felt that we were such an insignificant and powerless minority that the best thing for us to do was to go along with the prevailing policy of the country.

When I read my poems at the Jewish club, those written on biblical themes were greatly applauded. When I read the poem about Mussolini, I received applause only from the members who wanted peace with the government at any cost; but their applause was prolonged, vociferous, impressive. My thirteen years of age made me more crisp, brisk, and zestful after these moderate triumphs. But the story did not end there. The second part, and the one which for my personal life is the most significant, is now beginning. In all this I had forgotten my father.

My father was the opposite of an admirer of Mussolini. A physician by profession, he practiced on the periphery of Pisa, remaining aloof from the political scene, which he detested. He never took an actively rebellious role, for he believed he could do nothing against the overwhelming wave of nationalism and totalitarianism. While he was treating the poor and the needy, his attitude was one of silent protest.

But when he found out that I had written such a disgraceful poem and that I had had the effrontery to read it in public, he called me aside and soundly scolded me. His words were a severe punishment. He was very angry. How could I extol the enemy of freedom and democracy, the man who was subjecting everybody to his despotic power? My father's words were bitter and, because of my lack of understanding, sounded injurious to me. I oscillated between thinking that he was wrong and thinking he was right. When I felt he was wrong, I felt betrayed. While everybody, starting from my teacher, was praising me highly, my own father was knocking me down. Could everybody be wrong except my father? Probably he was clinging to the outmoded political ways of the nineteenth century and was deaf to the new ideals, blind to the epic greatness of the new times. On the other hand, he might be right; and if he were right, I had done a terrible thing, aligning myself with the oppressor. I felt punished, defeated, crushed.

My mother's love, even in that instance, was openly on my side. Although she agreed with my father that I should not have written and read such a poem in public, she pleaded in my favor, pointing out that I had been influenced by the environment. But my father, it seemed to me, was not making any such allowance, and did not accept this excuse. He felt I should have been able to discern and learn the truth, and not be so easily persuaded by the corruptors. I felt utterly confused and very unhappy. Of course, at that moment I was thinking only of myself. It did not occur to me until much later how great my father's sorrow must have been in seeing his beloved son in danger of becoming overcome by Fascist madness.

No mention was made of the episode for several years. Helped by my father's reproach I saw the light and soon became convinced of the absurdity and evil of Fascism. Throughout my subsequent life I have tried to spot oppression of any kind and expose it.

I became an adult, and early in 1939 I emigrated to the United States. During the Second World War I had no contact with my parents, and I did not know whether they were dead or alive. After the war I learned that they had miraculously been able to save themselves in spite of Mussolini and Hitler. A few times, while hiding in woods and mountains, they had almost fallen into the hands of the Nazis. My joy was immense. I was able to reestablish contact with them and visit them periodically as long as they lived.

On two occasions, however, to my chagrin, my father reminded me that when I was an adolescent I had written a poem in honor of Mussolini. It seemed to me that my father had not yet forgiven me for what I had done at the age of thirteen. I believe now that my father wanted to do a little teasing, to which he was certainly entitled. But in view of the holocaust and the terrible suffering that people had undergone in Europe because of Fascism, I felt not teased but ashamed and, at the same time, motivated to defend myself.

I still feel under the compulsion to defend myself. Although it is true that I knew my father was an antifascist, he was one of the very few persons known to me who had democratic leanings. During my late childhood and early adolescence my father did not have the time or the inclination to explain politics to me, but he assumed that the merits of democracy would appear as self-evident to me. Democracy was so to him because he had been raised in a completely different historical climate. He had grown up while Italy, shortly after her unification, was permeated by the spirit of the so-called Risorgimento (the unification of the country). When he finally became aware of the effects of the environment on me and started to explain important matters to me, he gave me insights for which I shall always be grateful. Today, more than ever, I revere his courage and steadfastness of purpose at a time when many were in doubt and it was easy to succumb. But he was no pedagogue or psychologist and did not fully realize the strength of the environment on children and adolescents. He did not know the phenomenon of endocracy.

Endocracy, in this case determined by the school and society at large, had at first been stronger than his influence. Should it have been so strong? For the sake of scientific accuracy I must say that my personal situation was more complicated than I have so far described. I really always knew in my heart that my father was an antifascist. But I chose not to hear his words, which he expressed stealthily because of the external danger. I did worse than Jonah; I did not go to Tarshish, but in writing that poem I extolled the merits of Nineveh.

During my psychoanalytic training I learned that, like most boys, I passed through the Oedipal stage of development. For that reason at a certain stage in life I probably had the desire to take a stand opposite to that of my father. During the First World War he was in the army fighting with the Allies against German and Austro-Hungarian imperialism. He came back when I was five, and for a few years it was difficult for me to share my mother's affection for him. But the Fascist environment not only did not help me solve my Oedipus complex, but reinforced it until the episode just narrated brought about a solution. Endocratic power, instead of helping to solve personal psychological problems, feeds on them in order to reinforce itself.

ETHICS, FALSE ETHICS, AND ETIQUETTE

We must reevaluate some ideas that have been current in ethical theory since Kant. According to this great philosopher "obligation" expresses a necessity which occurs nowhere else in nature. The moral will is by its very nature outside the chain of cause and effect that occurs in the phenomenal world in which we live. Duty, or obedience to the moral law, is something which cannot be explained. It involves recognition and submission to a supreme principle of morality. We are free to obey "the categorical imperative" which requires us to do our duty.

This freedom thus becomes an oughtness, a must. Kant's teachings do not explain oughtness in the personal phenomenal world; they reinforce it. For Kant, the origin of oughtness is in the moral nature of man, is "noumenal," something purely abstract, nonempirical, or existing in itself. But we have seen that oughtness is not noumenal but endocratic or psychological in nature. Endocracy is actually the psychological precursor to Kant's categorical imperative. Kant taught, "Act according to that maxim which can at the same time be a universal law." Translated into more common language, this means, "Do not do to others what you do not want to be done to yourself." He also wrote, "Act as to treat humanity, whether in your own person or in that of another, always as an end and never as means only." But Kant's teachings have often been misinterpreted, and this error has led to disastrous consequences. His maxims were replaced by others, so that the strong Kantian feeling of oughtness was applied to wrong principles of action.

Even Adolf Eichmann, during his trial in Jerusalem, invoked Kant for his defense. He said that his duty toward his fatherland transcended any other consideration and justified his crimes. Kant, of course, would be horrified at these misconceptions.

Oughtness is valid only when it is associated with a just and good principle. The dangerousness of this endocratic oughtness is not limited to that elicited by political systems. Religious dogmas, myths, beliefs of any kind may acquire a great endocratic power, which may lead even to the extermination of people. It is the power which during the Crusades led Christians to exterminate non-Christians; Catholics to massacre Huguenots on Saint Bartholomew's Day in 1572; Turks to murder Christian Armenians during the First World War; Germans to kill Jews during the Second World War, etc. History records a long series of barbaric acts, perpetrated by men on men, almost always through the intermediacy of endocracy.

Actions committed out of endocratic motives can assume a degree of horror seldom reached by other human behavior. The horror derives from the fact that endocracy decreases enormously in people the ability to will or to choose. It also mobilizes obscure tendencies toward violence and aggression which may exist in many people, but which would remain dormant were they not activated in this way. The person possessed by endocracy acts blindly, confusedly, and often with a false certainty of doing a good thing. The action reaches extremes difficult to conceive. These statements are not intended to minimize other factors, political and economic, which were behind these historical events. As a matter of fact, we shall examine these additional factors in subsequent chapters.

We have so far mentioned extreme cases. Actually, every culture imparts various degrees of endocracy to different aspects of life. It is often difficult to judge whether what is requested of the individual is a bad action or bad manners, a moral deed or a proper habit; that is, whether we are dealing with ethics or etiquette. Even great sociologists have confused these issues. In *The Rules of the Sociological Method* Durkheim wrote:

> When I fulfill my obligations as brother, husband, or citizen, when I execute my contracts, I perform duties which are defined, externally to my self and my acts, in law and in custom. Even if they conform to my own sentiments, and I feel their reality subjectively, such reality is still objective, for I did not create them; I merely inherited them through my education . . . Similarly, the church-member finds the beliefs and practices of his religious life ready-made at birth; their existence prior to his own implies their existence outside of himself . . . Here, then, are ways of acting, thinking, and feeling that present the noteworthy property of existing outside the individual consciousness.
>
> These types of conduct or thought are not only external to the individual but are, moreover, *endowed with coercive power, by virtue of which they impose themselves upon him, independent of his individual will* . . . (Italics added)[10]

What Durkheim calls coercive power is habit formation when it determines ways of living; it is endocracy when it determines oughtness.

Social forces impinge upon the individual not only consciously but also unconsciously. The individual often feels that he is free in making his decisions and in choosing courses of action. Actually, his freedom is reduced by the effect of these two psychological phenomena: habit formation and endocracy. The anthropologist Leslie White has emphasized that the cultural determinants of human behavior often act without the individual's being aware of them. He wrote:

> The unconscious character of the operation of culture in the lives of men can be demonstrated in many particular instances as well as in a general way. The determinants of ethical behavior—why, for example, one should not play cards on Sunday —lie in the external cultural tradition. The individual, however,

unaware of either the source or the purpose of the taboo, locates it in his inner self: his conscience is but the screen upon which the unconscious factors of society and culture project themselves.[11]

White is undoubtedly correct, but he too, like Durkheim, does not make a clear distinction between habit formation and endocracy.

The eliciting of endocracy is not restricted to great institutions, to religion, state, political party, or to great leaders. In the private life of many individuals certain persons have such power. Spouses, lovers, gang leaders, shamanlike individuals often have endocratic effect. The coercive capacity of these individuals is such that they are often thought of as possessing hypnotic power, persuasive strength, charisma, unconscious threatening ability, prophetic qualities, a sense of mission, a mystical spell, sex appeal, etc. These compelling people may even lead their followers to commit crimes, as Charles Manson did with the girls and boys who murdered the actress Sharon Tate and several others.

THE GOOD ASPECTS OF ENDOCRACY

Let us remember, however, that endocracy is useful in evolution and in the development of the individual, and is useful whenever it is connected with a good principle of action. It is generally good when it is connected with reason and logic.

But reason and logic are not enough when a great deal is demanded of the individual. Habit formation is also not enough because people drop habits, even if slowly, when they clearly lose adaptational value. Obligation rather than habit formation, and inner mandate rather than external command, have been more effective in guiding the individual through the tortuous paths of life.

Evolution perpetuated this mechanism of endocracy, which was useful in spite of its many and tragic shortcomings. We must also realize that man would learn endlessly and aimlessly unless society and its leaders tell him that certain things have priority over others. The things which have priority assume, like people, an imperative attitude. From the tribe to the organization of the modern state a patrimony of learning, imposed by imperative attitudes, has taken place which has made possible our complex social life.

Education and reason are feeble means of achieving desirable ends unless they are accompanied by other strong motivations. Endocracy is one of the strongest. If men did not have a sense of endocratic oughtness, they would behave like little children or like psychopaths. They would want immediate results, immediate satisfaction of their desires. They would not be able to dedicate their efforts to what they were not concerned with at present. "Après moi le déluge." "If the brook has already passed beyond my land, I don't care if its water becomes turbid." In other words, they could not act now for an end not immediately achievable. They would have no sense of *commitment*. Thus endocracy gives to the will not only the dimension of oughtness, but also of commitment.

Animals do not have endocracy. They have to rely on other motivational forces, which are even stronger. Inasmuch as we too are animals, we share these stronger and simpler motivational forces, which have to do with immediate survival and procreation. Hunger, thirst, sexual desire, need for a certain temperature range are very strong indeed. Nothing less powerful would have saved the animal kingdom. Let us assume, for the sake of argument, that at a human level nature had reversed the usual sequence of events and that sexual intercourse would be as painful as childbirth, and childbirth as pleasant for both parents as intercourse is. Nothing could be more disastrous for human survival. How many women would be willing to undergo an excruciating pain today for the sake of a pleasure to be experienced nine months afterwards? How many would be so committed to the preservation of the human race? A sense of commitment so strong as to take the place of present sexual pleasure would require the most tyrannical endocratic power.

Morality is generally not as strong as these instincts and physiological functions, but in general adds an effective motivation to the weak force of reason. If you are not disposed to do something because it is logical to do it, at least do it because you must. When it is not a question of survival and procreation, but of organization of men into groups and societies, imperative attitudes and endocracy are needed to maintain cohesion, stability, and regularity. Later these imperatives and inner mandates become a code of moral behavior to be applied to people of the same group. The prophets of the Old Testament and the evangelists of the Gospels advocated endocracy linked with good principles of action as a code of morality to be applied to all of humanity. This ideal has never been reached. Certainly there is reason to be discouraged when we think not only of the occasional criminals but especially of the great criminal leaders who throughout history have inflicted brutality and suffering on humankind.

We must not, however, let discouragement overpower us. Humanity has survived in spite of these errors and horrors. Positive endocracy has won. Even in periods of brutality the countless little good deeds of people have been able to overcome the tide on a global scale. Criminals and psychopaths have always been in a small minority, and the wicked and infamous leaders have been defeated by the soul of Mr. Nobody. The meek have won. I believe that this is the meaning to be given to that passage of the New Testament which states that the meek shall inherit the earth. It is the meek, endowed with positive endocracy, that make human survival possible. It is the meek who will prove wrong the dictum *homo homini lupus* ("man is a wolf to man").

PSYCHOANALYTIC INTERPRETATION OF THE MORAL SENSE

It may be useful at this point to reexamine the psychoanalytic view of morality.

Classical Freudian psychoanalysis has enlarged our understanding of this issue by interpreting morality as the introjection of external authority. This concept is extremely useful, but does not include some major facts.

In *Totem and Taboo* Freud explained his views. According to him, in the primitive clan as it existed in the early stages of humanity, the sons murdered their fathers in order to take possession of their wives. The murder was followed by remorse and identification with the father. The sons were held together by a feeling of loyalty based on their complicity in the primal crime. Although the necessities of the social group made morality useful, it was the expiation of the guilt connected with murdering the father that, according to Freud, gave origin to morality. Many anthropologists have disputed Freud's account of the primal crime. But even if the events took place as Freud described, conscience and morality must have existed before the crime. Otherwise the sons would not have been able to experience guilt and the need for expiation.

Later, Freud did not stress these early anthropological theories and based morality on introjection from the environment. The external authority of the father or father substitutes is transformed into inner authority. The aggressive attitude of the punishing father is incorporated and the child punishes himself. But the child also experiences some retaliatory aggression toward the father. Since he feels guilty about this aggression, he again turns this aggression, originally directed toward the father, toward himself. Thus, the strict superego which causes tension and guilt is the result of a double dose of introjected aggression.

In many psychoneuroses the superego is excessively severe. Psychoanalytic treatment can decrease its severity by eliminating the infantile wishes which mobilize the superego. Psychoanalysis does not, however, advocate that the ego should replace the superego. Freud did not say "Where superego was, ego should be," but limited himself to saying, "Where id was, ego should be."

Orthodox psychoanalysis has not been helpful in explaining other facets of oughtness. It is obvious that authoritarian rules are not introjected in the usual learning process. Introjection of the command presupposes the presence of such conditions as a climate of basic trust, symbolic reward and punishment, imperative attitude, and endocracy.

Neo-Freudians have been no more helpful than Freudians in explaining ethics. Fromm distinguishes "authoritarian" consciousness from "humanistic." The former is the internalized external authority—the parents and the state—and corresponds to the Freudian superego. The latter is not "the internalized voice of an authority whom we are eager to please and afraid of displeasing; it is our own voice, present in every human being and independent of external rewards and sanctions." [12] Humanistic conscience is "the expression of our true selves." It helps us to develop fully; that is, "to realize ourselves, to become what we potentially are." The "true self" is an ideal and not well defined in Fromm's theory. If listening to our true self implies a sense of oughtness, the result may be doubtful because we do not know that what we shall hear will be good instead of evil. The real or true self seems to be not what it is, but what it ought to be. Oughtness somehow enters the picture again. Hitler, too, may have felt that he was listening to an inner dictate coming from his real self when he was committing barbarous acts for the "greatness" of the Third Reich.

Like Maslow and Horney, Fromm seems to believe that the

highest ethic is the one which leads to self-realization. This point of view is fallacious on many grounds: firstly, there is really no preordained, specifiable potential in man which has to be realized. Man is indefinite and capable of unpredictable growth because of the multitude of possible encounters with different systems of symbols and concepts. As I have illustrated in greater detail in *The Intrapsychic Self*, man must aim at continuous growth or self-expansion, but not at a mythical realization of an assumed potential.[13]

Secondly, the feeling of "self-realization" is very deceptive as a subjective experience. Reading Mussolini's writings one thinks that, like Hitler, he was sure he was "realizing himself and his own destiny."

Thirdly and most importantly, self-realization leaves out the actual problem of ethics, the moral relation to others. Humanitarian ethics become a form of hedonism. Self-fulfillment is not an ethical aim. Certainly what Fromm and other authors mean by it may be a legitimate aspiration. However, when self-fulfillment is pursued, it is not on ethical grounds but for personal gratification. To remain ethically justifiable, it must not interfere with ethical principles. We certainly should aspire to our psychological growth and happiness provided they do not infringe upon the rights of others.

Karen Horney wrote in a similar fashion about listening to the real self and gratifying the real self. She also stressed the so-called "tyranny of the shoulds": we impose on ourselves codes of behavior or levels of aspiration that we cannot fulfill because they are too high. Thus we are bound to be disappointed and frustrated. We should give up the idea of satisfying unrealistic ambitions caused by a neurotic motivation to attain glory.[14] Whereas for Freud our neurotic secret wishes are infantile and mostly sexual in origin, for Horney they come from our attempt to be what we cannot be, to live in accordance with a grandiose image of ourselves that we have neurotically built. Freud and Horney correctly illustrated various types and various sources of wishes and aspirations. But while Freud never said we should do without superego, Horney seems to imply that we should live "without the shoulds." This position is never clearly stated by Horney and perhaps I misrepresent her. Reading her writings, however, one thinks that the non-neurotic style of life is reached when we do things because we wish to do them, not because we feel we should do them. Certainly it is much easier to do things when we wish to do them, but in life there is always a surplus of things that we have to do irrespective of our wishes. Again it is utopian to believe that we could eliminate duty altogether as a motivation. And yet many people are so afraid of endocracy that they *would* like to eliminate duty entirely. On the one hand, the chains of strict endocracy may certainly cripple man's will and immobilize it completely. On the other hand, complete absence of the shoulds or endocracy would not solidify man's will, and he would be left vulnerable to his wishes and to the immediate seduction by the environment.[15]

CHAPTER 6

Pinocchian, Alienated, and Newly Committed Youth

THE REVOLT OF THE PEERS

ACCORDING TO THE TALE, PINOCCHIO FUMBLED HIS WAY INTO trouble three times, and each time because of his associations with peers.

The first trouble was when Pinocchio went to see a puppet show, and was a member of the audience. The puppets performing on the stage recognized him as a brother puppet while he was sitting among people of flesh and blood. They stopped working and in a state of sudden excitement and irrepressible joy greeted him triumphantly, disrupting the show. The puppeteer, who, like all impresarios, believed the show must go on under any circumstances, was very angry at Pinocchio for causing that fracas and threatened to use the puppet as wood for his fireplace.

The second trouble occurred when Pinocchio met two unpleasant characters, the cat and the fox, and instead of listening to the talking cricket (the representative of his conscience) he immediately made them his friends. They made him believe that he would find a way to become rich without working, so that they could cheat him.

The third trouble occurred when, instead of trying to become a real boy as the Fairy with the Blue Hair had admonished him to do, Pinocchio joined his friend Lucignolo in a trip to the country of toys. In that country children were not required to go to school; life consisted of one amusement after another; no duties, but only games and play. Unfortunately, in that country children were gradually being transformed into donkeys. The story, like an ancient myth, repeats the theme of how easy it is to be persuaded by contemporaries, schoolmates, peers of any kind, to succumb to immediate pleasure and to avoid commitment.

If it is hard to resist one's wish, it is even harder to do so when your equals entice you to take the easy road. Were you to resist, not only would you feel deprived, but you would also feel alone, odd, isolated, ostracized. The sweetness of the enticement is added to the pleasantness of gratification.

There is a diversity and an increase in responsibility in the three instances reported in *Pinocchio*. In the first instance those who want not to work but to be merry are fellow puppets. The story is touching. The puppets recognize in the audience a brother puppet, a peer, and want to celebrate the momentous event in an act of spontaneous comradeship and solidarity.

In the second case the situation is more involved. The enticers are not just peers, and they are not motivated by brotherly solidarity. They have criminal tendencies. They remind us of those people who convince others that there is a way to make big money fast. These unscrupulous characters actually want to cheat the others of the little money they have.

In the third instance, a peer, Lucignolo, induces Pinocchio to go where other children have chosen to go: to the country of toys, where happiness is within one's grasp and school abolished; but also where the children lose their human status. They are literally transformed into donkeys. The story shows how hedonism in its deepest degrees brings about decadence and finally a purely animal-like status.

If Collodi were alive today he would hesitate to write a book like *Pinocchio*. In fact, Collodi was preaching obedience to his young listeners, but the term "obedience" has become a cursed word today. To be obedient means to accept the endocratic yoke, to submit to parental tyranny.

Do I imply that the youth of today, the peers who rebel, are like Pinocchio and his friends? Not at all; such coarse categorizing would be absurd. When the aim of youth is—as we shall see in the later part of this chapter—to decrease excessive endocracy, to challenge conformity and petrified principles, to resist some but not all repercussions of scientific expansion, we must welcome them and see in them signs of more advanced development. We must see in them the founders of a movement with a new commitment.

On the other hand, we must distinguish a second group of young people who are not only uncommitted but are also in an unnatural state of estrangement called alienation. And there is a third group that forms what I call the "Pinocchian subculture." Its members are those who unleash the id, abandon the road to maturity, disregard education, and take easy trips to artificial toy-counters which ultimately lead to dehumanization.

Many authors confuse these three categories, and the confusion is made easy by the fact that some young people present mixtures of traits of two or all three of these categories. Nevertheless, it seems to me that we must separate these groups. If we are to find hope and salvation in the new generations we must be able to make these fundamental distinctions.

To confuse these three categories has disastrous consequences, as the worst may be confused with the best; the innovator may be mistaken for a regressing, decaying person. It is true that in some cases regression and innovation are mixed together to produce creativity; but this fact should not bind us to the recognition of actual or potential abnormality.

Roszak, who has deeply studied today's young generation, in his recent book has confused these three categories.[1] A distinguished and lucid author who did not make this confusion is Keniston.[2] Although I differ from Keniston on one or two points, I consider his contributions very significant. Keniston has directed his studies to the groups of alienated and to the newly committed, but not to the Pinocchians, to whom he refers only in passing and calls impulsive.

Throughout history generations of young peers have been in revolt. Even if Freud's description in *Totem and Taboo* of sons rebelling against the father is not historically correct, he has created a psychological model which represents the perennial conflict between generations, in the manner of a myth. Focusing on sexual problems, Freud limited the scope of his myth by fitting it to the theoretical frame of the Oedipus complex. The sons rebelled because they were sexually repressed. We have seen in Chapter 4 that Marcuse added a socioeconomic interpretation to this myth. In our own time the revolt against the fathers is to be included in the vast revolt against the Establishment.

THE PINOCCHIANS AND THE PROBLEM OF SCIENCE IN OUR DAY

One of the basic tenets of the Pinocchian philosophy can be summarized in two short sentences: "Be. Do not become." In other words, spend your time in being and enjoying the way you are now, and not in trying to become something else tomorrow. Live to the fullest possible extent now; expand your awareness and your pleasure. Whoever tells you to direct your life in accordance with what your future demands of you is to be distrusted. Living for the future is like saving money in the bank. You live less today, you die a little bit today, saving for a possible adulthood and old age when, depleted of vital energy, you will no longer be able to savor the pleasures of the flesh. The reader will remember that some of these statements are similar to those we considered in Chapter 4.

In this chapter we have to reconsider some of the same issues from the point of view of the group or subculture which I call Pinocchian. The subculture teaches "not to wait." Why wait until you are an adult to have fun? Why struggle for a career, the full benefits of which will be available to you only in your declining, decrepit years? Thoughts of tomorrow dilute the beauty, intimacy, and intensity of the act of love. In these situations we must be fully involved with the present moment.

But intense involvement with the present does not imply that we should give up "becoming" altogether. As a matter of fact, it is mainly in the process of becoming that our human nature distinguishes itself from that of animals. A cat, a dog, a horse change very little throughout their lives. They, too, are affected by the course of life and grow old, but these changes are very limited in comparison to those of human beings. Animals have practically no symbolic functions and therefore must remain within the limits of what is immediately offered to their senses. Relatively speaking, their psychological growth through life is very small from youth to death. They are as they are; they do not become.

Man, on the other hand, is always becoming because he is

constantly affected by a universe of symbols. Today he is somewhat different from the way he was yesterday, and tomorrow he will be different from the way he is today. He listens, reads, learns; he observes daily events which are personal or collective, private or public, scientific or experiential, practical or theoretical, rational or irrational, moral or immoral. There is no definite end to the possible growth of man.

The reader remembers that in Chapter 2 we described the importance of the temporal dimension in the development of the will. No mature will is possible without the ability to postpone. Only an ability to overrule the present makes us capable of making choices and of "becoming." *Giving up becoming means returning to an immature stage of will.*

A second characteristic of the Pinocchian subculture is the desire to enjoy the material objects (cars, color television, motorcycles, etc.) produced by technology, and at the same time to have a very strong antischolastic and antiscientific attitude. To put it differently, the Pinocchians hate science but crave scientific products. This attitude of the Pinocchians gives us an opportunity here to reevaluate the role of science in our society.

Undoubtedly science has some aspects which are dangerous when and if they are applied indiscriminately to human life. One of them is actually what the Pinocchians like about science, the technology that fills the world with material things which give pleasure. Our economic system exploits these technological advances in order to increase manufacturers' profits. The aim is to transform every consumer into a Pinocchian, to make merchandise irresistible to him. At times it is impossible to distinguish between a Pinocchian and a hardworking man who believes he is entitled to an air conditioner, a color television, an electric toothbrush, a new car every two years. In such cases consumerism replaces all other values. Obviously, the trouble is not in science *per se* but in those social factors which allow science to degenerate into consumerism.

Some authors, like Roszak, see in science the roots of many other evils. They condemn science totally and by so doing reinforce the general antiscientific attitude of many youngsters who would like to burn the books of scientific knowledge.

It is necessary to stress the difference between being an actual evil and being a possible evil. Scientific knowledge and control of nature do not necessarily lead to evil results. They may lead to the conquest of polio as well as to the construction of gas chambers, to man landing on the moon or to the dropping of the bomb on Hiroshima. Whether scientific methodology will be used for good or evil is determined not by science itself but by the use men (scientists and nonscientists alike) make of it.

In our twentieth century reason and science have been used on the side of evil, and results such as penicillin, polio vaccine, and reaching the moon are pale in comparison to such catastrophes as two world wars, the murder of six million Jews by the Germans, and the use of the atom bomb. What was at fault in these cases was not science itself, but the way science was used. Somebody could say that although technology offers an increasing number of opportunities for good and evil, the balance always will fall on the side of evil. In fact, if science opens destructive possibilities, somebody will avail himself of those possibilities sooner or later, and the effect will be felt by the whole world.

Again, the bad use of science cannot be attributed to science itself or to scientists. When Pasteur gave the world the new science of bacteriology, he intended to help his fellow human beings from diseases which had reached at times epidemic proportions. He never thought that the findings of bacteriology would one day be used for germ warfare. The many physicists whose work in previous generations led to enormous progress in their field did not think that their discoveries would eventually produce the atomic bomb. Science increases the range of human action. It increases the range of a Pasteur, a Salk, a Schweitzer, a Barnard, as well as that of a Hitler and a Stalin. It also increases the range of action of the multitudes who may follow somebody like Pasteur or like Stalin. In a system of freedom and moral values science is likely to benefit mankind. In a system of tyranny and exploitation science is likely to oppress.

Scientific innovations bring about unpredictable social consequences. New technical apparatus creates new forces which cannot be arrested. No matter how much we understand what we have done in the past, there is always an irreducible element of uncertainty in future applications. At the beginning of the industrial revolution nobody conceived the possibility of global pollution. And nobody now knows whether traveling to the moon will be dedicated to the benefit of mankind or to its destruction. These doubts are justified, but we cannot deal with them by wanting to abolish science. Science and its advances are here to stay. Being against science is like being against sex. It is an attempt to solve a problem merely by suppression or unsuccessful repression.

· Science is said to cause a special mentality which is not desirable. If influenced preponderantly by science, the individual would come to appreciate efficiency exclusively and to disregard the subjective and private aspects of himself as well as other values. This criticism is valid only when acceptance of science has led to an exclusive commitment to a scientific world view. Much of American education has been seriously at fault in teaching scientific subjects almost exclusively and neglecting the humanities.

The scientific methods of analyzing and quantifying are valuable when they are applied to scientific areas. When they are applied to the whole life of the individual and statistics reign supreme, individualism is lost and depersonalization occurs. Those qualities of life that are not reducible to the rigor or exactitude of science are allowed to wither.

As a scholastic discipline, science leads to these extremes *only if* separated by other cultural forces and *only if* it appropriates to itself the roles which belong to other fields. In other words, the *progress* of science must be recognized as progress; but it should not be accompanied by a *regress* of the humanities. For several decades in many American colleges education has been so disproportionately scientific that it is no wonder that many people have tended to become technicians, technocrats, and slaves of technocracy. The opposite should have occurred. Emphasis on science should have been paralleled by a stress on humanities. The objectifying caused by science reaches an extreme and harmful degree unless compensated by a reverence for the individual. The more scientifically oriented the education, the greater is the need for reaffirming the ethical and aesthetic values of the individual.

With apparent plausibility somebody could retort that there is no time in the curriculum for both scientific and humanistic education. Educators must indeed reorganize and revitalize the course of studies and determine what is expendable and what is of lasting value for the whole man and not just for his future profession. A person with a Ph.D. in a scientific field is not likely to become a technocrat or a technician if he has come to know Isaiah, Homer, Sophocles, Shakespeare, Giotto, Bach. Among the great scientists were Leonardo da Vinci, a painter, and

Goethe, a poet. Science alone does not encompass the human spirit.

The forced separation of science from the humanities is not only unnecessary, it is the cause of a disastrous dichotomy. History teaches us that disastrous dichotomies have occurred when important cultural forces have been allowed to depart from each other and even assume irreconcilable positions. For instance, for many centuries the Judaeo-Christian influence was in opposition to Greek culture. In the early Christian era these two cultural currents spread apart; then in the West the Judaeo-Christian subjugated the Greek. Whatever appeared Greek in spirit was destroyed, repressed, or suppressed for approximately one thousand years in Western Europe. In the separation of these two cultural forces we can recognize one of the major causes of that turbulent era of regression, the European Middle Ages. Only at the time of the Renaissance could the two major branches of Western civilization merge and lead to what is glorious in the modern world.

The reasons the growth of science has been accompanied by a regrettable decrease in the cultivation of humanities are not to be found in questions of time, curriculum, feasibility, etc., but in socioeconomic conditions and the rise of certain ideologies. I have already mentioned the economic factors which have to do with industrialism and commercialism.

One modern antihumanistic ideology goes back to Auguste Comte (1798–1857). This French philosopher believed that human thought and knowledge passed through three stages: the theological, the metaphysical, and the scientific. Comte thought that the highest society is one founded on only the third or positivistic stage. Comte introduced the new science of sociology. According to him, the passing of the theological and metaphysical stages was not merely to be witnessed, but accelerated.

Comte's influence has been enormous, although it has not been equally strong throughout the century or so since his death. In spite of Comte's great contribution in his battle against obscurantism and in his creation of the new science of sociology, we must recognize that his positivistic approach has been adopted by some to an extreme and dangerous degree.[3]

In fairness we must add that if some aspects of science have a negative potential, some others, among the collateral ones not often mentioned, have positive potential. As dangerous as is a culture based on the objectivity of science, more dangerous still is a culture which completely eliminates objectivity and relies on extreme subjectivity and violent passions. A culture dominated by violent passions and primitive motivations creates such occurrences as the Armenian genocide.

Science also accelerates the process of "demythologizing," which, in a nonscientific society, is extremely slow. Many ideas and principles of action which, as we have seen in Chapter 5, we accept and introject with disastrous results, are unmasked and eventually displaced by the findings of science. Moreover, science brings about a climate of change which is a great antidote to the stagnation of old ideas and to the petrification of traditional ideals.

Science has an additional inherent value. Involuntarily, but nevertheless profoundly, *science has unified mankind more than any religion, philosophy, law, or power have so far done.* Science discovers laws that are valid for the aborigine of Australia as well as for the Harvard professor, for the starving children of the underdeveloped world and for the lady of leisure of Park Avenue, for a Hitler and for a Francis of Assisi. Although science has learned that space is larger than we ever imagined, the cosmos has also become smaller because it is now more accessible to man in imaginative terms as well as physical. Earth is now the size of a nutshell in cosmic space, and we all have to live in it together. Our ideologies, religions, philosophies, and credos seem parochial in comparison to the universality of man expressed by science. When these systems of thought advocate the universality of man they can collaborate with science; when they lead to political-religious-philosophical parochialism, they work against science. When they are examined separately, their meaning seems ridiculously petty in comparison to that of the newly acquired universality of man. Who is now ready to fight and die for them? Who is now ready to be killed for the possession of the nutshell?

It seems to me that the important conclusion to be reached from this discussion is that science and technology, like everything else pertaining to man, are not value-free, as some people contend. By the obvious fact that they are necessarily connected with human action, they must and do have either a positive or a negative value. When science and technology aspire to a value-free state, they are value-negative and will lead to the deformation or alienation of the self, as we shall see in another section of this chapter.

As an antidote to the supremacy of science and technocracy, Roszak advocates a return to *shamanism*. Actually, in their vain attempt to obtain quick results and knowledge effortlessly, the Pinocchians do resort to shamanism, as well as to astrology, palmistry, and cultisms of various kinds.

Shamanism is a primitive form of religion. A high priest, the shaman, is supposed to have supernatural gifts which make him not only a medicine man but a prophet and a leader. Communication with the spirits is a common practice and is supposed to be achieved by beating drums. States of possession and trances are elicited through rituals. The trance is a sleeplike state of altered consciousness and dissociation, also characterized by reduced sensitivity to stimuli, marked decrease of awareness and understanding of what is happening, and abolition or decrease of voluntary activity. The person has the feeling of being possessed by, or under the control of, an alien spirit, a dead person, a deity, a shaman, or an enemy shaman. Voluntary behavior is replaced by automatic behavior or by behavior imposed by the will of whoever possesses the individual. The explanation often given is that the soul of the individual is absent or has been stolen and has been replaced by the spirit who possesses him. Shamanism requires special susceptibility on the part of the individual who falls under its power. The majority of people, however, seem to be susceptible if raised in an environment which has made them receptive to these procedures.

These phenomena thus are not only psychological in nature but sociocultural as well. The work of Erika Bourguignon [4] reveals that possession and trance states are very common in many parts of the world, such as Siberia, Central and South America, Africa, Liberia, India, Alaska, Greenland, etc.

It is hard to imagine how a practice or institution which requires giving up one's will can be recommended. Going under the domination of an alien is not an act of liberation. Moreover, as we have already mentioned in Chapter 5, shamanism, psychic possession, and trance, uncontrolled by normal adult thinking, may easily lead to exploitation and even to induced murder.

The only type of trance which modern Western medicine has accepted is hypnosis, introduced by Mesmer. Hypnosis consists of an induced trance or altered state of consciousness during which the subject automatically and uncritically carries out the suggestions of the hypnotist. In medical hypnosis the purpose is to carry out an action or a function which in a normal state of consciousness could not be fulfilled: the revelation of a forgotten memory, the stopping of smoking, etc. The hypnotist loses importance, as he becomes only an instrument for the implementation of the therapeutic task.

At any rate, even if it were correct, as Roszak advocates, that science should be devalued and shamanism installed in Western culture, he seems to indulge in a *non sequitur* when he recommends that society should empower *only* young people to implement these changes. Firstly, we must be sure that there is no predominance of Pinocchians among the reformists. Secondly, the problem of age has to be more fully understood.

All societies and cultures age and die unless they undergo modifications and periodic renewals. The changes have to be proposed and implemented by persons of great vision and courage, irrespective of their age. Keats wrote his best poems at an extremely young age, and Einstein was less than twenty-five when he advanced the theory of relativity. On the other hand, Socrates and Galileo were of advanced age when they rose against the Establishment. If the young dissenters are people with great vision, let us learn from them; if they are Pinocchians, let us not be influenced by them.

Roszak benevolently accepts all the young dissenters and calls them "centaurs"; that is, half-horses. But Collodi, in the wise symbolism of the tale, tells us that Pinocchians become not half-horses but full donkeys. Roszak tells us that "the young, miserably educated as they are, bring with them almost nothing but healthy instincts." He relies, apparently, only on the healthy instincts and not on reason and learning. It is true that we are still half-barbarians, but we would be complete barbarians without something in us which comes from Abraham, Moses, Buddha, Isaiah, Homer, Plato, Sophocles, Jesus, Francis of Assisi, Kant, Spinoza, Rousseau, and many others.

A total rejection of culture (no school, but a country of toys!)—"the Great Refusal" as Roszak calls it—would send us back to primitive times. Undoubtedly there are *many* things that we should refuse in our culture, but let us not put our whole cultural heritage into one wastebasket.

Roszak seems also on the side of the Pinocchians in their condemnation of parents. Parents are not evaluated in a psychiatric context, as possible originators of psychodynamic conflicts, but considered responsible as adults for the evil contained in the culture. Such accusations may be correct in some cases, as with the generation of Germans who legally elected Hitler when free elections were still possible, and who later permitted his atrocities. But many youngsters today condemn their parents as if

they were the founders of the culture and not just its trans-
mitters. Along with parents they condemn great men, too, for
having failed to purge complicated and imperfect man of his
barbaric side. Barbarism must indeed be removed, but not by
going to the country of toys or by following the cat and the
fox, as Pinocchio did. We shall see later how the newly com-
mited youngsters deal with these great issues.

In 1954 William Golding's *Lord of the Flies* received immediate popularity and retained it for more than ten years. This
book was called "a parable of our times." It was more than a
parable. Written in the early fifties it was a prophecy of what
would happen in some places in the sixties. Marooned on a
desert island, two groups of children govern themselves. The
bad group, whose members were characterized by immature
instinctual and aggressive behavior, gains supremacy and brings
about moral decay, pain, death. In the absence of adults the
forces of the id take over, in all their virulence. The two good
boys, Ralph and Piggy, who symbolize maturity and intellectu-
ality, are eventually destroyed by the unrepressed aggressivity
of the Pinocchian group. Suffering soon prevails on the island
until adults suddenly and unexpectedly reappear and restore the
forces of morality and reason.

The book was an enormous success, with several million
copies sold. Part of the pleasure the book gave was a vicarious
gratification in reading about the wildness of the group "liberated from the forces of reason and morality." Its greatest interest, however, lay in Golding's unfolding of the decay that this
"liberation" brought about. The book seemed to convince the
reader that this "liberation" was not to be welcomed at all, but
avoided. And what a sense of relief when, at the end of the
book, adults land on the island and bring real liberation from
anarchy, chaos, death, and despair. I wonder whether the book
would have had equal success on campuses had it been published in the late sixties, when the craving for id-liberation became stronger and stronger.

The youngsters of today who believe only in being and not in
becoming want to intensify their being. They live for an expansion of awareness or intensification of the senses. This is the
principle on which they justify their use of drugs. Some traditional drugs like heroin and morphine become addictive in a
very short time. The individual loses his ability to resist the
craving for the drug. The will is thus impaired, even if the
cognitive functions remain intact. Other, newer drugs, like

mescaline and especially LSD, produce a widening of experience; but unless taken in minimal amounts they also produce damage to the nervous system. What a price to pay for the widening of experience! The experience, moreover, although at times beautiful, is illusory and does not produce growth. What remains is only the memory of the pleasant (and sometimes horrifying) experience. The person who has taken LSD may believe he is reaching God, or the absolute, or platonic universals. For instance, a patient of mine told me that while he was under the influence of LSD he drove to the shore of a lake. He did not know the name of the lake, but he said to himself, "This is Lake"; in other words, that lake had become the real lake, the universal lake, and a specific name was no longer necessary. Again, the patient looked at a tree, whose botanical name he did not know, and said to himself, "This is Tree." What he saw appeared to him as universal reality.

If such experiences were not illusory and would add in a constructive way to the life of the person, it would be a marvelous event. But the experience of reaching the absolute *is* illusory and similar to the experiences of delusional schizophrenic patients who, with complete certitude, believe they have attained knowledge or intuition of the absolute truth. Once the individual is over the effect of the LSD trip, he returns to the modest world of particulars. But the worst occurs when he does not return to this modest world. A not unsubstantial number of LSD users develop psychoses, which are difficult to treat.

The only controversial issue in this field concerns marijuana: whether it is really dangerous and whether its use should be legalized. Many researchers have reached opposite conclusions, some affirming that it is a harmless drug, others insisting that it produces psychological damage. Part of the controversy about marijuana stems from the fact that it is legally but wrongly classified as a "narcotic" producing physical addiction. Marijuana is not a narcotic and does not produce physical addiction unless it is mixed with different drugs.

Marijuana, however, presents some dangers. If used in excess, it does produce a kind of dependence: the person who stops taking it after excessive use feels depressed or apathetic, unwilling to attend to his work, less willing to face the unavoidable anxieties that life presents. Vagabondage and inactivity are promoted. An additional danger consists in its users' not finding it completely satisfactory or strong enough, which may lead them to use more dangerous drugs. Many psychiatrists have recognized that the use of marijuana is particularly inadvisable in adolescents.

This insatiable hunger for the purely sensuous, for physical and material pleasure, is not an exclusively youthful phenomenon. It has roots in the life of decadence that some of the adults of today have transmitted to the new generation, so well represented in Federico Fellini's film *La Dolce Vita*. This film was remarkable not only because of its aesthetic value but also as a portrayal of the life style of certain segments of society. It depicted an absurd life characterized by easy enjoyment and absence of any orientation to the future. Fellini's characters were adults or young adults, and the social classes involved were predominantly the aristocracy and the plutocracy. But their disciples are the Pinocchians of today, who want to emulate their elders without waiting. In the words of a disturbed adolescent, "If you can make love already at thirteen, why wait?"

There are other groups of young people who join the Pinocchian subculture although they do not belong to it. These people have always existed. They are the chronically antagonistic. It does not matter whether they are against their parents, the government, society, school, their neighbors, their coworkers. They are always against somebody or something. It is by fighting, arguing, or being against that they feel alive and able to hide their emptiness or their difficulties. Either an antagonistic character disorder, or rigidity of thinking, or a false search for absolute standards, or paranoid attitudes, or in some cases even a latent or manifest paranoid psychosis places these people against whatever is accepted by the majority. The origin of these difficulties as a rule is found in abnormal relations within the family.

It is not in the group of the Pinocchians that we must find hope and inspiration for a solution to the problems of our society. On the other hand, we should not simply condemn these people. We must recognize that their craving for an easy life hides a deep uneasiness, and their craving for immediate comfort hides an inner and more important discomfort. We must find out why they have become the way they are and why they are more numerous today than when Pinocchio was written. We shall attempt to do so in this chapter, after we have examined the other two major groups of dissenting young people.

THE OLD AND THE NEW ALIENATIONS

The alienated constitute a second group of young people who are not in a state of harmony with their elders. Much has been written about them. Kenneth Keniston has probably given us the best book on the subject.[5] He rightly feels that psychology alone cannot explain the condition of those who estrange themselves from society, and that sociological factors are very important. The unfairness of our economic system, the disillusionment with all utopias, and especially the supremacy of technology over all of life are for Keniston what lead to alienation. The alienated young person, whom he calls "the new Ishmael," has to be understood in Keniston's terms as the agent of his own alienation; he chooses to be alienated because for him it would be too difficult to be at one with society. The natural relation of one person to others is replaced by rejection. At times it is the individual who rejects society, while at other times it is society which excludes the individual. Whatever the cause, the result is generally "uncommitment." But can a life find fulfillment in alienation and without commitment?

Alienation is a word with different meanings. Marx used it in reference to the worker who, separated from the means of production which belong to the capitalist, becomes emotionally disconnected from his own work. In psychiatry alienation at first meant "estrangement from the world of reality"; that is, insanity. The insane (generally the schizophrenic) was the alienated, and the psychiatrist was called the alienist. This type of psychiatric alienation will not be considered in this chapter. More recently in psychiatry and psychology alienation has come to mean disconnection of a part of the self (or of the psyche) from the rest of it. The self does not feel or undergo experiences as it should. A part of the self is dissociated, and remains a foreign body. In different language we could say that in alienation there is a mutilation of the soul (or of the psyche). The alienated individual has to live with this mutilated self.

There are three types of this alienation. In the first type, the part of the self which is mutilated, or not experienced as fully alive and sensitive, is the part that makes us relate to others. Thus the alienated person is the withdrawn individual, the schizoid, the introverted, the aloof or detached person. A second type of alienation, described by Horney, the early Fromm, and by some novelists, like Camus in *The Stranger*, consists of disconnection from one's own feelings in spite of the facts that there is no .insanity and that the behavior of the person is apparently not grossly abnormal. There is a third type that I want to describe, one which, although not yet fully reported in the psychiatric literature, has become very common.

In this type, the part of the psyche which is in contact with the external environment is very efficient. Thus the individual does not seem alienated at all. He makes thousands of contacts, has many acquaintances, and is aware of myriad stimulations. He seems to experience all that the environment offers and to want to experience more. But the part that he does not experience (or which has undergone some mutilation) is his *inner self, his inner life.* In other writings I have described in detail the origin and development of this inner life.[6] From approximately the ninth month of life the child retains mental representations of external objects, events, relations, and the feelings which are associated with these psychological events. The inner self is the result of a constant reorganization of past and present experiences. Its development is never completed throughout the life of man, although its greatest rate of growth occurs in childhood and adolescence. It is based on the fact that perceptions, thoughts, feelings, and other psychological functions do not cease to exist completely once they have occurred, but remain in the psyche, where they are constantly reelaborated. They do not remain as they were experienced but as components of the inner life.

Inner life represents, substitutes, distorts, enriches, and impoverishes the reality of the external world. Although it has many exchanges with the environment, it has an enduring life of its own. It becomes the essence of the individual. But the person who suffers from the new type of alienation is not in contact with this part of his psyche. Instead of being in touch with himself, he is in contact only with the external world.

In this new alienation the inner conflicts are neither acknowledged nor even denied. Inwardness is frowned upon, as if it would be the enemy of relatedness, cooperation, human friendliness, solidarity, and feelings for others. To be called an introvert is an offense. The journey homeward to the self is seen as a detachment from the world and not as a source of life, inspiration, or as an entrée into a universe of personal values and depth. Extension replaces profundity. To meditate on one's inner problems or resources is considered strange. The thing to do is to plunge oneself into what is immediately offered by the mass media, the habits of others, and especially one's peers. One must be in contact, react, respond. Let the environment affect you but not penetrate you; bathe in it. Rather than learning to build yourself through acquisition of concepts and values, you learn the superficial forms of behavior to deal with the habits of others and adapt to the always changing environment. The inadequacy of the inner self will predispose the individual to stress that part of the psyche which deals with the external world. A vicious circle is thus established. Whatever still urges the individual to recapture the inner self is promptly dismissed as neurotic. For instance, any sense of guilt is labeled "neurotic guilt."

Other authors have also observed this new form of alienation, but have described and interpreted it differently. Marcuse describes it in *One-Dimensional Man.*[7] Twenty-five years ago Riesman gave a scholarly report of what he called the other-directed personality.[8] Extreme degrees of other-directedness, in my opinion, are abnormal conditions and constitute the new form of alienation. In Riesman's conception the other-directed person takes peers as models, not the older generations. But in the advanced forms of the third type of alienation even the peers are not lasting agents of stimulation. The individual becomes immediacy-directed, or directed by circumstances. If the young man loses a girl friend, he easily replaces her with another. The role, the function, is more important than the person; dependency on external sources reaches extreme degrees. A Saturday night without a date or a weekend without companionship is a tragedy, intolerable to endure. Rather than recapture the inner self the individual seeks artificial means to find what he senses he is lacking. The profundity which other people find in thought, he vainly searches for in the intensification of sensuousness; he uses drugs, or psychedelically colored garments, and he immerses himself in an electronic world. *Responding* becomes for him even more important than *conforming*.

This person has great difficulty in finding a suitable self-image. He has not learned long-range ideals and goals. He is incapable of orienting his life toward the distant future. He cannot borrow sustenance for the present from any faith in the future. When he recognizes that his self is empty, or unidentifiable, or unacceptable even to himself, he may collapse. In some serious cases schizophrenia results. In other serious cases depression follows.[9]

How are these three types of alienation to be interpreted? What causes them? Psychologists and psychoanalysts (for instance, Guntrip) [10] have interpreted the first two types as a flight from life based on weakness of the ego, and on deep-seated fears originated in infancy. We have seen that Keniston gives great importance to social factors, especially in those cases (the majority) which do not reach extreme psychiatric proportions.

In my opinion the third group of alienated people occur in greater number in a social climate characterized by technology, consumerism, and especially the electronic world described by McLuhan. These people are under what Keniston calls "the dictatorship of the ego," or "hypertrophy of the ego." They have to train their ego to accept and cope with the heavy demands of reality, especially to the constant pace of continual change. The ego has to overexert itself to the detriment of the other parts of the psyche. Many skills have to be learned, and the person will end by identifying or defining himself in terms of his ego, not of his whole personality. I prefer to say that the ego of these alienated people is not hypertrophied or overdeveloped but has become deformed or warped. In some respects it may even be underdeveloped.

Another cause of all the types of alienation, according to Keniston, is the decline of utopianism which has occurred in our time. The great ideals, or the concerns for something bigger than ourselves, for something which will promote or actualize human betterment on a large scale, are now considered myths and no longer cherished. New ideals exist but have short prospects.

Some people think that the young are relativists and do not believe in absolutes any more. Einstein's theory of relativity, pertinent in science, has mistakenly been applied to human life. If everything is relative, nothing is valuable enough to become an ideal. Now many old ideals, in fact, had to be debunked. The trouble does not lie in their demise, but in the fact that they have not been replaced by others. Moreover, even if we believe that absolutes are no longer recognizable as such, we are not justified in assuming that total relativism is the logical alternative. Some ideals may still be valuable for our times or our life. Society has not yet been able to find an acceptable or authentic "relative relativism."

Certain philosophical and psychological trends also contributed to the creation of an intellectual climate conducive to alienation of the third type. A philosophy of life based on empiricism and operationalism tends to give importance almost exclusively to what comes from the external environment. Only what comes from the external environment can be subjected to a set of operations or experiments which permit verification. Most of what comes from the inner life is debunked as non-operational.

The strongest apostle of operationalism, Bridgman,[11] advocated that all "concepts of which we cannot give an adequate account in terms of operations" be no longer used as tools in our thinking. Unfortunately society has followed only too well Bridgman's teaching!

According to Von Bertalanffy [12] some of the new schools of psychology are partially responsible for having perpetrated a form of functional "decerebralization or menticide." They have adopted a positivistic, mechanistic, and reductionistic approach which can be called the *robot model of man*. There is no doubt that academic psychology shares some responsibility in this externalization of the psyche, and has thus contributed to some extent to this third form of alienation. Whether the focus has been on Pavlovian conditioned reflexes, on the principles of reinforcement, or on aversion therapy and Skinnerian machines, the main concern has been on the part of the self which is in contact with the external world. In addition, those currents in psychoanalysis which concern themselves exclusively with environmental factors and do not include intrapsychic functions do not help to combat this new form of alienation.

THE NEWLY COMMITTED

Many young people today are not given to immediate pleasure like the Pinocchians, nor do they settle for an impoverished life. They are the ones whom Keniston calls "the committed"; they are those on whom Charles Reich relies for the "greening of America."

According to Keniston these newly committed young people "have developed a sense of inner identity; have demonstrated a capacity to work, love, and play; have a commitment to their Movement; have a sense of solidarity with others; feel joined to a radical tradition; and they have more of an ideology in the broad sense than do most adults in America." [13]

I wish to add that these young people are engaged in fighting excessive endocracy and in challenging conformity and petrified principles. They warn against those results of science which, by being wrongly applied, contribute to a total objectification of life, consumerism, and loss of basic values. They are against preferential status, unjust wars, and gigantic power structures which subordinate the individual. They think that laws should not protect vested interests but have moral aims and enhance the satisfaction of human needs. They want to fill the gap between law and justice, between what is professed and what is practiced.

These young people easily recognize that some old valid principles are retained, but in forms which are almost caricatures of the original. "To be free" has become equivalent to be free to own a refrigerator, a car, a television set, etc. To live better in a material sense has become the ideal of the masses. The rise in the standard of living does not seem a worthwhile achievement to many youths unless the individual has also more time and inclination to pursue spiritual ideals. It is worthwhile to conquer technology, provided technology does not conquer us. There is nothing wrong in possessing many things, provided we are not possessed by them. If we allow material goods to replace spiritual goods, we regress, but our regress is masked as progress. Life as a whole becomes a masquerade.

THE CAUSES OF YOUTH'S UNREST

Why have so many young people joined the band of the Pinocchians, the group of the alienated, the movement of the new commitment? On the other hand, is it true that already in the early seventies their number is decreasing?

The various forms of alienation seem relatively easy to understand. In the old types, early intrafamilial psychodynamics played a fundamental role. When something goes very wrong in the early relations with one's parents, the individual grows up with an excessive burden of fear. He becomes alienated in order to withdraw from the adverse psychological environment.

Keniston has tried to understand why some young people become radicals or newly committed. He critically examines what he calls "two inadequate hypotheses." The first hypothesis argues that "the position of today's young radicals reflects a violent rebellion against and hatred of all male, parental, and societal authority." The radical would place the responsibility for the conflicts in his family on society. According to the second view —"the red diaper baby hypothesis"—young radicals come largely from politically radical families, and since early childhood have been exposed to radical ideas about social reform and political action.

Keniston points out the inadequacy of these two hypotheses. Both "overlook the actual complexity of radicals' development, and both posit either a total break with the past or total acceptance of it, which rarely occurs in human life." I have already discussed in this chapter the causes of the third alienation, which, in my opinion, is becoming more frequent.

There are some common conditions that seem to have predisposed young people to join either the Pinocchian or the newly committed groups. This apparently common origin is disconcerting since we must discourage the occurrence of one group and encourage the other. In both groups many parents seem to have been confused in their parental roles. Uncertainty and confusion are, of course, understandable in a period of transition. These parents were afraid to adopt the methods of their own parents and felt uneasy about new ones. Being afraid of making mistakes or of asserting themselves, they maintained a distance or detachment from their children which predisposed them either to a Pinocchian or to an avant-garde position. In some families of radicals, a tradition of liberalism was transmitted in spite of the emotional distance between the generations.

When we try to understand the behavior of large groups of people, we must find explanations based at least partially on sociocultural conditions. These conditions may not manifest their effects immediately but will sometimes do so even after a delay of a whole generation. Some people have attributed the Pinocchian phenomenon to the consciousness of living in the atomic era. Tomorrow we may all be blown up; let us live in joy and merriment today! The verses of Lorenzo de' Medici, called the Magnificent, acquire particular poignancy in our days: "Let him be glad who will be. There is no certainty in tomorrow."

I do not agree with this interpretation. From my dealing with many young people, especially those who were in psychoanalytic treatment, I have become convinced that the awareness that the world may blow up at any minute is not a vital part of their psychological makeup, either consciously or unconsciously. As a matter of fact, I believe that a more realistic concern with this possibility would be more appropriate and would confer a deeper grasp of the relevant issues of our times. But most people, and especially the young, think of this possibility as merely theoretical, as an improbable event which is not going to happen. Some readers may believe that this attitude of unconcern is only on the surface and that at a deeper level, perhaps unconsciously, there is a concern with this terrible reality. I must repeat that in my deep analysis of many young people, especially Pinocchians, there is no such unconscious preoccupation. Why such an astonishing denial of reality is possible is too vast a question to be discussed in this book.

That some major disturbances began at the same time might seem to indicate some historical event was their catalyst. Student rebellion and radicalism have occurred increasingly since 1964. To interpret them as a protest against the Vietnam war is contradicted by the fact that these revolts have occurred also in West Germany, France, Italy, and other countries not involved in the war. It seems also unlikely that even such a disturbing event as the assassination of John Kennedy in November 1963 could induce masses of young people to revolt, althought it deeply shook their conscience.

Also, to attribute the readiness to revolt to the sad state of the world does not seem convincing. Firstly, the unpleasant state of the world and the capacity or willingness to revolt, although related, are different phenomena and do not always go together. The world is indeed in a sad state, but history teaches that it has always or almost always been in this state or even a worse one. Wars, massacres, oppressions, injustices have recurred almost without interruption.

In what follows I shall discuss two different factors which seem to me responsible for the readiness of young people to revolt in either a Pinocchian or new-commitment form: the first consists in the increased intolerance of people to adverse conditions; the second consists in the psychological preparation for confrontation.

Greater intolerance for whatever is unpleasant has many causes. People living today have been protected from pain much more than previous generations. Medicine has indulged and kept people from pain in thousands of ways, from the use of aspirin to anesthesia for surgical operations. Also, progress on a sociopolitical level makes people more intolerant. People used to tolerate child labor and even slavery. When oppression and injustice diminish, the ability to fight against remnants of oppression and injustice increases. For instance, a completely subjugated minority will not have the possibility of revolting on a large scale. If the minority is to some extent emancipated, it will be easier for its members to fight for their complete liberation.

Young people also believe that material scarcity is no longer necessary in the world. Satisfaction of any desire now seems a possibility and therefore want of any kind is not to be tolerated. Victory against poverty, illness, brevity of life, and long work hours, and the production of large masses of goods seem to many youngsters past achievements. The possibility of gratifying desires in a general sense appeals equally to the Pinocchians and to the new committed. The young intellectuals see in it an end to unpleasant competition. The Pinocchians see in it the opportunity for complete id satisfaction.

The second factor which makes it easier for young people today to initiate and implement confrontation is found in predominantly psychological phenomena. The youngsters who are involved in confrontation come from middle-class families which have adopted new systems of education. Educators like John Dewey and Maria Montessori, psychoanalysts of the Freudian and neo-Freudian schools, and pediatricians like Benjamin Spock have all advocated a regime which does not use traditional strict discipline. Both in the family and in school they have recommended liberalism, which often has been allowed to change into permissiveness. After the Second World War many American parents, through the inaccuracies of intermediate popularizers, have misunderstood Dewey, Freud, and Montessori and have allowed themselves to be of little or uncertain guidance to their children. In some schools progressive methods of education have been wrongly applied and have degenerated into a "blackboard jungle."

In defense of parents and educators we could say that it was difficult to adopt new ways and replace the old ones which had a tradition of thousands of years. It was easy to go too far in a way which Dewey, Freud, and Montessori never intended. The pedagogues who were influenced by psychoanalysis stressed only the avoidance of unnecessary anxiety, frustration, and harsh discipline. Montessori, Dewey, and other leaders in the field of education intended to increase the power of motivation and to stress freedom and individualism. Misinterpretations and exaggerations resulted in confusing the parental role. Endocracy was viewed as a yoke, but in reality the "yoke" became so light that it could be easily thrown off. The overthrow of endocracy favors the production of either Pinocchian or newly committed youth. In other words, it may facilitate either weakening or strengthening of the will.

What can we do to prevent the first outcome and to favor the second? The analysis of some social phenomena, which we shall examine in the next chapter, may help us in this difficult problem. Here we have to bring up, however, another point we have already referred to. Dissenting young people, no matter to what group they belong, seem already to be declining in number since the late sixties. Many people welcome this decline; others are alarmed.

Is this decline actually taking place? It could be that the obvious characteristics of these groups have altered or been dropped, but that the seeds for social change that some of these groups have planted continue to grow in a less visible manner. Many historical movements which have taken three steps forward, in a second phase took two steps backward.

The newly committed youth are gradually dissociating themselves from the Pinocchians and the alienated and have become an even smaller minority, still in search of a mass following and of ideological syntheses.

CHAPTER 7

Endocratic Surplus
and Other Adverse
Sociopsychological
Factors

BREAKING TRADITIONS

MANY PEOPLE CALL THE STUDENTS WHO REBEL ON VARIOUS CAM-
puses in America and Europe iconoclasts. Labeling them this
way implies that they only destroy old icons or idols but do not
offer anything new to replace what is destroyed. It is not a
minor accomplishment to remove what is archaic, fossilized,
obsolete, absurd in our times, and maintained only by the
inertia of unchallenged traditions. We have seen in Chapter 5
that not only persons, but also ideas, institutions, and traditions
engender endocracy in the psyche of the individual. Their
validity and sometimes even their sacred origin are often taken
for granted. Fallacious ideas and obsolete institutions become so
ingrained that only two categories of people are able to eradicate them from our system: great innovators or revolutionaries
or people raised with less endocracy.

Geniuses have always been very few: a handful in the whole
world for each generation. We cannot blame the dissenting stu-

dents for not having many of them in their ranks. I am not even referring to men like Michelangelo, Shakespeare, and Galileo, but to a different category of greatness that includes people like Rousseau, Luther, and Pope John XXIII, who dared to change the established order of life.

As an example, let us examine Pope John XXIII. He advanced a doctrine of the brotherhood of men of all faiths and an attitude toward the Jews in particular which stood in sharp contrast to the Roman Catholic Church's official position. His attitude ultimately produced the declaration of the Vatican Ecumenical Council of October 15, 1965, which deplored antisemitism and declared that the crucifixion of Jesus Christ "cannot be attributed to all Jews, without distinction, then alive, nor the Jews of today." It is important to remember that for many centuries Jews have been killed because they were thought to have been related by blood to those who had condemned Jesus Christ. During Easter Jews were frequently the object of violence by enraged crowds, whose hostility was excited by the reenacting of the Passion of Jesus Christ.

Although John XXIII had already died when the declaration of the Ecumenical Council was made, he must be considered its real author. In a series of actions he tried to change rapidly the attitude of the church toward the Jews and to prepare the ground for the declaration. In March 1959, in the church of Saint Mary in Jerusalem, in Rome, the Good Friday prayer was read in his presence for the first time omitting the word *"perfidi Judaei"* ("perfidious Jews"). Pope John was in contact with the famous French historian Jules Isaac, who wrote *Jésus et Israel*, and he asked Cardinal Boa to study the book. He also requested that those lines of Matthew, according to which the responsibility for the blood of Jesus must fall on Jews and on their children, be omitted from any prayer. Pope John also organized a Secretariat to study the relations of Catholics toward non-Christians and, especially, Jews.

Let us take another look at the historical declaration of the Ecumenical Council. It says that the crucifixion of Jesus Christ "cannot be attributed to all Jews, without distinction, then alive, nor to the Jews of today." This is the same as saying that no Greeks living today, nor all Greeks living in 399 B.C., were responsible for the trial and execution of Socrates. And it is the same as saying that no Italians living today, nor all the Italians living in 1498, were responsible for the trial and execution by burning of Girolamo Savonarola. In other words, these three statements present not only truths, but truisms, something which not just the man in the street, but a man with less than average intelligence could understand. Do I then believe that Pope John XXIII had no merit? On the contrary; it is my profound conviction that John XXIII was a great man. His greatness did not consist in discovering something new, but in being able to take the first necessary steps toward removing the endocratic power of a myth which was transmitted for almost two thousand years, and caused discrimination, persecution, and great suffering for many innocent victims.

It is true that John XXIII was helped by circumstances; his merit remains great nevertheless. His virtue lay in the fact that his heart and determination were stronger in him than the endocratic tradition of the church. To show how strong this endocratic yoke was, it is enough to mention that when the declaration of the Ecumenical Council was finally made, it was not approved unanimously. Fourteen percent of the bishops voted against it.

This example that I have reported in detail shows that unusually great or unusually courageous men are needed to eradicate the endocratic power of absurd myths and false beliefs. But if we rely on these great men to free society of myths and dismantle fossilized traditions, we are in very bad shape indeed, and history will continue to proceed at a snail's pace. These men are very few; moreover, they must be born at the right time and place and be located, by an unusual combination of chances, in a social position which permits them to affect the world. We also need many people, not necessarily great men, willing to struggle against myths and social injustices. These are the people without a heavy endocratic yoke, like the newly committed youth of today. Let us remember that removing institutional endocracy is like moving mountains. That is why people have resorted to revolutions for this purpose. Although some revolutions can be historically understood, they have generally caused disasters. In terms of suffering, death, and violence, they are very expensive ways to correct the errors of history. But today a way to correct these errors is becoming more common and more effective: confrontation, unrelenting and continual (what in Europe is generally called "contestation").

Confrontation is much more likely to occur when endocracy has already been diminished. If the young people who protested in the late sixties had not been raised in an atmosphere of reduced endocracy, they would not have been ready for confrontation. If we evaluate these newly committed youth in this new frame of reference, we are able to recognize their full historical significance.

THE ENDOCRATIC SURPLUS AND ITS PREVENTION

We have seen in Chapter 5 that a certain amount of endocracy is necessary, for without it we become Pinocchians or, as we shall see in Chapter 10, psychopaths. What has to be eliminated is what I call *endocratic surplus*. Endocratic surplus occurs when authorities, traditions, laws, principles, and mores are internalized not because of their intrinsic worth, but solely because of their imperativeness. Endocratic surplus is incompatible with free will. It is this surplus which cripples the will of man by making him subservient, submissive, conformist, unwilling to change or even try unfamiliar paths, and therefore obligating him to become stereotyped and uncreative. At a sociocultural level the endocratic surplus slows progress and keeps moribund systems alive. I wish to clarify that although the word "surplus" is often connected with Marx and Marxian theory, in the present context it has nothing to do with Marx: it is a psychological and not an economic concept.

What can be done to eliminate not endocracy, but endocratic surplus? The task is not easy, as shown by the fact that society has failed in this respect most of the time. Here I shall offer some preliminary suggestions.

1. Parents should not exert endocratic power on their children when the latter have reached an age which permits them to understand what is discussed. Except in very early childhood parents should give advice, not orders; and even when they give advice, they should explain the reason behind it in terms that the child is able to understand. When parents are psychologically introjected, they should be as givers of love and enlightment, not as controllers of will. In other words, what I advocate is decreasing the comprehension-action gap—the gap between the principle of action and the suggested action itself. We have seen in Chapter 4 that this gap is a large one when children are very young and cannot understand. With increasing age, the gap should decrease. The child and the adolescent should not be told, "Do so-and-so because I told you so," or "Do so-and-so because the book says it is the right way," but that this action leads to good results from a moral or practical

point of view. The child will learn thus to see authority as flexible and based on rationality.

2. The motivation for the action involved must be based on reason. It must come from the goodness associated with the action and not from endocratic power. Of course, this formulation is unclear because it presupposes that we know what is good. But a tyrant, or anyone, may convince himself that his action, prompted by his wishes, is a good one when instead it is evil. Nevertheless, even without a clear definition of what is good, most people, *unless victims of endocratic surplus,* are able to evaluate whether an action is really desirable or is only being made to appear so.

3. A constant reevaluation and challenge of known principles of action should take place. For instance, a principle followed for many thousands of years is that it is proper to kill your enemy in war. Is this position compatible with the inalienable rights of a member of our species? If it be granted that one has to defend himself from enemies, should not a civilized humanity devise defenses which do not require taking the life of a fellow human being? International organizations should develop humane defenses.

4. Without the accumulated learning which comes from the experiences of previous generations, culture would not be possible. The experience of the past, however, should not be transmitted in the immutable form of commands but in the changing form of education. Moreover, the older person, the expert, and the individual who learns from a book should recognize that any situation is different in a new set of circumstances. The difference should be taken into account, too, when the old principle is suggested.

The reason the concept of "authority" brings about an unpleasant resonance to many newly committed young people lies in the fact that this term is connected or identified with power, external or endocratic. The word "authority" is generally used to connote legal or rightful power, the right to command or to act. "Authority" comes from the Latin *auctoritas,* which, in its turn, is a derivative of *auctor. Auctor* means "author," a word which derives from the verb *augere* (to make things grow, to increase, to produce). "Authority" should mean "capacity to make others grow by sharing knowledge." The genuine authorities are those who share their knowledge with other human beings who did not have the opportunity or the ability to acquire this knowledge or wisdom.

The person with genuine authority is authoritative, not author-itarian. He does not have the power to enforce actions or to intimidate other people into making special choices. By impart-ing knowledge or understanding to others he increases, not decreases, their range of action. The person with genuine au-thority may indicate what he believes is the best choice, but the final decision remains with the individual who acts. The individual must choose for himself and not be constrained by fear of punishment from authority or its internalization.

Authority thus ceases to be rational or irrational. Whereas until now authority was considered irrational when commanding an action which was connected with a bad principle, now au-thority is deprived of the power to command actions at all. Genuine authority becomes always powerless in this sense but always rational since it has the ability to instruct and "make grow."

In our times, however, people, and especially the young, have become frightened of anything resembling authority because they automatically react to the old concepts. Often even good advice imparted to a young person is considered an imposition, pressuring him into a certain course of action. Weak and neuro-tic persons are prone to feel this way. In psychoanalytic prac-tice we often hear young daughters-in-law who resent advice from mothers-in-law as intrusions into the private life of the young couple. It is true that autocratic mothers-in-law some-times disguise as advice what is meant to be proof of their greater wisdom and experience in life. But in many cases the advice is sincere. Nevertheless, the insecure daughter-in-law in-terprets it as a command which, instead of increasing the range of choices, will restrict it to only one: her mother-in-law's.

The advice is experienced as charged with such endocratic power that it can be resisted only with great effort. The daughter-in-law resents having to make this effort and therefore considers the mother-in-law an intruder, an invader, a domineer-ing old woman. Were the daughter-in-law able to experience the advice only as advice, resentment would not occur.

Until a few generations ago paternal advice had endocratic power in making some decisions—selecting a wife, an occupa-tion, a career. In Western countries the selection of a spouse in accordance with parental wishes has gradually become less common and in the last two or three generations a real rarity. Choosing a profession or trade in agreement with one's father's wishes was the rule before the industrial revolution. It was assumed that the agricultural or artisan father would educate his sons in his work. In some environments children were mainly sources of labor for their fathers.[1] In most of Western society the father has lost this function. He is no longer recognized as the expert and, consequently, has lost his position of authority. Even today, though, there are a few families which experience a sense of professional tradition as strongly endocratic. The sons must follow their fathers and grandfathers and be bankers, lawyers, physicians, industrialists, etc. Changing the family pattern, however, is no longer seen as an unforgivable sin.

CULTURAL AUTHORITY AND HISTORY

Not only living persons and institutions, but culture in general and history in particular, elicit surplus endocracy and are therefore under attack from the members of the new commitment.

Even more than in modern times, cultural endocracy prevailed in the Middle Ages. *"Ipse dixit"* ("He himself said so"), teachers would say as final proof in reference especially to Aristotle, but also to other great men like Thomas Aquinas. And the students had to accept what the great masters had said. Needless to say, neither Aristotle nor the other thinkers who became endocratic authorities ever wanted to be in that position. Whereas a critical attitude would have permitted the student to distinguish their valid doctrines from those which could not pass the test of time, the endocracy attached to their names required and imposed a total acceptance.

What happened is that the forces of the Establishment—church, monarchy, state, army, etc.—incorporated all the tenets of these great men, rigidly enforced them, and enhanced their internalization. In other words, they used these tenets to consolidate their power. External power, as we have already seen and as we shall see more fully in Chapter 9, often seeks reinforcement from endocratic power. The confrontation that has recently taken place is not really against culture, history, or even tradition, but against endocratic surplus engendered by them. I refuse to believe that even the most extreme radicals want to eliminate culture in its totality. Without it the human being would return to an animal-like state. I refuse to believe that even extremists would want to renounce Homer, Plato, Sophocles, Dante, Shakespeare, Michelangelo, Galileo, Newton, Beethoven, Pasteur, and similar men. The vociferous or militant minority who would like to burn the books, as the Nazis did, do not belong to the newly committed but to the Pinocchians, who want to quit school and go to the country of toys. I have already mentioned in Chapter 6 the effect of the rejection of the classical culture at the beginning of the Christian era. Religious people, with their prejudice against everything from pagan times, joined forces with the barbarians in destroying the classic world and helped to bring about the Middle Ages. After approximately a thousand years, the Renaissance rediscovered the classical world.

On the other hand, there is no doubt that cultural endocratic surplus is also damaging. It is the force which fights a Galileo or a Darwin, is against contraceptive pills and most kinds of innovation.

As an example of endocratic surplus, I shall discuss the teaching of history, a subject which is taught to every student, and which is important in shaping the personality of the student and his identity as a citizen. Let us examine some of the criticisms often made.

Is the study of the past relevant to the here and now? The proof of its relevancy must come from those who believe in it. History seems to prove that history is irrelevant. Has history in the past really led to a better understanding of humanity? Has it modified human life in such a way as to prevent evil? What good has it done to study history if in our own times we had a Hitler, a Stalin, a Hiroshima? The old Latin saying, *historia magistra vitae* ("history, teacher of life"), has not proved its validity. Although it is true that a certain progress has been made since the time men were cannibals, the progress has been too little and too slow. And yet such great thinkers as Thucydides, Tacitus, and Machiavelli, and, in our time, Jaspers, have insisted that history has much to teach. I believe that the study of the past is indeed very important and relevant to the issues of today. I think, however, that changes must be made in the teaching of history to make it really useful. In most schools history has been more a sanctification of the past than a quest for truth. Teachers of history have transmitted cultural slants of which they themselves were not aware. In many countries an elite of thinkers has apotheosized national character and national destiny and has rewritten history in accordance with their basic premise. What they wrote was always an account and interpretation of facts and events which justified their ideology. According to Plumb [2] John Foxe (1516–87) rewrote English history to see in it the great work of Christian salvation. Hegel (1770–1831) saw greatness in German history. Vincenzo Gioberti (1802–52) saw the primacy of Italy among all the nations of the world, and Giuseppe Mazzini (1805–72) saw in Italian history proof of the religious mission of the Italian people.

History has not been rewritten only by those who had an ideology to sponsor. History has been rewritten many times to minimize or to softpedal all the atrocities which have been committed by men. What the crusaders did to the non-Christians, the Catholics to the Huguenots, the Turks to the Armenians, the Germans to the Jews, although reported in history books, is generally minimized.

History is almost a constant series of barbaric acts perpetrated by men on men, from prehistoric times to our days. The times of relative peace are like oases in a great desert of ferocious brutality. The books of history do not reveal the full extent of these barbaric acts, either "to protect" young readers from psychological traumas or because they are not deemed the most important facts in the context. But what could be more important than to reveal man's major recurring crimes in order to increase the desire and the ability to prevent their recurrence? I believe that the real reasons historians or, to be more exact, teachers of history, conveniently forget the full extent of these atrocities is to protect from utter shame and dishonor either some specific groups of men or the human race as a whole. These teachers unconsciously or half-consciously succumb to the social and psychological pressure of the Establishment, which wants them to ignore (or psychologically deny) the events which incriminate some basic institutions.

History should portray events as they occurred. I realize that objective history is impossible because historians have biases of which they are not conscious. But every effort should be made to unveil the unconscious prejudices, and every conscious reworking should be eliminated. When history becomes a thesis, an ideology, it acquires great endocratic power. It is absorbed by men who will continue to support the historical biases which they have introjected. Not only the triumphs of men, but also the horrors and the barbarous acts should be reported. If the unpleasant facts are reported, incorporation of false values will be more difficult. An unedited history will be less likely to strengthen a decaying establishment. It will make us less liable to succumb to nationalism and chauvinism. It will make it easier for us to transcend the parochialism of our own culture and will put us in a better position to see the universality of man. These remarks do not imply that we should not have a feeling of love and solidarity for the group to which we belong. But our group, political or ethnic, should be seen as part of a harmonious variegated humanity, not as one of the contending forces in a bloody arena.

Some philosophers and historians, like Hegel, Spengler, and Toynbee, saw history as having a natural outcome, as an unfolding process, or as a representative of divine will. For Kant history is the progressive actualizing of right; for Hegel reason rules the world and history must therefore unfold rationally. Of course, it is not clear why Hegel believes that this universal reason should select Prussia to rule the world. Special pleading and attempts to hide personal, national, or class interests can be recognized even in the theories of these great authors. The people of the new commitment, be they young students or persons my own age, are rightly disturbed by these attempts.

Explanation should not be confused with justification. Historical events should be justified when they deserve to be; but most of written history is inadequate and inexcusable. Furthermore, there are some historians and great thinkers, like Benedetto Croce, who believe that history should not be approached or evaluated from a moral point of view. History is the study of facts, and transcends moral considerations. In other words, if I understand Croce's view, history should be studied as a natural science; for instance, as biological evolution is studied. According to him, every historical event produces subsequent events and therefore should not be condemned. I cannot agree with this point of view. Whenever the will of man enters, moral issues enter.

When we study evolution and learn, for example, how horses have changed in size and bone structure through evolutionary stages, we pass no moral judgment. Only when man appears on earth are moral judgments possible. Even the history of horses changes, since men have used them for work, transportation, and in the practice of war. How is it possible to study the history of Nero, Hitler, or Stalin without passing moral judgment? A detached attitude would be artificial and harmful. Ultimately all the theories which argue against moral judgments of history conclude by justifying history and help to endocratize history. The role of the will of man should be restored to its proper place in history.

Another important fact has disturbed people of the new commitment. The historian and history teacher stress the importance of emperors, popes, kings, and despots in the shaping of human life. But does this representation really show how the obscure peasant, the merchant, the artisan, the housewife, the serf, and the billions of unknown people were involved in the drama of history? Neither possibility (that their participation was not noted, or that they did not participate at all) is going to be relished by the newly committed.

Finally, an additional point which has disenchanted some students from studying history has to be mentioned. History has become in some places knowledge of what is archaic or unimportant. I do not want to be misunderstood on this point. If someone wants to do research about a forgotten dynasty which reigned in Tibet or Ethiopia or over Indian tribes thousands of years ago, he should be allowed to do it. There should always be room for the antiquarians of history; but if they are teachers, they should not impose their hobbies on multitudes of students.

History, as a subject, has also failed to show adequately to the student that periods of great human progress and human regress have almost always been caused by sociocultural factors, prominent among them the presence or absence of endocratic surplus. Has history adequately answered such questions as what kind of human beings are likely to live in a given society at a given historical time? Has this society or that historical era supported or undermined human fulfillment?

As a biological entity man can be considered a constant. The Greeks were as biologically fit before and after the period of Greek splendor as they were during that period. Italians were biologically the same before and after the Renaissance.

The reader must by now be aware of the major point made so far in this chapter, in contrast to what was discussed in Chapter 4. There we pointed out how primitive impulses, especially aggression but also uncontrolled sexuality, may prevent the exercise of mature will and lead to impulsive action. Here we point out that systems of ideas, when allowed to acquire endocratic power, may also cause great suffering and distort the will.

The examples that we have given may give the impression that only social, political, and religious ideas may delay progress. It is not so. Even science has been delayed by endocratic surplus. Generally it is assumed that science unfolds according to an undisturbed rhythm. For instance, an Einstein presupposes a Newton, a Newton presupposes a Galileo, a Galileo presupposes a Euclid, and so on. This is true. The length of intervals, like the one between Euclid and Galileo, however, requires a different kind of explanation: it is to be ascribed to the endocratic power of the prevailing culture. Galileo himself was almost totally silenced by the tyranny of his cultural milieu.

In 1952 [3] I attempted to demonstrate that there were no scientific prerequisites which made it possible for psychoanalysis to appear on the world scene only at the end of the nineteenth century. A man like Freud could have made the same discoveries twenty-three centuries earlier. The delay in the onset of psychoanalysis was determined only by the endocratic power of certain sociocultural forces. In general medicine, similar telling examples are available. Galenic medicine dominated the medical schools for twelve centuries, long after physicians of various countries should have realized its ineffectiveness. Society owes it to a courageous rebel (and still-controversial figure), Paracelsus, that the obsolete books of Galen were eliminated from medical education. Paracelsus lived from 1493 to 1541. The medical profession had to wait for his appearance to be told the simple fact that blind subservience to traditional authority should be removed and nature should be observed directly.

In fields other than medicine, delays caused by the endocratic power of tradition have continued to occur. When a Galileo or a Darwin makes a revolutionary discovery which subverts basic beliefs about man's nature and destiny, a delay of at least half a century is not uncommon before public acceptance is obtained.

Anthropology teaches us that we share with primitive men not only the capacity for error but the capacity to internalize and endocratize error. For instance, Cro-Magnon men, who lived about 70,000 years ago, attributed to a certain red powder the function of blood and therefore the capacity to make people live. They used to sprinkle the bodies of dead relatives with ochre in the hope that the red color would restore them to life. It seems from different excavations that this practice persisted for at least 20,000 years, long after everyone should have been convinced of its futility.

CAN FALSE VALUES BE VALUABLE?

Some say that false values are better than no values or a scarcity of values. This statement may seem obviously absurd, but it requires some consideration. Firstly, we have seen that people with little internalization of values may develop the third type of alienation, consisting of extreme contact with the external world and loss of touch with oneself. Secondly, as we shall see in Chapter 10, those without values tend to become psychopaths more frequently than others. Thirdly, some historians remind us that false values, like the confusion of military ambitions with great patriotism of the ancient Romans, led to the diffusion of Greek civilization, which was a good thing. Vico, Jung, and Fromm have tried to demonstrate that myths, too, have positive values. Some anthropologists teach us that even magic has a beneficial effect in a primitive society inasmuch as it gives hope to people and satisfies their need for knowledge.

Although false values and false knowledge occasionally lead to good outcomes, we cannot and should not count on this possibility; it is too risky. We know of many instances where false values led to a great deal of suffering. For instance, when values are founded on myths, we are on shaky ground. Some myths had a definite beneficial influence, for they extolled virtues, renewed hope, and stimulated men to help the community. But we have also seen that some myths, like that of the deicide, have inflicted tremendous suffering. If a myth has a potentiality for good effects, its potential goodness can be transmitted in different, less risky ways; for instance, in artistic-literary forms, not as historical testimony.

If I have belabored the effects of false values and false ideas, it was to counteract views expressed in some psychoanalytic circles. There the view is held that it is naive to attribute to myths, ideas, systems of thought, and ideologies the cause of war, barbarism, suffering, etc. There is in man an innate need to hate, to be aggressive, to hurt, and to overpower which is the cause of these unpleasant events. In other words, the thanatos instinct is there, and myths, ideologies, etc., are only pretexts for the discharge of the instinctual drives. This theory is misleading. Certainly the human being is endowed by nature with the capacity to be aggressive, enraged, and harmful. This capacity, shared with other animals, should be actualized only when the need for it emerges. In a civilized environment this need should seldom occur; it is, instead, artificially created by ideas and endocratic systems which promote hate and aggression. No need ever exists for murdering millions of people.

Some may see other dangers in abandoning old values, cultural mores, and habits of living. The change may be too rapid and may subject the human psyche to undue stress. After all, there is a certain security in sticking to our beliefs, in considering them eternal truths or absolute principles, in relying on what we have learned, in not having to look at the world afresh, and in not having to cope with new and complex situations. If the teacher who first imparted such values and principles to us had "imperativeness" and charisma, it will be even more difficult to relinquish his values.

Change becomes increasingly difficult with advancing age. Many who in youth were progressive and liberal tend to become conservative, set in their ways, and at times even dogmatic and opinionated as have age. Most will not admit that their ability for absorbing the new is diminished. They prefer to believe that age has increased their wisdom and ability to appreciate the old values. But the individual has to make a constant effort to remain open to the new. Unless he is ever vigilant, sooner or later he will succumb to the endocratic power of the old. Obviously he should not embrace the new just because it is new, for this tendency, too, may be a poorly disguised form of conformism.

If it is difficult to remain open to the new, how will the human being manage in the future where he will encounter a rapid flux of new things? Will he be able to endure it? Will he succumb to mental illness? Are not these risks worse than surplus endocracy? Would we have to resort to artificial methods like operant conditioning, brainwashing, brain implants, and computer psychotherapy?

These problems are very important and cannot be disregarded. They are too new to permit us to have a solution for them. Hopefully, the mental energy now required by endocratic surplus will be diverted to the new demands and challenges.

OTHER ADVERSE SOCIOPSYCHOLOGICAL FACTORS

Endocratic surplus is not the only sociopsychological factor which affects the psyche adversely. In recapitulation I shall review here the other two, described in this book, which reduce greatly our margin of free will. *Primitivization* consists of all the mechanisms and habits which foster the primitive functions of the psyche at the expense of higher level functions. Prominent among these mechanisms are decontrol of the sexual and aggressive drives, craving for immediate satisfaction, and return

to magic and shamanism. Primitivization on a grand scale seldom occurs in isolation. Not only is the effect of the mob
very important, but primitivization is also generally promoted
by the other two sociopsychological factors. For instance, massacres of millions of people would not have been likely to occur
without the concomitant effect of endocratic surplus (incorporation of false ideologies and leadership). The disinhibition of
sexuality on a grand scale has also been helped by the teaching of some well-known thinkers, as we have seen in Chapter
4. The Pinocchian craving for immediate satisfaction of worldly
pleasure is enhanced by deformation of the self.

The adverse sociopsychological factor which I have called
deformation of the self and Keniston has called "dictatorship of
the ego" has increased tremendously in the last fifteen years.
The application of the scientific model to all aspects of life, the
actual reduction of people's feelings and ideas into numbers,
mass production and consumerism—all have brought about a
gradual but steady deformation of the self. This social attitude
is often disguised under the name of democratic laissez faire.
A competitive frame of reference, masked as free enterprise,
leads to contempt for the losers. Begin better than your neigh-
bor replaces the ethic of brotherhood. Manipulated or persuaded in hidden ways, the individual acquires the habit of
reacting, not acting. His will becomes atrophied while he retains
the illusion of freedom. Reaction is confused with spontaneity,
promiscuity with romance, intrusion into one's privacy with
sincerity and comradeship. The self is deformed and tends to be
alienated, and addictive drugs are used to combat alienation.
When the "ups" or the "trip pills" are used, an attempt is made
to escape deformation through primitivization. When the "down"
pills are used, alienation is supplemented by increased passivity
and false contentment.

If we try to interpret these three adverse sociopsychological
factors in reference to Freudian terminology, we can say that
primitivization expands the id at the expense of the other parts
of the psyche; deformation of the self warps the ego; and endocratic surplus overburdens and distorts the superego. Freud, of
course, was aware of the importance of society on the individual's psyche, but was not aware of the three mechanisms described in this book. He felt that society acted predominantly
by summoning the service of the superego for the repression of
the id. Thus for Freud the superego was an ally of society and
of the ego insofar as it controlled the undesirable aspects of

the id. He did not see endocratic surplus of social origin as constricting the will of the individual and thus as injuring the whole personality. Sexual repression was the ultimate inhibiting force, and the search for power was not important enough to be considered.

According to Freud, the ego was the part of the psyche which deals with reality. He did not see how "reality"—that is, the social environment—might warp the ego. For Freud the id was a cauldron of instinctive energy ready to erupt in spite of the restrictions or demands of morality and society. In the Victorian world in which he himself was brought up, Freud could not conceive that society itself at times promotes eruption of the id.

Other adverse effects of society have not been examined so far because, although very harmful, they act upon the individual as external forces and are not internalized. They may even paralyze man's behavior, but do not affect predominantly his psyche.

If in exposing these three adverse sociopsychological factors we have criticized our society, it is not because we believe that other societies in different countries or different times have been or are more like paradise. Utopia is not around the corner. Even periods of decadence have their own beneficial effects inasmuch as they eventually activate need for change. Every society reflects or even magnifies the imperfections of man, and therefore to some extent hurts the individual and stunts his growth. On the other hand, without some kind of society no human being could survive, mature, and expand. It is in man's nature also to overcome the static social forces and to improve his condition. Of course sociologists have studied the effects of society on the individual, but, except for a few outstanding examples, their work has been predominantly sociological and not psychological, as is this book.[4]

CHAPTER 8

The
Origin
of the
Power Drive

POWER

PREVIOUS CHAPTERS HAVE SHOWN THE INDIRECT, COMPLICATED, and unconscious ways by which some social forces hinder man's inner self and ability to will. But social factors need not be subtle to injure the human spirit. As a matter of fact, they can be as conscious, as manifest, and as blatantly oblivious of human feelings as tyranny and the institution of slavery demand. They do so when they resort not to endocratic power but to *external power*.

According to Bertrand Russell, power is "the production of intended effects." [1] In other words, it is the ability to bring about the satisfaction of one's desires. If a man relied only on his own ability to satisfy his desires, power would be a synonym for personal ability. Any achievement would be the result of one's performance, but this is seldom the case. In order to bring about intended effects, people need other people; they must exert an influence on them so that the latter will help attain the desired results.

Let us take the case of a physician who discovers a cure for a fatal illness. He will have the power to achieve the recovery of many ill people, which is the intended effect. This "power" is an ability of the physician; it is not the external power we are referring to. It does not coerce the will of other people. The words "power" and "external power" will not be used in this book in all their possible connotations. By external power we mean only the faculty of changing by direct means the actions of others. Inasmuch as the individual prefers to be the master of his own desires and actions, he generally experiences this external power as thwarting, deflecting, inhibiting, or arresting his own will and freedom. Endocratic power and external power can be separated only artificially, for the sake of analysis. They are in fact almost always associated. Any external action has an intrapsychic counterpart without which it would not take place. When the intrapsychic counterpart of an action is relatively minor, we shall overlook it in our discussion. Moreover, for simplification's sake, we shall use the word "power" to mean external power only. When we refer to endocratic power we shall designate it as such.

Power has not yet received adequate consideration from the psychological point of view. It has generally been studied only in a sociopolitical frame of reference, but since it affects the will of man it is susceptible to psychological inquiry at an individual and at a social level. Individually, the drive for power has characteristics of its own not found in the primitive needs like hunger, thirst, sleep, sex, etc. These biological needs we share with other animal species are indeed powerful, but also self-limiting. A man cannot eat more than a certain amount of food, and cannot have sexual relations with more than a certain number of women. Even very large harems, as they exist ·in some countries, signify prestige and wealth more than sexual prowess. Unlike sexual ability, the drive for power is potentially endless and boundless. Some people in search of power cannot conceive any limitation to it. Such people as Alexander the Great and Napoleon could have had all the wealth and sex they wanted in the early period of their political life, but they continued to seek more and more power. Even the meaning of money has to be reinterpreted in relation to power. If money is a means to obtain food and sex, it cannot go beyond physiological satisfaction. But money can buy status, prestige, and power.

Marx's economic interpretation of history needs revision. It is true that the nineteenth-century bourgeoisie wanted an economic position in which it could prosper and exploit the masses. The whole theory, however, can be understood in terms of the dynamics of power. In a capitalistic society in which birth privileges are not important and the aristocracy plays a minimal role, the most common way to increase power is by amassing capital. If we cannot be aristocrats, we can become plutocrats. Marx's ideology can conceive a classless society as far as economy is concerned, but certainly the system by which the ideology is supposed to be fulfilled does not lead to equal distribution of power. We shall discuss this issue in Chapter 9.

THE ORIGIN OF THE POWER DRIVE

A power drive exists in many people. Can we draw the conclusion that this drive is an inherent part of human nature, like sex and aggression, and that the only alternatives open to man are dominating others or being dominated? Science has explained the power drive in two ways: by resorting either to ethological or to psychoanalytic theories. Ethology is the science of instincts. In Chapter 4 we discussed how some ethologists, like Konrad Lorenz,[2] explain a great deal of human behavior, including domination of others, as part of the instincts of aggression. For the sake of continuity I shall mention again briefly some concepts examined in Chapter 4.

The ethological theories focus on the fact that the human being tries to adapt to the environment with the same mechanisms used by subhuman species. Animals are endowed with aggressive capacities with which they fight other animals, secure food, maintain territorial rights, compete sexually, and defend their progeny. The capacity for aggression is very important for the preservation of animal species. Evolution has preserved this capacity with many selective mechanisms. One of them is to make aggression pleasant for the aggressor. Aggression is not as pleasant or as important as sexuality, but it nevertheless has a major role biologically and psychologically.

Athough these biological facts are undeniable, they can explain neither the full range of human hostility nor the power drive. The neurophysiological functions of rage and physical aggression in man have become only part of larger mechanisms. Many elaborated aspects of human hostility do not include or disclose these elementary forms. Freud and the Freudian school included aggression in the theory of thanatos, or the death instinct. According to Freud, this instinct is in some ways the opposite of eros, or the love-sex instinct, and aims at reducing organic matter to an inorganic state.

Neither Freud nor the ethologists could give us adequate theories because they disregarded the fact that, at a certain point in the life of man or in the history of the human race, new factors emerge that completely change the aim and potentiality of aggression. To view some of man's complex psychological processes purely as behavioral manifestations of instinctual aggression is a reductionistic approach. The complex functions of man that range from rage to hostility have at least five aims, often combined: self-defense, or elimination of fear; hurting others; depriving others; revenge; dominating others. We are interested here only with this fifth function, which is manifested especially when aggression bypasses the other four aims. Power is the result: the ability to manipulate, control, deflect, exploit, crush the will of others. The aim is to dominate irrespective of whether domination or the means to achieve it hurts or not.

Power affects every personal relation and tends to disturb it to such a point that a state of trust or communion between two or more people is no longer possible. When two people are together, an unequal distribution of power—that is, unequal abilities to exert one's will—tends to develop unless strong measures are taken to maintain the equilibrium. The result is that one person will be dominant and the other submissive. This need to dominate may disturb the relation between parent and child, husband and wife, teacher and pupil, employer and employee, and so on. A relation which is meant to be based on love, affection, learning, or cooperation becomes corrupted by power seeking—most of the time implemented not only by conscious mechanisms but also, and in many cases predominantly, by unconscious maneuvers. Society generally sanctions the more common unequal distributions of power, which may thus remain unchallenged for thousands of years, or until liberation movements occur.

When people live together, the life of each changes as a consequence of their living together. It is therefore unavoidable that people who live in proximity will exert a certain *control* over each other. In other words, they influence and restrict each other's behavior. This necessary, and in many respects, spontaneous control, is and should remain moderate. The more the climate of basic trust is approximated, the less control is required. In most cases, however, basic trust is present to a limited degree and more than moderate control is exerted, even within the realm of the family.

Many psychiatrists have studied the flow of power within the family and have done remarkable work in elucidating the intricate relations.[3] Because of the special aims of this book we shall focus on how society determines positions of power among people.

Unequal distribution of power gives rise to a hierarchy, then to control, finally to potential or actual subjugation. I repeat that the aim of power is not necessarily to hurt, but to dominate. Nevertheless the dominated person is hurt. The person's autonomy and individuality are attacked; as a result the individual may become a rebel, or an Uncle Tom, or even willing to be a slave. When the dominated seems to accept his domination, he does so in order to avoid even stronger fears and anxieties or because he cannot conceive other ways of living. Thus excessive power almost always ends up becoming evil.

In the fields of psychology, psychoanalysis, and related sciences, Alfred Adler [4] is the author who first realized the importance of power in human life and who advanced meaningful hypotheses about its origin. According to Adler, the child starts to feel inferior when he finds himself as a little person in a world of adults. Later he learns that "to be human means to feel inferior." He wants to overcome his inferiority and become superior by exerting power over others. This explanation is plausible but leaves many questions unanswered. Why does the individual continue to feel inferior when he grows up? Why does everybody feel inferior, even kings and presidents? And why is inferiority compensated for by domination of others?

In my opinion the search for power is a reaction to a double set of anxieties: anxiety caused by fear of others, and anxiety caused by dissatisfaction about oneself. I shall consider these two anxieties separately. The fear of others will be discussed from a social point of view.

According to Keith [5] and other anthropologists the first groups of men were very small. Among them a feeling prevailed which we can call basic trust, corresponding on a social basis to the one described by Erikson in the individual child growing in the secure family. The members of these small groups did not fear the others in the group but regarded them in a spirit of cooperation and reliance. An unwritten code of mutual help was strictly observed, just as it is today among the Eskimos. Had the law of the jungle prevailed within these small groups, their members would not have been able to survive, as they were less equipped than other animals to cope with the hardships of the environment. It is thus not correct to say that primitive man was ferocious. Keith asserts that within his own clan primordial man was highly ethical. The individual understood that if he wanted to live and enjoy life he also had to help his fellow men. It was a natural and spontaneous activity to help those in whose proximity one lived, for they were one's allies against the environment, they were one's brothers, protectors, and friends. When the groups increased to the size of a tribe, new conditions developed. In those times there was no means of production with which to provide for the needs of the increasing population. The scarcity of food perpetuated a state of hunger among people and a state of rivalry among tribes over the source of food, especially concerning hunting and fishing rights. Men conceived humankind as divided into two categories: the little group or tribe to which the individual belonged, and all the other groups to which the individual did not belong. Whereas basic trust prevailed within one's own group, all other groups were mistrusted. The individual was afraid that the other tribes might not have enough food and might even satisfy their hunger by capturing and eating him. They might not have enough women for their sexual needs, and they might kidnap women of his own tribe. It was thus important to learn to fight. Contrary to other animals, men directed aggression toward members of their own species, although to persons belonging to different tribal groups. It is difficult to determine whether the urge to fight came more from a desire to have the goods of other tribes or from a mistrust of other tribes. It seems to me that mistrust was probably the more important motivation. Had trust existed, the tribes would have learned to establish among themselves the rules of cooperation which prevailed within a single group, and all men would sooner or later have realized that every group would benefit from abiding by them. But as long as mistrust and fear of the others existed, this cooperation was not possible. It became necessary to acquire power: in other words, to combine the aggressive capacities of the members of the tribe, which included the ability to defend one's group, to hurt others, to deprive others, and to retaliate. Many tribes learned that it was easier to fight than to work. Moreover, they learned that their possessions and their capacity to continue to fight increased in proportion to the number of people whom they had overpowered, enslaved, and compelled to work for them.

In the long run, however, even mistrust, as a motivation to acquire power and to fight, would have been conquered by reason, and people would have learned to strive in an atmosphere of cooperation and intertribal loyalty, if another difficulty had not complicated the human situation. This difficulty is intra-psychic in origin, grounded in some intrinsic properties of the human psyche.[6] I am referring now to the second type of anx-iety, that caused by dissatisfaction about oneself. This dissatis-faction, in my opinion, goes beyond the feeling of helplessness of the child, to which Adler attributed the complex of inferiority. This dissatisfaction is based on conceptual processes which be-come more complicated with the progressive organization of human collectivities.

In my studies I have become increasingly aware that cogni-tive processes—e.g., such complicated structures as so-called philosophies of life, or what the sociologist Gouldner[7] calls "domain assumptions"—are responsible not only for constructive events but also for destructive motivations and may become a cause of anxiety. The beliefs that we have about ourselves, our fellow human beings, life and its meaning, and the world in general become *psychological facts*. When the ideas remain clear and fully conscious, they constitute in my own terminology not domain assumptions but "cognitive domains." I restrict the term "domain assumptions" to ideas which need not be con-sistent or logically coordinated. They may not even be fully verbalized or even recognized, and yet their validity comes to be taken for granted. Cognitive domains and domain assump-tions shape our personality and direct our actions. When domain assumptions are fully unconscious, or are at least kept at the periphery of consciousness, they determine actions for which man cannot assume full responsibility.

Sociologists and politicians have stressed the role of hunger in human motivation. Under the influence of Freud, psychia-trists and psychoanalysts have given great importance to the role of instincts and bodily needs in determining human be-havior and have minimized the role of ideas. My cognitive ap-proach does not deny that a lack of satisfaction of biological needs may unchain powerful dynamic forces and lead to con-flicts. It asserts, however, that many emotional factors affecting men favorably are by no means consequences of this type of deprivation but rather of ideas and their unconscious ramifications. Since prehistoric times a great part of human behavior has been motivated by suppositions which are part of elaborate intellectual structures. Some of them have prevented man from finding more rational solutions to the problem of hunger and have been disguised as remedies to hunger, although they were only urges to dominate others. Let us try to recognize some.

Because of the expansion of his conceptual processes and of a philosophy of life which he fabricates in his contacts with other human beings, man becomes aware that a discrepancy exists between the way he sees himself and the way his thinking permits him to visualize what he could be. He is always falling short of what he can imagine; he can always conceive a situation better than the one he is in. He conceives an ideal state, but he is imperfect and, in relation to the ideal, inferior. When he sees himself less than what he would like to be, he believes others, too, are dissatisfied with him. He faces a theoretical infinity of space, time, objects, and ideas which he can vaguely visualize but cannot master. On the other hand, he becomes aware of his finitude. He knows he is going to die, and that the range of his experiences is limited. He cannot be better than he is capable of being and he cannot enjoy more than a certain amount of food and sex.

Being able to conceive the infinite, the immortal, the greater and greater, he cannot accept his littleness. If frustration were not such a weak and misused word, we could say that he feels frustrated about his own nature and desperately searches for ways to overcome his condition. At a certain period in history some religions have offered him compensations in another life after death. These conceptions of immortality, however, are relatively recent acquisitions. In early prehistoric eras the only way to obtain an apparent expansion of the prerogatives of life was to invade the life of others. This method has remained the prevailing one. My life will be less limited if I take your freedom, if I make you work for me, if I make you submit to me. Thus, instead of accepting his limitations and helping himself and his fellow men within the realm of these limitations, man developed domain assumptions which made him believe that he could bypass his finitude and live more by making others less alive.

These assumptions ramified and built up networks of rationalizations. If one's life was limited it was only because others infringed upon him, restricted his potentialities, and limited his will. If he succeeds in ruling others he will expand and live intensely; he will have the pleasure of exerting an unbounded will; he will increase his ego and decrease his superego. The conception of the superman, which reached full consciousness and distinct formulation in the philosophy of Nietzsche, has existed in related forms since prehistoric times in the psyche of the masses of men as an unconscious domain assumption. Because of it the individual tends to confuse the concept of freedom and of individual autonomy with the irrational illusion of infinity, and by doing so he diminishes the freedom of others. Thus the human being has searched for an identity acceptable to himself, not by relying on his inner worth or on feelings of human equality, but by changing his relationship to others. He has chosen power, not communion.

I must stress once more that most of the time these conceptions are not fully conscious. Whatever is not acceptable to the self tends to be repressed or to be kept at the periphery of consciousness, whether it comes from primitive, ordinary, or unusually high levels of the psyche. Again I must stress that this interpretation does not rule out more primitive motivations for dominating others, such as the need to hurt, to deprive, to revenge, or to remove fear and anxiety. *The unconscious aim to overcome the human limitation may become the ally of the pleasure principle and of what some authors call id motivation.* It certainly becomes the ally of the tendency of mistrust and gives almost a mortal blow to the original cognitive domain of basic trust which may have existed in the primordial small groups of men. It will be up to the slowly emerging ethical cognitive domains to eventually reestablish some degrees of basic trust and mutual aid.

Throughout history contrasting cognitive domains have coexisted. Moreover, to make the situation even more confusing, they have been, and are, also mixed with domain assumptions. The dissonance produced by these sets of cognitive elements and their accompanying sentiments determines special sociocultural climates and brings about conflicts in the individual. Unless a voluntary and very difficult effort is made, the individual or the group succumbs to the domain which exerts the strongest pressure and which has been more solidly endocratized. We must, of course, distinguish between the cognitive domains and domain assumptions which tend to affect all groups of men, constantly or whenever a particular situation develops, and those instead which are related to specific sociocultural contingencies. The former, which I call primary domains or assumptions, are related to the human condition in general. The latter, or secondary ones, are connected with particular circumstances. In this chapter we shall continue to discuss only the primary domain determined by man's reaction to the concept of his own limitation.

When man discovered the predicament of his finitude in the midst of the infinite, theoretically he could have reacted in four possible ways. He could have accepted his finitude with the proviso that by following the ever increasing realm of ideas he could continue to grow as long as he lived. He could have recognized that his fellow human beings shared the predicament of his finitude and therefore could have tried to help them by fostering justice, equality, and individual growth. He could have become overcome by fear, given up freedom, and delegated his responsibility to others. Or in a futile attempt to overcome or decrease his finitude he could have tried to overpower others and make others even more limited.

History clearly shows that with rare exceptions man has selected the third and fourth possibilities as the acceptable domain assumptions.

The details of this horrendous choice will be described in Chapter 9. Obviously the fourth choice was the easiest and most gratifying; it was the one which permitted him to be aggressive in a deflected way; it was the one by which he felt he could get quick admiration and approval from others. The tendency toward his choice was certainly reinforced by fear of others. If you do not dominate others, they will dominate you. Thus we return to the problem of the presence or absence of basic trust. We enter a circular process in which it is impossible to distinguish the initial from the subsequent steps.

When the search for power is accepted, other subsidiary mechanisms are facilitated. For instance, man convinces himself that he should hate those he wants to dominate. Whether they are a group, or a few persons, or an individual, they become his scapegoat. The would-be dominator not only perceives the scapegoat in an altered way but projects onto it the worst qualities of himself. Thus he assures himself that his hate is justified. Even ethical principles are used for the pursuit of power. Darwin wrote, "When two tribes of primeval men, living in the same country, came into competition, the tribe including the greater number of courageous, sympathetic, and faithful members would succeed better and conquer the others." [8] Competition thus favored also the tribes which had cooperative qualities. Kropotkin [9] has also stressed (and perhaps exaggerated) the value of mutual aid in evolution.

The search for power is attributed also to a neighboring tribe and therefore an atmosphere of threat is maintained. With the development of technical abilities, and especially with the advent of agriculture, scarcity of food decreased as incentive to conquer and fight. But the search for power became stronger. When man is less harassed by hunger, he meditates more about his nature, becomes dissatisfied, and develops the urge to dominate others. Not all men want to dominate a large number of other persons, but those who do affect the life of many. Seeking power becomes more important than fair distribution of the necessities of life. Land becomes a crucial issue. The power drive interferes with territorial distribution in accordance with people's needs. Some groups (and later nations) which never cultivated all their land did not want other people to use it.

A disequilibrium in power between two neighboring tribes reproduces the law of the jungle. Darwin wrote, "When of two adjoining tribes one becomes less numerous and less powerful than the other, the contest is soon settled by war, slaughter, cannibalism, slavery, and absorption." [10] Mistrust does not permit tolerance of a disequilibrium of power. No group wants foreign groups to be or to become stronger than itself. If the alternative is to conquer or to be conquered, almost everybody will choose to conquer.

History justifies the mistrust which has existed from the era of primitive tribes to the great nations of today. If a disequilibrium exists, a tendency exists on the part of the stronger to defeat or destroy the weaker. This is equally true whether the contenders are small tribes or big nations. The aim of the United Nations is to guarantee peace by international justice and not to permit the destruction of one contender or of one alignment of contenders. The uncertain balance, however, is now maintained not by international justice but by the balance of nuclear terror. In a few years many small nations will be as capable as a big nation of blowing up the world. Then we may be in the paradoxical situation that neither love nor ethics may bring peace on earth but an equilibrium based on terror! Can a new universal basic trust rely on terror? It is hardly believable.

CHAPTER 9

The Brutality of External Power

POLITICAL POWER

ANY ACT OF WILL HAS, IN ADDITION TO A PSYCHOLOGICAL DIMENSION, a sociopolitical one. I can view any action of mine as eliciting a neutral or partial response in others. Are people indifferent to my action? Are they approving? Are they disapproving? Are they going to encourage or inhibit me? Are they going to remember or forget me? Society passes judgment on any and all human action. Even such disparate actions as smoking a cigarette, having sexual relations, going to school, working, not working, buying, selling, and defecating are regulated or at least judged by society. The very few actions which seem not to have a sociopolitical dimension may also be considered sociopolitically if only for the very unusual fact that they lack sociopolitical implications.

Actions often acquire a political dimension either because we delegate our attitude towards these actions to others or because others appropriate to themselves the right to tell us what attitude we should have toward these actions. In other words, when we live in any group of people, our actions become regulated. We thus become less free and delegate power to others, to whomever regulates our actions.

Political science and sociology study how power is organized. Since Herodotus it is generally seen as distributed in three ways, according to whether the rule comes from one, the few, or the many. No matter how distributed, power should always be used for the benefit of those who have relinquished it, or for the sake of the collectivity, and not as an end in itself or for special personal interests. Delegated power should be used to promote as much freedom as possible for everybody—justice, dignity, knowledge, and happiness to all the members of the group. The minimum power required to achieve these aims is the preferable one because it will interfere as little as possible with the will of the individual. Any acquired power which is beyond this minimum or which is not used for the promotion of these community goals is, in my opinion, best designated as *surplus power*. Delegated or appropriated power often becomes surplus power and instead of being used to promote civilization is used to gratify the power drive that we described in Chapter 8. People who have this impelling drive take advantage of the fact that social living requires the delegation and accumulation of power. For them power becomes an end in itself. The persons who succeed in accumulating enormous amounts of surplus power are relatively few in proportion to the general population, but inasmuch as they affect the will of the masses, it is of extreme importance for us to study how they operate. The desire for naked power is generally dressed and disguised in ideological clothes. One of the first who approvingly admitted that power is sought for power's sake was Machiavelli. We shall start by discussing briefly this theoretician of power; we shall then proceed to study the great practitioners.

MACHIAVELLI

Niccolò Machiavelli used (or misused) his genius teaching princes and other leaders how to acquire, retain, and increase political power. He wrote that it is advisable for the prince to do good things for the people because this is an efficient method of preserving his power. If, however, in order to retain or increase his power, the prince must perpetrate injustice and crime, these actions must be considered a political necessity. The end justifies the means.

If Machiavelli is considered a dispassionate analyst of politics who reveals how the game of power is played and how it needs to be played to achieve victory, then we cannot help but admire his genius. The five centuries that have elapsed since he wrote *The Prince,* including, of course, what we have witnessed in our generation, prove that the same game is played with the same ruthless rules that he described. But can he be considered a dispassionate analyst? It seems obvious that his passion is on the side of the ruthless prince.

The admirers of Machiavelli insist that he was an Italian patriot who hoped that a prince of the Medici family would follow his teachings, unify Italy, and chase away the foreign oppressors. As a matter of fact, at the end of the book Machiavelli, by quoting the poet Petrarch, expresses the hope that under the leadership of the ideal prince, "Virtue will fight against fury, and the fight will be short, because the ancient value has not died yet in the Italian hearts." [1] Further, shortly before the end of the book Machiavelli quotes Livy: "Only those wars are just which are necessary, and pious are those arms when there is no hope outside of them." [2]

The admirers of Machiavelli who ask us to evaluate him as a patriot and an advocate only of "necessary wars" make an impossible demand. More than patriotism and justification of necessary wars is requested. Firstly, if the only aim which counts is to acquire power, any war becomes, or can be made to seem, necessary. Secondly, Machiavelli requests that we ignore any ethical consideration. For instance, he wants the reader to admire his idol, Cesare Borgia, popularly called Valentino. Machiavelli describes with admiration [3] how Valentino sent to death all those who had conspired against him except the powerful Orsini family. Faking feelings of friendship for the Orsinis, he enticed them to his side in order to exploit their political machine. Valentino then reduced to submission the Italian region called Romagna. With the help of Remirro de Orco, a cruel and efficient man, he subdued all insurrections, subjugated opposition, and imposed peace on the region.

Later, in order to placate the discontented people and to keep them under his rule, Valentino used Remirro de Orco as a scapegoat. He attributed to this henchman all the crimes which had been committed to repress the insurrection. Valentino then proceeded to have Remirro executed in a public square. His body was exposed next to the dagger with which he had been killed and which was still stained with his blood.

Machiavelli considered the episode not only noteworthy but also worthy of being imitated as a way of conquering a region and then making the population displace the hate from the prince to the man second in command. Throughout *The Prince* many similar suggestions and examples are given to the would-be ideal prince. These methods work. The second man in command, be he a vice-president or a hatchet man, is expendable when the first man no longer needs him. He does not have to be necessarily murdered; he may be fired.

Machiavelli's most brutal advice was accepted only by tyrants. If Machiavelli's aim was to unify Italy, no Italian leader succeeded by following his teaching. Giuseppe Garibaldi and Camillo Cavour, the two men who, with their combined efforts, succeeded four centuries later in unifying Italy, did not resort to the unethical Machiavellian precepts. The Italian who not only followed Machiavellian principles but also praised and recommended them without reservation was Benito Mussolini. In an essay called "Prelude to *The Prince*" [4] he agrees with the Florentine's pessimistic view of man. Machiavelli stated more than once that people regret the loss of their own property more than the death of a father or of a brother because there is no remedy to death, but property can be restored.[5] Mussolini states that subsequent history has demonstrated that the human being is worse than Machiavelli had depicted.

When Machiavelli is descriptive, in many respects he is right. His writings are not only important as historical and political documents, but also as psychological insights into the worst qualities of men when they are engaged in a race for power. When he becomes prescriptive, he is not right, if ethics is to receive its due consideration. He teaches how it is possible for a prince to retain or increase his power by exploiting either the fear or the greed or the selfishness of the masses. He is concerned with the preservation of power, not with the salvation of man. Although in his private life he was an honest and decent man, in *The Prince* he seems to have forgotten his ethical ideals and to be completely uninterested in making the world a better place for everybody to live in. He is not interested in seeing in man the image of God or in helping him to become more like that image. On the contrary, he seems interested in seeking the image of the devil, both in the prince and in the subjects, and in extolling and exploiting those devilish qualities for the sake of the prince and the subjugation of the people. When the purpose of the prince is too obviously selfish and therefore repulsive to man's humanity, it is transformed, made to appear noble and sanctified. In other words, the prince must adopt not only external power but the capacity to induce endocracy. The prince's purpose is now to be recognized as the purpose of the state or the good of the country. In his "Prelude to *The Prince*," Mussolini goes along with the game.[6] He wrote that although Machiavelli referred to the prince, by prince he really meant the state. The tyrant repeatedly confuses himself with the state and his will with the people's will. Although this at first is a conscious deception, it becomes a confusion in the mind of the tyrant himself, and finally an endocratic, patriotic belief in the mind of the subjects. The final result is that will is taken away from the people.

MARX, COMMUNISM, AND POWER

Marx and the Marxists give a different interpretation to the boundless desires of man. They describe inequalities among men not in terms of power but in economic terms. In a nutshell, Marxian theory is as follows: the capitalist class exploits the laboring class and maintains or increases its large profits. The capitalist class is able to do so because it owns the instruments of production and operates through special unfair marketing practices. According to Marx the value of a commodity is determined by the quantity and quality of labor needed for its production. But a laborer is paid less than the value of his work. The capitalist, after paying the laborer a subsistence wage, is able to keep the rest of the value of the laborer's work for himself, the so-called *surplus value*. Let us assume that a laborer works ten hours a day and receives payment equivalent to the commodity value of five hours. The rate of surplus value is 100 percent of the laborer's wage and 50 percent of the product's value.

According to Marx and Engels, the appropriation of unpaid labor is the basis of the capitalistic mode of production and of the exploitation of the worker. Surplus value creates a division of people into a minority of exploiters and a mass of exploited. The mass is progressively impoverished and the elite is progressively enriched.

The genius of Marx and Engels clarified the importance of economics in human history—an approach previously minimized or misunderstood. In the opinion of many people, however, it would be a mistake to base all the social inequalities of men on the mechanism of surplus value. In my opinion surplus value is only a variety of the mechanism of *surplus power*.

Surplus power may be based on wealth, but also on other circumstances involving the life of men, especially on the ability to coerce the will. Alexander the Great, the Roman emperors, Napoleon, and Hitler were motivated more by the acquisition of political power than of material goods. Many people, however, obtain power through wealth and, therefore, try to become richer by exploiting others. In many cases, but not always, the searches for power and for wealth connect in a vicious circle. Marx is right to the extent that in a capitalistic society the bourgeoisie uses predominantly economic means in order to gain power. It was not so for the French aristocracy, which based unequal distribution of power on hereditary rights prior to the French Revolution. It is not so for any form of society which devises different methods for unequal distribution of power.

Communist countries have tried, at least to some extent, to follow Marxian principles and to eliminate the inequities caused by surplus value and unequal distribution of wealth. They have not succeeded in reaching their utopian goals because they have neglected to consider surplus power and the unequal distribution of power. In the Soviet Union wealth is distributed more evenly than in capitalistic countries, but power is much more unequally distributed than in Western democracies. Stalin had practically all the power of the nation. His will reigned as supreme as that of a Roman emperor.

In a capitalistic country, too, of course, power is unequally distributed, especially in Fascist countries. When we compare a Fascist and a Communist country, we find, as a matter of fact, that although the two differ very much from the point of view of their economic structure, they are similar in the distribution of power: either the chief or an elite have all the power. The country is divided into two classes, the powerful and the powerless. The class of the powerful is in its turn divided into at least two subclasses, one formed by the leaders or by the government; the other, by all the bureaucracy which, in a hierarchical structure, supports the government. In both communistic and capitalistic countries, politics is based on maneuvers to increase or preserve power. Inasmuch as economic conditions increase or decrease power, they may become intimately connected wtih power struggles. Struggles for power existed even in primitive societies before the advent of capitalism. In the bourgeois world money is not used only to buy comfort and pleasure, but to attain power. Comfort and pleasure are self-limiting concepts: it is not physically possible to obtain more than a certain amount of them. But power is unlimited; and the more money is available, the greater is the possibility of acquiring power.

If a person is rich enough, he may even fulfill his aspiration of marrying the young and beautiful widow of a president of a great country. The ability to make such a marriage ultimately denotes power exerted through money. Love, sex, and even money appear intermediaries to the ultimate factor, power. In some instances money seems to have the power that the combined Greek army needed to win back the beautiful Helen of Troy. We must conclude that the economic and sexual motivations Marx and Freud so well elucidated are at times ends in themselves, but often are also intermediary means or collateral means to the power motivation. Adler seems vindicated except for the fact that, as shown in Chapter 8, he did not understand fully the origin of the power drive. I want to clarify at this point that I do not imply that the search for power is man's only motivation. Man has many other motivations in addition to the powerful ones of sex, hunger, wealth, and power.

The bourgeoisie resorts to many methods to obtain power through economic means. Psychiatrists know that these methods invade the family, too. Thus many husbands keep their wives in a state of submission through economic control; and some parents, by financing the education of their children, want the latter to make certain decisions in life which agree with parental wishes.

Marx believed that men enter into definite "relations of production" and that these relations constitute the structure of society, a structure based on economics. He believed that the mode of production in material or economic life determines the character of the social, political, and spiritual processes of life. Marx certainly uncovered many ramifications of economic power in life, as Freud later uncovered many ramifications of sex. Strangely enough, however, he did not see that, especially in political life, economics was one of the species under which the genus power presents itself. Consequently the study of noneconomic power and surplus power has received only secondary attention in Communist theory; a great deal of attention, however, in Communist practice!

In their famous *Manifesto*, Marx and Engels wrote, "When, in the course of development, class distinctions have disappeared, and all production has been concentrated in the hands of a vast association of the whole nation, the public power will lose its political character. Political power, properly so called, is merely the organized power of one class for oppressing another." [7] This, of course, is not what has happened in the Soviet Union or any other Communist country.

Marx and Engels were very much interested in protecting civil liberties and the inviolability of the person, but early in Communist history such aims became subordinate to the interests of the revolution. Perhaps the shift in position was marked by the approval that Plekhanov, one of the founders of Russian Communism, gave to Posadovsky in 1903, during the conference of the Russian Social Democratic party.[8] Posadovsky had asserted that the revolutionary party may require the subordination of all democratic principles, including the fundamental liberties of men. The assent of the authoritative Plekhanov made this attitude official. Plekhanov's assent was a formal betrayal of Marx's idealism. *It was the official acceptance of surplus power to combat a system in which surplus value prevailed.*

A few years later, Lenin not only followed the same principles, but extended them to a point where he could disregard civil liberties. He accumulated surplus power to such an extent that he could exert actual terror. On January 27, 1918, he said in Petrograd at a presidium of the Supreme Soviet, "We cannot obtain anything if we do not use terror." In a proclamation made on September 5, 1918, and entitled "Red Terror," he declared that it was necessary "to protect ourselves through terror." Cultural terror was already exercised at the time of Lenin by removing from libraries books which did not agree with Communist ideology. According to Lenin, Engels did not literally mean that the proletariat, in assuring the state power, "puts an end to the state as the state." [9] Violent revolution, according to Lenin, is a necessity to suppress the bourgeoisie and to bring about the dictatorship of the proletariat. Actually, the dictatorship of the proletariat meant dictatorship of a few, or of one (Lenin, and later Stalin). Lenin and Stalin became the new Machiavellian princes.

If Lenin practiced an unequal division of power, Stalin brought it to its extreme. Lenin saw the Communist party as the embodiment of unity of will. In *The Foundations of Leninism* Stalin wrote,

. . . iron discipline in the Party in inconceivable without unity of will, without complete and absolute unity of action on the part of all members of the Party . . . Unity of will and unity of action of all Party members are the necessary condition without which neither Party unity nor iron discipline in the Party is conceivable . . . The existence of factions is incompatible either with the Party's unity or with its iron discipline. It need hardly be proved that the existence of factions leads to the existence of a number of centers, and the existence of a number of centers connotes the absence of one common center in the Party, the breaking up of the unity of will, the weakening and disintegration of discipline, the weakening and disintegration of the dictatorship.[10]

The words "dictatorship of proletariat" actually meant "Stalin's dictatorship," and the words "unity of will, incompatible with the existence of factions" meant "the existence of other independent wills is incompatible with the supreme will of Joseph Stalin." *Will thus, in any form, is taken away from the people.*

In his famous speech, delivered to the Twentieth Congress of the Communist party of the Soviet Union, Khrushchev said,

The negative characteristics of Stalin, which, in Lenin's time, were only incipient, transformed themselves during the last years into a grave abuse of power by Stalin, which caused untold harm to our party.

We have to consider seriously and analyze correctly this matter in order that we may preclude any possibility of a repetition in any form whatever of what took place during the life of Stalin, who absolutely did not tolerate collegiality in leadership and in work, and who practiced brutal violence, not only toward everything which opposed him, but also toward that which seemed, to his capricious and despotic character, contrary to his concepts.

Stalin acted not through persuasion, explanation and patient cooperation with people, but by imposing his concepts and demanding absolute submission to his opinion. Whoever opposed his concepts or tried to prove his viewpoint and the correctness of his position was doomed to removal from the leading collective and to subsequent moral and physical annihilation. This was especially true during the period following the 17th Party Congress, when many prominent party leaders and rank-and-file party workers, honest and dedicated to the cause of Communism, fell victim to Stalin's despotism . . .[11]

Khrushchev, in his speech, tried to exonerate Lenin. He said that Vladimir Ilyich (Lenin) had called Stalin excessively rude.

The position of the Secretary General should be given to a person who would differ from Stalin in being more tolerant, kinder, less capricious, and more considerate. In the same speech Khrushchev said that whereas Lenin had resorted to extraordinary methods (that is, to violence) only against the opponents of the party, Stalin resorted to brutal methods against everyone. Khrushchev seems correct in characterizing Stalin, but he accepts without hesitation terror against the opponents of the regime, and seems to forget that Lenin, too, resorted to terror (although on a much smaller scale and only against political opponents).

Incriminating only Stalin and not Communism, as Khrushchev did, is like incriminating some Roman emperors like Nero and Caligula, but not the institution of the Roman Empire, which permitted the people to be at the mercy of such emperors. If the emperor happened to be a good man, like Marcus Aurelius, the population was safe. Khrushchev ignores the fact that in a classless society, the individual freed from the inequalities of capitalism may become even more cruelly enchained by the dictatorship of the state (not of the proletariat).

Stalin could openly say that

> the state is a machine in the hands of the ruling class for suppressing the resistance of its class enemies. In this respect the dictatorship of the proletariat does not differ essentially from the dictatorship of any other class, for the proletarian state is a machine for the suppression of the bourgeoisie. But there is one substantial difference. This difference consists in the fact that all hitherto existing class states have been dictatorship of an exploiting minority over the exploited majority, whereas the dictatorship of the proletariat is the dictatorship of the exploited majority over the exploiting minority. Briefly: the dictatorship of the proletariat is the rule—unrestricted by law and based on force.[12]

Stalin thus said that the dictatorship of the proletariat was unrestricted power based on force and protected by law. Everybody knows, however, that what was supposed to be dictatorship of the proletariat was in fact the dictatorship of Joseph Stalin; and we know what kind of dictatorship that was. If Robert Conquest in *The Great Terror* is correct, and there is no reason to doubt his accuracy and honesty, Stalin was responsible for the death of 20 million Russians. Conquest calculated that in the years 1937 and 1938, 800,000 persons were executed in Russian prisons by Stalin's order. In the so-called work camps approximately 30 percent of the prisoners died, making a total of 17 million victims between 1936 and 1950.[13]

In the famous speech to the Twentieth Congress of the Communist party, Khrushchev said that Stalin felt this terror was necessary for the defense of the interests of the working class against the plots of enemies and the attacks of imperialists. Again the end is supposed to justify the means in a Machiavellian way: terror is implemented in the interest of the Party and in the defense of the revolution.

As Conquest shows, the truth is that Stalin had an endless will to power. He wanted to be more powerful than his former enemies, the czars, more powerful than the man with whom he secretly competed and whom he admired, Ivan the Terrible. The least suspicion that someone would threaten, hinder, or resent his absolute power was enough to unchain the desire to annihilate the potential or fantasy enemy, and he had the power to do so. Craving for power, when unchecked by any restriction, may assume absurd, fantastic, and morbid degrees beyond the conception of the common man. Stalin had also devised a method by which the political prisoner almost always confessed to crimes that he had not committed, and for these "crimes" he was later executed.[14]

All this is remote from the humanitarian considerations of the two great theoretical founders of Communism, Marx and Engels, and antithetical to the truths that they revealed about men and society. The system which was supposed to bring about the brotherhood of the proletariat and the elimination of economic injustice gave birth to a terrifying machine and permitted the acquisition of total power on the part of one of the most criminal men who ever lived. This monstrous outcome is not a necessary consequence of the teachings of Marx and Engels. Nevertheless, these two thinkers cannot be exonerated either, since an error was implicit in their theory that made such an aberration possible. They interpreted history only economically and disregarded everything else. They did not recognize that their formula "surplus value" was only a species of the genus "surplus power."

Communism permits accumulation of power not only in the hands of one or of a few leaders, but also in the party bureaucracy and the managerial group. The proletariat as a whole or the single citizen has no voice over the policies which are adopted by the government or the Party. When we consider the accumulation and preservation of power at an international level, we can easily see that there are no basic differences between Communist imperialism and the others.

For example, it was the aim of imperialist Czarist Russia to cross the straits of the Bosporus and the Dardanelles, thus to expand into the Mediterranean Sea. The great powers which dominated Europe—England, France, and Turkey—were determined to keep the straits closed to Russian expansion. Communist Russia has succeeded much more than the Czars' Russia. Not only has Russia already secured free access into the Mediterranean, but it is now trying to obtain control of the Suez Canal and to expand its influence into the Indian Ocean.

FASCISM AND NAZISM

Unlike Communism, theoretical and official Fascism does not try to disguise its inequities in the distribution of power but represents them in a heroic masquerade. On theoretical grounds Fascism is incomparably inferior to Communism. While we immediately recognize the greatness of Marx and Engels even if we cannot forget their mistakes and their consequences, we easily assess the insipidity of the Fascist theoreticians.

Fascism, too, in the words of its main theoreticians, Alfredo Rocco and Benito Mussolini, pretends to put the welfare of the collectivity or the state above the welfare of the individuals. In a well-known speech delivered in Perugia, Rocco said that whereas in the doctrines of democracies the fundamental problem is the question of the rights of the individual, for Fascism the fundamental problem is the right of the state and the duty of the individual. "Individual rights are only recognized insofar as they are implied in the rights of the state. In this preeminence of duty we find the highest ethical value of Fascism." [15]

According to Rocco, in the Fascist concept of liberty the individual was "allowed to develop his personality in behalf of the state." Freedom therefore is due the citizen and the several social classes on the condition that they exercise it in the interest of society as a whole. Freedom is not a natural right but, "like any other individual right, is a concession of the state." What we consider to be a natural inalienable right becomes for Rocco a concession. While theoretical Communism focused on economics and neglected power, theoretical Fascism focused on power and neglected economics. As far as economics is concerned, Fascism accepted capitalism because it believed that it was the best economic form for the state.

As a theorist Mussolini is even weaker than Rocco. To rationalize his theoretical weakness he classified himself as a *tempista*. This Italian word is used by Mussolini to mean "capable of grasping the opportunity as soon as it presents itself, without losing time to formulate theories for the present or the future." He wrote that "for the Fascist, everything is in the State, and nothing human or spiritual exists, much less has value, outside the State. In this sense Fascism is totalitarian, and the Fascist State, the synthesis and unity of all values, interprets, develops, and gives strength to the whole life of the people."

Mussolini wrote that Fascism is opposed to democracy, "which lowers the nation to the level of the majority." He wrote that the purest form of democracy is really the most powerful idea "which acts within the nation as the conscience and the will of a few, even of One." The One, with a capital "O," means, of course, Mussolini himself. Concerning international relations his theory is the following: "Fascism rejects universal concord, and, since it lives in the community of civilized peoples, it keeps them vigilantly and suspiciously before its eyes." [16] In another passage of the same article Mussolini expressed the idea that struggle and competition are natural states of the animal kingdom, which includes man.

In the already mentioned and infamous "Prelude to *The Prince*," Mussolini wrote,

> The individual tends to evade continuously. He tends to disobey the laws, not to pay taxes, not to fight wars. Few are those— heroes or saints—who sacrifice their own self to the altar of the State. All the others are in a state of potential revolt against the State. The attribute of sovereignty applied to the people is a tragic farce. The people, at most, delegate but cannot exercise any sovereignty. Systems of representation belong more to mechanics than to morals . . . To the people remains only a monosyllable, to say "yes" and to obey. . . . Sovereignty graciously directed by the people is taken away when needed. It is left to the people when it is harmless or reputed as such; that is, during ordinary administrative practices. Can you imagine a war proclaimed by referendum? The referendum is appropriate when it deals with the selection of the most suitable place to locate the fountain of the village.[17]

In other words, people are spoiled children and are interested only in avoiding their duties. They break the laws, object to paying taxes, and do not want to fight wars. Their judgment is limited. At most they may be consulted on where to locate the fountain of the village. The rest of the power has to be delegated to the state. But the state, of course, means Mussolini and his henchmen. Since the spoiled children do not want to fight wars of conquest, we have to educate them to fight by creating a climate of war. I have already mentioned in Chapter 5 that even medical students in Fascist Italy had to learn "military science." The climate of war had to be created even when there was no war, in order to prepare for war and possibly to provoke war. Mussolini felt that a climate of war changed people and ennobled life. There is no doubt that he was right about people being changed. Whether they are ennobled remains to be demonstrated. This climate does give different horizons to life. Any means becomes justified to reach the supreme goal: winning a war of conquest. Unscrupulousness, paranoid tendencies or at least suspiciousness, and ruthlessness will increase and finally prevail everywhere in life. The desire to find a common ground or at least a basis for understanding between people or a reconciliation between nations is frowned upon. The only acceptable aim becomes that of overpowering, conquering, or annihilating those who do not think as you do, who do not recognize your power or add to it, who interfere with your dreams of earthly greatness. External power thus becomes endocratic, too. Jerusalem and Athens are sold out to Sparta and Rome.

The Fascist party even promulgated "the Fascist decalogue," presumably to compete with the biblical Decalogue. It is not necessary to enumerate here all the "commandments" that the good Fascist was supposed to obey; the first, eighth, and tenth are good samples of the whole.

1. Know that the Fascist and in particular the soldier must not believe in perpetual peace.
8. Mussolini is always right.
10. One thing must be dear to you above all: the life of the Duce.

Unequal distribution of power reaches unbelievable climaxes and brings about brutal consequences in German Nazism. Hitler had no compunction about advocating war, inducing people to believe in strength and conquest rather than right, and demanding complete reliance on the will of one person, the Fuehrer himself.

The following excerpts are taken from Hitler's speeches.[18] More strongly than Mussolini, Hitler equated human society with the life of the jungle and argued that this was the natural and desirable state. He wrote:

> . . . The power which nations can bring to bear is the decisive factor. It is evident that the stronger has the right before God and the world to enforce his will. History shows that the right as such does not mean a thing unless it is backed up by great power. If one does not have the power to enforce his right, that right alone will profit him absolutely nothing. The stronger has always been victorious. The whole of nature is a continuous struggle between strength and weakness, an eternal victory of the strong over the weak. (*Völkischer Beobachter,* April 15-16, 1923).
>
> . . . Unfortunately, the contemporary world stresses internationalism instead of the innate values of race, democracy, and the majority instead of the worth of the great leader. Instead of everlasting struggle the world preaches cowardly pacifism and everlasting peace . . . (*Völkischer Beobachter,* November 26, 1926).
>
> . . . The inventions of mankind are the result of eternal struggle . . . The struggle against the great beasts is ended, but it is being inexorably carried on against the tiny creatures— against bacteria and bacilli. There is no Marxian reconciliation on this score; it is either you or I, life or death, either extermination or servitude. From [various] examples we arrive at the fundamental conclusion that there is no humanitarianism but only an eternal struggle, a struggle which is the prerequisite for the development of all humanity. (*Völkischer Beobachter,* April 5, 1927).
>
> . . . If men wish to live, then they are forced to kill others. The entire struggle for survival is a conquest of the means of existence which in turn results in the elimination of others from these same sources of subsistence. (*Völkischer Beobachter,* March 17, 1929).
>
> . . . There is no distinction between war and peace. Struggle is ever present. A latent peace is only possible when one is either a free lord or a slave. The final decision lies with the sword. (*Völkischer Beobachter,* May 4, 1928).

These short excerpts reveal the whole of Hitlerism: no humanitarianism; only eternal struggle. It is ridiculous to think of living in peace. "If men wish to live . . . they are forced to kill others. Force alone is decisive. Therefore I, Adolf Hitler, must have power, power, power, so that I be your Lord and either extermi- nate you or reduce you to my servitude. It is either you or I."

It may seem incredible that the nation who gave the world perhaps the greatest of all ethical philosophers, Immanuel Kant, should have brought this monster to power. Monsters exist in any place, but the fact remains incredible that the free descendants of Immanuel Kant in 1933 should freely elect to power such a man when at least for ten years he had already made his abominable beliefs known to everyone. He called con- science "the circumcision of the soul." For him humanitarianism, which, as the etymology of the word indicates, is characteristic of man, is to be discarded. Men must be like animals in the jungle where the stronger wins. From what happens in nature (that is, in the jungle), Hitler concludes that the stronger has the right before God and the world to enforce his will. To descend to the animal status of the jungle is for him man's greatest achievement.

Perhaps we do understand now one of the main sources of Hitler's antisemitism. He is against the basic philosophy of the Hebrew prophets of the Old Testament. They were for right, not might. They felt right had to be defended, even if might temporarily wins. And whereas the prophets of the Old Testa- ment were advocating times when swords would be changed into ploughshares, the Teutonic monster was preaching that ploughshares be transformed into swords. The two philosophies could not be more diametrically opposed. Christianity, too, of course, upholds the ideals of the prophets, but Hitler conven- iently forgot that minor point.

A clarification is necessary. I do not mean that Hitler was conscious that his hate for Judaism was based on the fact that it had an ideology about human life opposite to his. He had vaguely sensed this opposition in his contacts with the Judaeo- Christian tradition. But he could not hate the Christians, who were holders of power, as much as he could hate the weak sharers of this ideology. Other cultural-historical factors and many rationalizations, personal in origin, permitted him to vent his hate.

In theoretical as well as in practical Nazism, the leader, the Fuehrer himself, is seen as the embodiment of the collective will of the people. In the words of Ernst Huber, one of the main theoreticians of Nazism, "The will of the people is realized" in the Fuehrer's will. In reference to the Fuehrer, Huber wrote,

> He shapes the collective will of the people within himself, and he embodies the political unity and the entirety of the people in opposition to individual interests . . .
>
> . . . His will is not the subjective, individual will of a single man; but the collective national will is embodied within him in all its objective, historical greatness . . .
>
> Such a collective will is not a fiction, as is the collective will of the democracies, but it is a political reality which finds its expression in the Fuehrer. The people's collective will has its foundation in the political idea which is given to a people . . .
>
> The state does not hold political authority as an impersonal unit but receives it from the Fuehrer as the executor of the national will. The authority of the Fuehrer is complete and all-embracing; it unites in itself all the means of political direction; it extends into all fields of national life; it embraces the entire people, which is bound to the Fuehrer in loyalty and obedience. The authority of the Fuehrer is not limited by checks and controls, by special autonomous bodies or individual rights, but it is free and independent, all inclusive and unlimited.[19]

Just as, under the pretext of representing the collective will of the proletariat, Stalin came to be the only person in Russia possessing his own will, Hitler, under the pretext of personifying and embracing the will of the whole people, came to be the only person with a free will. *Again will, in any form, is taken away from the people.*

Huber gives himself away in many ways without realizing it. In the quoted excerpt he wrote that the collective will of the democracies is fictitious and only the will of the Nazi state is a political reality. But in the next sentence, he said that "the people's collective will has its foundation in the political idea which is given to a people. . . ." In other words, the Fuehrer gives the political idea to the people. The people accept it as a consequence of deceptive persuasion, brainwashing, or fear of being executed. When the people have accepted the idea (and they cannot reject it), they return it to the Fuehrer, who will embody it and actualize it. A greater fallacy is hard to conceive.

Another important issue has to be considered before concluding this section. Many authors have tried to analyze the socio-cultural conditions which have prepared the ground for Fascism, especially in its Nazi variety. Such factors as the background of Prussian militarism and profound sense of duty toward the fatherland, the philosophy of Nietzsche, the Teutonic sagas rediscovered by the German Romantics from Herder to Wagner, the theory of the Frenchman Gobineau on the inequalities of human races, which was accepted much more in Germany than in France, would have made Nazism almost inevitable. Undoubtedly this cultural preparation facilitated the success of Nazism. This cultural milieu, however, constitutes what in Chapter 8 we have called a *secondary cognitive domain,* and in no way disproves the existence of the underlying primary cognitive domains and the domain assumptions which determine the power drive. Special secondary cognitive domains make it easier for the power drive to gain supremacy, but are not necessary in an absolute sense. As a matter of fact, they did not exist in other countries where Fascism prevailed. Only fanatic theorists could, for instance, find in the writings of D'Annunzio or of Marinetti preparations for Italian Fascism. These writings had very little impact on the masses.

More pertinent is Erich Fromm's theory that the Germans succumbed to Nazism in order to escape from freedom, of which they were afraid.[20] That the Germans gave up freedom and submerged themselves into the totality of the state there is no doubt. As I mentioned in Chapter 8, this renunciation of freedom seems to me, however, not to be determined by fear of freedom but by fear of not achieving freedom because of one's human limitations. If you feel discontented about yourself, it will be easier for you to succumb to the influence of those who claim they can take over your prerogatives for your own benefit. Moreover, if you identify with the leader, or oppressor, you have the illusion not of giving up your will but of acquiring part of his will. His will becomes yours, too.

THE CHARACTERISTICS OF UNCONTROLLED POWER

Many authors, from Thucydides to Berle in our own day, have studied power in its various aspects.[21] My discussion will be devoted to extreme or uncontrolled power. I have differentiated five main characteristics of it. Although they are interrelated, I shall describe them separately.

The first characteristic which makes uncontrolled power so dangerous is its *self-accruing* quality. Uncontrolled power tends to grow like the snowball which becomes an avalanche. The self-accruing quality has at least two major causes. On the one hand, the more power a person possesses, the easier it will be for him to acquire still more. On the other hand, getting feebler and feebler responses from his opponents, the holder of power will feel increasingly capable of making demands and will be greedier and greedier in his requests. Moreover, since nobody dares to criticize him, he comes to believe that he is always right.

As a rule, the first steps of a would-be dictator are not strong or resolute and could be arrested by an alert, vigilant opposition. Arbitrary interpretations of law (like some loopholes in the constitution of the Weimar Republic of Germany or of the decadent monarchy in Italy) permit an early accumulation of power if there is no watchful attitude on the part of the people and their free representatives. When Mussolini became premier in 1922 he did not ask for dictatorial power but only for some special rights. In 1925, only three years later, he was already a dictator. Hitler's power became so extraordinary that in less than five years his theoretician, Ernst Huber, could openly and approvingly define the authority of the Fuehrer as "complete and all embracing" and extending "into all fields of national life." There is no need to describe here the analogous situation concerning Stalin.

Uncontrolled power is like a fatal disease which finally invades every cell of an organism and sucks all vitality from it. The will is concentrated in one man, and the masses are reduced to things without will of their own; they become commodities used by the leader. Marx was correct in describing the abusers of surplus value, but surplus value is a pygmy evil in comparison to uncontrolled surplus power. The most successful, most callous, and most rugged capitalist is a pale figure in comparison to a Hitler, a Stalin, or even a Mussolini, who was the least dangerous of the three.

The second characteristic of uncontrolled power is implicit in the first. *Uncontrolled power tends to become uncontrollable.* It is impossible to say when the disease will become uncontrollable, but sooner or later it will. When I say uncontrollable, I mean within the system which permitted its growth. For instance, Nazism was eventually controlled, but only by a foreign force. Because of these characteristics, citizens must be on the alert and be unwilling to grant special power to their chiefs. Even what seems a moderate request for unusual power on the part of a political leader must be considered by the citizens not just with caution, but also with suspicion. Many dictators were able to receive unusual power under the pretext that it was needed to save the nation in a moment of danger or crisis; naturally the same dictators were later unwilling to relinquish their power. As a matter of fact, dictators generally retain power until they die a natural death, are killed, defeated in war, or compelled to go into exile. If, in extreme circumstances, unusual power is granted, it must be with guarantees, even for the shortest period of time, and always with the possibility of revocation. During the period for which the special power is granted, the citizens must know whether the chief puts into operation various mechanisms which will enable him to retain power indefinitely. If allowed to do so, not only will he use external power, but also all the methods which elicit endocratic power, as we noted in previous chapters. He will resort to false ideologies embellished by myths, like the grandeur of imperial Rome, the superiority of the Aryan race, and the return to the natural state of the jungle. All ideologies, teachings of history, philosophies, and political creeds which try to persuade people to renounce their will must be examined suspiciously.

The third characteristic is the *potentiality of power*. In other words, *power does not have to be actualized in order to produce effect*. The oppressor does not need to put his physical instruments of power into actual operation. The knowledge on the part of the victims that the oppressor has the means with which he can injure is enough to coerce their behavior. They maintain a submissive attitude in order not to be further victimized. So power is also effective as a deterrent, in its capacity to threaten or elicit fear. The deterrent quality of power has been used in international politics since ancient times to control foreign nations or special blocs or alliances. This quality, however, exists also for internal affairs in totalitarian or police states.

By either actual or potential power strong nations and strong alliances have been able to control weaker nations. The United Nations has the aim of diminishing or controlling the power of the various countries. Ideally this organization would ensure a fair share of power to all nations, no matter whether they are big or small. But of course it does not have the power to implement this division of power. What has resulted instead is the emergence of superpowers, each acting as a deterrent against the other, and each having a group of followers or satellites. At the end of Chapter 8 we have already mentioned that with the advent of the atomic era, the time is approaching, however, when even the smallest country will have great deterrent power, a power which could destroy all the other countries. Equality may thus be established among nations—not an equality based on peace and harmony but on the *equal* capacity to produce the world's destruction. This diabolic equality may at first seem to have pragmatic value. If the result is peace, this is all for the good; but there is no guarantee that this will be the result. First of all, an unscrupulous or megalomaniacal leader, like Hitler or Stalin, may not care about saving the world if he himself is going to perish. He may delude himself into thinking it is good for the whole of humanity to perish, and he may push the button. Secondly, knowing that these methods are not going to be used because they imply world destruction, governments of some nations may, by tacit consent, engage in non-nuclear warfare. Since the advent of the atomic bomb, many not-so-small wars have occurred or are still being waged throughout the world.

A fourth characteristic of power is its *creation of an artificial and unnatural but nevertheless effective distance between the holder of power and the power-deprived citizens.* The chief, dictator, despot, or president becomes invested with superior attributes. He becomes the depository of everybody's will and is supposed to have the ability to represent everybody and to include everything. *"L'état, c'est moi,"* said Louis XIV. Rudolf Hess, introducing the Fuehrer at one of the Nürnberg Nazi meetings, said, "Germany is Hitler and Hitler is Germany." As Huber and other Nazi theoreticians repeatedly stated, these words meant that Hitler did not stand only for contemporary Germany but for past Germany and the Germany of the next thousand years. Hitler was supposed to include even such spiritual giants as Kant, Goethe, and Beethoven.

At the same Nürnberg meetings other party leaders addressed Hitler in the following ways: "When you act, the people act." "The German youth is shaped in your image." "The supreme Fuehrer, the supreme judge." In those rituals the chief may be deified, as in imperial Rome, or may be considered to be "always right," like Mussolini. The chief ends by believing that he really has these attributes. On the other hand, the other citizens, unless they identify with him or feel approved or loved by him, consider themselves worthless and lose human dignity. They live only for the sake of being instruments of his power. The *arcanum tremendum* which religious leaders were reputed to possess is transformed into *arcana imperii*. The subordinates cannot see the leader. The leader knows everything. The notion will prevail that if people are reluctant to obey it is because they do not know all the facts. If they knew, they could not help but obey. Incidentally, this persuasive technique is resorted to, to some extent, even by chiefs of so-called democracies when they want to induce people to go along with their requests. The leaders recreate artificially the situation which existed in early childhood and which only in early childhood was justified: the gap between thought and action (see Chapter 2). The leader says that information is not given to the people because it has to be kept secret for reasons of security. He asks that people obey on account of what is implied in that unrevealed information.

Watergate?

The leader's supposed superior knowledge becomes totally ridiculous when it is extended to specific fields whose mastery requires special training. A Stalin becomes a superior authority on such subjects as agriculture or evolutionary theories, as during the famous Lysenko controversy. When Stalin fell into disgrace after his death, the attribute of omniscience and the responsibility for all innovations and advancement was to a large extent restored to Lenin, and to a lesser extent to Marx. The following is an example from a subject familiar to me.

Thought disorders in schizophrenia and other mental illnesses present difficult problems and are studied by many psychiatrists and psychologists who have devoted years of work to it. It has been one of the major areas of my research. I recently learned that a new Russian book by B. V. Zeigarnik on schizophrenic thinking had been translated into English. Of course I bought it and read it. In the first pages of the book, Zeigarnik referred several times to Lenin as the inspiring author who, together with Marx, opened the road to the psychological and psychiatric study of thinking processes. For instance, on page 24 Zeigarnik gives the principles of the Marxist-Leninist philosophy of cognition, on which subsequent Russian studies of thinking are purportedly based.[22] Lenin's words are, "The dialectical road to the recognition of truth, to the recognition of objective reality, runs from living contemplation to abstract thought, and from these to practical activity. . . . All scientific (true, serious, not trite) abstractions reflect nature more profoundly, more truly, more fully." [23] For Marx, language is the "very essence of thought." [24] Zeigarnik concludes, "These general principles of Marxist-Leninist philosophy form the basis of the views of Soviet psychologists on the nature of mental processes, including thinking." [25] These "general principles," even if expressed in high-sounding words, are statements of little value and no originality.

Although the omniscient leader may be dead, the general directive imposed by the party is to acknowledge his omniscience. If the leader's alleged superiority is extolled, the common citizen's ability, other than that of obedience, is minimized. Let us remember once more that only two years after he gained power, in his infamous prelude to Machiavelli, Mussolini said that the citizen is capable only of expressing *an opinion* about the location of the fountain of the village. And this was the Duce at the beginning of his career.

The distance between the leader and common mortals is constantly increased. The leader is gradually but rapidly deified; the citizen is gradually but rapidly transformed into a thing.

A fifth characteristic of uncontrolled power is the *ability to change drastically the personality of the subordinates.* We have already seen how society can inflict on the individual psyche the changes that we have called primitivization, deformation of the self, and endocratic surplus.[26] We shall add now a few alterations of personality connected with external power which may have an endocratic and deforming effect, but which are nevertheless better considered separately.

In situations where uncontrolled political power prevails, obedience becomes the greatest virtue of the citizen. The religious precept, first enunciated by Tertullian, *"credo quia absurdum"* —"I believe because it is absurd"—is also applied to political matters. The act of believing goes through four (or sometimes five) stages. In the first stage the citizen cannot believe a certain statement or ideology because *it is absurd.* In the second stage the citizen forces himself to believe it, even though it is absurd. But this is too much to ask. Reason does not permit it. In the third stage the citizen finds great merit in believing something *because it is absurd.* There is no merit in believing things which are obvious, logical, or rational. It is not necessary to be a good citizen in order to be able to believe the obvious. This third stage is a period of stress which would be impossible to endure if it were not rapidly followed by the fourth stage in which the citizen comes to believe that the belief is *not absurd* at all but is true. The acceptance of the belief removes anxiety and conflict and brings about peace, tranquility, and security. Thus the citizen convinces himself that the leader or the party is right: it is good to believe! The former anxiety was felt as a conflict between a fear of punishment if you do not obey, and a betrayal of conscience if you do obey.

In the fifth stage, which occurs only in some cases, the citizen develops the *habit* of believing any absurdity coming from the leader without questioning it. Thus, either through an act of will or through habit, the citizen ends by obeying. Only a few strong ones are able to resist. The feeling of peace and security that most citizens attain during the fourth stage is false, of course, but it brings about relief from terror.

It is impossible to summarize here all the alterations that un-controlled political power will produce on people because effects vary according to circumstances. Some specific situations, such as colonialism and slavery, will be considered later in this chapter. When the individual sees all the prerogatives of life that are generally expressed through his will removed one by one, he may feel utterly deprived. He may see his life as being gradually stripped of meaning and consequently may become depressed. On the other hand, he may decide to surrender to this meaninglessness. In either case the solution necessitates a stultification of his existence. What he undergoes is different from the deformation of the self described in Chapter 6 and 7. Stultification is a consequence of the person's giving up all the functions of life which require free will. Stultification will be complete in most cases of slavery; it will be less pronounced in cases of so-called benevolent despotism.

Stultification may be arrested to some extent if external conditions will permit the individual to receive some love, either from his companions in submission or from institutions or religious ideas. Vicious circles, however, are formed because at times pseudoreligious ideas are exploited to perpetuate the intolerable situation. For instance, when a slave is made to believe that it is the will of God (and not of men) that he is a slave, or that he will be compensated in paradise if he behaves like a good slave while he is alive, tragic paradoxes are created.

EXTREME FORMS OF POWER

Power may reach extreme degrees in such special situations as colonialism, slavery, and concentration camps.

Colonialism is probably the mildest of these extremes. It is defined as the establishment and maintenance of rule over a foreign people.[27] In its modern Western form it started with the Portuguese explorations in the fifteenth century.

Colonialism implies the belief, not explicitly expressed, that a nation superior by virtue of its race and culture, more powerful because of military power or industrial equipment, better provided economically, and Christian in religion, has the right to dominate foreign countries inferior in race and culture, not powerful enough to resist successfully, not equipped industrially or economically, and not Christian in religion. At times, the colonization went to the extreme of almost totally exterminating the indigenous population. Often the conquerors professed to be there to save the souls of the natives by converting them to Christianity. While they were trying to save the natives' souls, they were busy dispossessing them of their goods, natural resources, land, and personal freedom. The conqueror was depicted as a person reluctant to conquer, but who accepted this heavy responsibility, the White Man's Burden, in a spirit of altruism, to spread culture and the true religion. The truth was, of course, that the conquering nation wanted to increase its power militarily, economically, and politically.

If colonialism improved during the last few centuries to the extent that it became possible for a man, let us say, under French rule in North Africa or English rule in India, to acquire a limited freedom of action, it was only because it was more advantageous for the conquering nation to grant that relative freedom than forcibly to impose harder conditions of living.

The colonial status was always detested by the subordinate societies. Frantz Fanon, in *The Wretched of the Earth*, has described very well the condition of the colonized people.[28] The person who is colonized undergoes adverse changes in his personality similar to those which I have called stultification of the self. The few defenders of colonialism have repeatedly stated that it was necessary to spread by military conquest spiritual values and scientific achievements. It seems hardly believable that such aims should require these methods. If the Europeans wanted to spread Jesus' message of love, subjugation and extermination do not seem to be the most appropriate procedures to do it. At any rate, religious proselytism through colonization was very limited. The only aspects of life which could be transmitted were the scientific and technological. But the example of Japan shows that it is better not to subjugate a nation militarily in order to make her participate in scientific progress. Nevertheless, despite its terrible qualities, colonialism is not the worst institution of extreme power. Slavery is infinitely worse.

Slavery has existed since ancient times. According to the Bible, kidnapping and selling a man was a capital offense. If the master had injured the body of his slave, the slave could obtain his freedom. If a slave ran away, he could not be returned to his master. Deuteronomy 23 : 15-16, says, "You shall not give up to his master a slave who has escaped from his master to you; he shall dwell with you, in your midst, in the place which he shall choose within one of your towns, where it pleases him best; you shall not oppress him." What a difference from the fugitive slave law that existed in America, which permitted the tracking of runaway slaves by bloodhounds!

Many books have been written about the horrors of slavery and especially of American slavery, the most brutal and inhuman which has ever existed. For an adequate account of this tragic institution it is necessary to read at least the book by T. D. Weld, published in 1839,[29] and the recent one by Elkins.[30] Only a few facts will be summarized here.

Certain African native chiefs in league with whites staged raids on neighboring tribes. The captives were frequently taken by surprise while peacefully living in their villages. After the shock of being captured, the prisoners found themselves in the hands of foreigners, brutal masters who could not understand their languages and in any case did not care to understand them. The second episode was the long march to the sea. Under a scorching sun and unbearable climatic conditions, fed a minimum of food, tied together like cattle, barefooted and barely clothed, they were driven to the coast. Many died, as hundreds of skeletons on the caravan routes have attested. Those who survived had to undergo inspection. If they were not well enough to be sold, they were abandoned on the coast to die of starvation. Those who were sold had to cross the ocean in ships reminiscent of Dante's infernal pits, where filth, disease, crowding, and cruelty prevailed. The captives had undergone such terrible experiences that when they arrived in the New World they were eager to be sold. The new owners at least were motivated to promote their survival.

The sold slave was completely uprooted from those who shared his language and habits, from those he loved and had lived with, and from the land he was accustomed to. Everything was strange and incomprehensible to him except the whip of his master. He was reduced to a tool, a valuable tool which would increase the power of the master. The first shipload of Negroes arrived in Virginia in 1619, but it was much later before slavery was regulated by law. While the lot of white servants progressively improved, that of Negro slaves became worse. Elkins, writes:

> The rights of property and all other civil and legal "rights" were everywhere denied the slave with a clarity that left no doubt of his utter dependency upon his master . . . A slave is in absolute bondage; he has no civil right, and can hold no property, except at the will and pleasure of his master . . . He could neither give nor receive gifts; he could make no will, nor could he, by will, inherit anything. He could not hire himself out or make contracts for any purpose—even including that of matrimony—and thus neither his word nor his bond had any standing in law. He could buy or sell nothing at all, except as his master's agent, could keep no cattle, horses, hogs, or sheep, and, in Mississippi at least, could raise no cotton . . . It was obvious, then, that the case of a slave who should presume to buy his own freedom—he being unable to possess money—would involve a legal absurdity.[31]

Elkins describes in detail many other regulations by which slavery was perpetuated. Every Southern state except Maryland and Kentucky forbade teaching slaves reading and writing because education might promote insurrection and rebellion. In North Carolina it was a crime to distribute books to them, including the Bible. The law also clearly established that embracing Christianity did not remove the state of slavery. The conjugal state of a slave was not recognized and had no legal standing. Elkins quotes a North Carolina judge who, in 1858, ruled that "the relation between slaves is essentially different from that of man and wife joined in lawful wedlock . . . for with slaves it may be dissolved at the pleasure of either party, or by the sale of one or both, depending on the caprice or necessity of the owners."[32] Only mating, not marriage, was compatible with the condition of slavery. Children could be separated from their parents at the whim of the owner, who could sell them. Paternity was not acknowledged for slaves. They derived their status from being born from mothers who were slaves. If the children had derived their slave condition from their fathers, the many mulatto children—born from the concubinage of white fathers and slave mothers—would have been lost to their owners and would have constituted an embarrassing situation to their fathers. Thus these men, after having enjoyed sexual relations with black women, permitted their own children to grow into a state of slavery.

Since the Civil War generations of white people have criticized some blacks for their relatively lax sexual and marital habits. Here again is proof of how easy it is for the powerful to confuse cause and effect. The majority inflicts a certain characteristic or trend on the powerless minority; it then condemns the minority for having the characteristic. On the contrary, blacks should have been praised for having been able to rid themselves to such a marked degree of the habits imposed on them.

American slavery was a closed system. There was no possibility for a person born a slave to free himself, and all his children and his children's children were doomed to be slaves. In Latin America, slavery did not reach the same degree of barbarism as in the United States. The church and the crown had more power to protect the slaves. The slave was respected in his basic personality traits and the possibility of redemption really existed. Slavery was thus an open system.

In addition to enormous suffering, slavery inflicted damaging characteristics on the personality. It undoubtedly produced a certain amount of primitivization of the self in the owner, and deformation and stultification of the self in the slave. The Negro was Sambo: an infantile character, submissive, docile, irresponsible, loyal like a dog, lazy, a half-person, and given to lying and stealing. Again the cause was confused with the effect. The Negro lost all his native resourcefulness. He was deprived of his human characteristics, the aim to fulfill himself, and yet was expected to have a sense of responsibility, responsibility towards a fellow man who professed a belief in human brotherhood and reduced him to a tool.

The phenomenon of slavery in America is difficult to reconcile with the tenets of civilized man. We cannot say that slavery always existed and it was automatically imported to the American colonies. Although it is true that some slavery existed in some countries, Western civilization as a whole had abandoned slavery on a large scale long before. Serfdom in the Middle Ages was a much more benevolent social state, and even slavery in Greek and Roman times was less cruel than American slavery. It is hard to believe that spiritual and political leaders could remain indifferent to this human tragedy or make only weak or token protest, if any, against the institution.

How could such revered people as George Washington, Thomas Jefferson, and Benjamin Franklin say, "We hold these truths to be self-evident, that all men are created equal, and that they are endowed by their Creator with certain inalienable rights. . . ," and still uphold slavery? How could Christians induce non-Christians to love their neighbors like themselves, when their neighbors made them their slaves? Some explain that the institution of slavery was the result of unopposed or unrestrained capitalism. Certainly the desire to be rich at others' expense was part of the problem. But much more was involved. Even if one was to believe (which I do not) that the only aim of the slaveowner was to be rich, what must be explained is the willingness to attain this aim by transforming a human being into a tool, an instrument of another, reducing him to a thing, and then blaming him for having the characteristics of a thing. This way of becoming rich was much worse than ordinary stealing, for it was a crime not to property but to human dignity. Thus, no matter how strong the desire to become rich is, the willingness and readiness to reduce other people to the condition of slavery shows an incredible moral turpitude. To what decadence must society have fallen to permit such a depraved means to be justified for the end of being rich? Let us focus on the turpitude and deprivation rather than on the aim of becoming rich, which is not so contemptible. Moreover, was being rich the real ultimate end? What about the desire to be powerful?

In England some people were powerful by reason of inherited nobility. The aristocratic tradition perpetuated a powerful caste. When nonaristocratic Englishmen came to America, they found ways to emulate the aristocracy from which they were excluded. They could achieve a different privileged status by enslaving men and by the methods of unrestrained capitalism. Slavery made the free man feel powerful by giving him undisputed control over other human beings and enabling him to use them so that he could become even more powerful. In other words, the slaveowner could cover up his many limitations by exerting the most extreme form of surplus power over some of his fellow men. Thus the slaveowner was not free either: he too was a psychological victim of the depraved practice of slavery.

Once a few power-seeking people succeeded in making slavery and its brutal implications legal, it was easy to implement and increase to a large scale its practices. The institution was sanctioned by the law of the land and supported by the privileged class. Only a bloody civil war could change the system. In South American countries, where slavery had never been so entrenched in the social system, no civil war was necessary to abolish it.

Power can also manifest itself as the capacity to exploit others for sexual or sadistic pleasures. Although sadism was inherent in the use of the whip on the part of the slaveowner, it was much more pronounced in another terrible institution created by men, the Nazi concentration camps. At first the camps were used as instruments of terror. The prominent enemies of the Nazis were to be intimidated by knowing of the mere existence of such camps. If they protested, they would end there. When these enemies were eliminated, the camps continued to function, receiving all potential and imaginary enemies of the state. Most of them were Jews who had not succeeded in emigrating to other countries. Six million of them were imprisoned and either worked to death or else simply killed. Most were kept hungry and thirsty, undernourished, dirty; they were beaten, tortured, kept uncertain of life and death, compelled to give up moral values in order to survive another day or to be the last in the group to die, brutalized in previously unconceived ways, and finally stripped and taken naked to the gas chamber to die. After their death their gold teeth were collected, their bones used to manufacture soap, and in some cases their skin used to make lamp shades. Pregnant women in labor had their legs tied to prevent them from giving birth, and children were killed in front of their parents. Only a few Jews survived, among them pretty girls used by Nazi leaders as sexual objects.

It is impossible to explain this horror in terms of capitalism, or in rational terms of any kind. Even if you believe the Jews were enemies to be eliminated together with their wives and little children, why make them suffer before killing them, to unheard of extremes of cruelty? Power, to the degree to which the Nazis reached it, included the possibility of an extreme sadistic, perverted pleasure. Such an extreme degree of power permits the release of the most depraved tendencies in man. Primitivization at its acme is the ultimate consequence of uncontrolled power.

THE WATCHERS OF EVIL

The Nazis' treatment of the Jews was similar to what happened earlier in our century, though on a smaller scale. I am referring again to the massacre of the Armenian people by the Turks.

The young Turk triumvirate consisting of the nefarious Talaat, Enver, and Djemal went to power and joined Germany in the First World War, hoping to restore the crumbling Ottoman

Empire to greatness. The Armenians, a persecuted Christian minority in an Islamic country, demanded basic rights. The war provided the opportunity for the government of Turkey to eliminate the Armenian problem by eliminating the Armenians.

A systematic plan of annihilation was put into motion by Talaat Pasha. First, the able men were inducted for military service and obliged to work mercilessly until they died of starvation or exhaustion or were killed outright. Next, the Armenian leaders, intellectuals, teachers, and clergymen were killed. Finally, the masses were robbed of all their property, tortured, deported, and finally murdered in the first great genocide of history. Although the Turks did not reach the same degree of sophisticated sadism of the Nazis, they were criminal enough to horrify the world. And yet the world did nothing. There was no punishment for the guilty. Although the Nürnberg trials were a ludicrously feeble response to the Nazi horror, at least they were a symbol of the world's protest. There was no sign of protest during or after the Armenian massacre. While it would have been difficult to stop a Hitler or a Stalin from perpetrating their massive crimes, since the power of the systems which they had built had become uncontrollable, it would have been relatively easy to stop the Turks. The Turkish government did not have enough strength to remain callous to an outside appeal. On the other hand, it had enough power to control its citizens.

The Germans and the Austrians did not lift a finger to dissuade their allies from massacring two and a half million Christians. England was powerful enough to do something indirectly, even as a belligerent, but she did not interfere. After the war, the Allies, although victors, never bothered to punish those responsible. Although it is impossible to predict what would have happened if the responsible Turks had been punished, it is reasonable to suppose that their punishment might have been a deterrent later for Hitler when he planned a massacre of even greater proportions. The fact that the world did not even make a gesture to help the Armenians or to punish their murderers reinforced Hitler's conviction that the law of the jungle is the one which prevails among men. As he revealed his plan for genocide to his general staff on August 22, 1939, Hitler remarked, "Who, after all, speaks today of the annihilation of the Armenians? . . . The world believes in success alone." [33]

The attitude of the world toward the Armenian massacre suggests that there are four roles men can play in relation to evil. First, there is the victim. Then, there is the evildoer. Next, and these are by far the fewest, is the opponent of evil. Finally, and as a rule the most numerous, is the evil watcher: he who witnesses evil and does nothing to stop it. It is this fourth category that we must examine at this point.

A few years ago, a young woman, Kitty Genovese, was brutally assaulted and stabbed to death in the borough of Queens, New York City, by a criminal who was later apprehended. Thirty-five people heard her screams for help. None of them went to help her; no one even called the police. In this case, the evildoer was a man, probably mentally unbalanced; therefore, the power represented by his mental aberration is not typical of the evildoers described in this chapter. Nevertheless, like the Nazis, this man robbed the victim, raped her, and gleefully stabbed her to death. Like the Nazi victims, Miss Genovese was the innocent victim of the utmost brutality.

By the highest principles of Western civilization we must believe, and rightly so, that her position was morally more enviable than that of the man who perpetrated the crimes against her. The two great branches of Western civilization have taught us to think so. In the Judaeo-Christian tradition, represented by the Old and the New Testaments, it is better to suffer evil than to do it. In the Greek tradition, the opinions that Plato attributed to Socrates are outstanding. In the *Gorgias,* Socrates' eloquent words demonstrate how it is better to suffer evil than to commit it. But there is another situation in which man often finds himself: witnessing evil. How should we judge the evil watchers, those who see Kitty Genovese or millions of people massacred and do nothing? Somebody might rightly say that it is too dangerous to oppose or even expose the evildoers. Can we expect people to be heroes and face death? How can we expect the individual to oppose the slaveowner when a terrible civil war was necessary to do so? To oppose Hitler and Stalin meant to sacrifice one's life and, in some cases, the lives of one's family as well. Only military defeat in one case, and natural death in the other, could put an end to their terrors.

It is too much to expect people to be heroes, and the supreme sacrifice of one's life should *not* be required to oppose tyranny. What we can do is prevent it—make sure that no person, however harmless or highminded he seems, obtains surplus power—more power than he is entitled to. The power-seeking person or institution should be stopped at the start. Americans allowed slavery to grow from an infrequent occurrence in early colonial days to a recognized and legalized institution. Germans allowed Hitler to become a criminal tyrant although they had ample evidence from his previous writings and speeches of what he intended to do.

Particularly reprehensible in the role of evil watchers are those persons who have a special power to stop evil and do not, or those persons who have been empowered by the people as guardians of liberty and yet do not live up to this trust. Even Jonah, when as God's prophet was charged with conveying the message to Nineveh and yet refused to go, ran the risk of becoming an evil watcher. But finally he helped to stop the evil.

We have seen in this century many leaders who, with their silence, have permitted evil to run its disastrous course. Some of them who held important positions of political or spiritual leadership have already been the object of much discussion and controversy. I wish to discuss here one of them who, as a watcher of evil, became a major cause of international disaster far beyond what could have been predicted from his position. I am referring to the infamous king of Italy, Victor Emmanuel III, who will be remembered in history for his demerits, which had repercussions even outside the borders of his unfortunate country. To understand his role we have to evaluate him in the context of the constitutional monarchy of the House of Savoy. The monarchy seemed a benevolent institution, devised to keep the country together after Italy was unified for the first time since the fall of the Roman Empire. The monarchy was supposed to guarantee the principles of freedom and self-government which had been formulated by the Italian liberals.

The first two kings after the unification in 1865 indeed were benevolent monarchs. The first, Victor Emmanuel II, was fortunate enough to live at a time when such great men as Camillo Cavour and Giuseppe Garibaldi were active and the intricate political situation of France permitted the unification of Italy to occur formally as a kingdom under the House of Savoy. The greatest interest of Victor Emmanuel II was not Italy but the favors of his mistress, the beautiful Countess Rosina di Mirafiori. The second king, Humbert I, killed in 1900 by an anarchist, was almost illiterate. He hardly ever read a book. He, too, was mainly interested in his paramours, and especially in the seductive art of the duchess Litta, whom he made live in a home built in the park of his royal palace. Except that for the benefit of the credulous Italian people an aura of greatness was artificially created around the name of Victor Emmanuel and an aura of goodness around the name of Humbert, these two men did not do much damage.

The trouble started with the third king of Italy, Victor Emmanuel III. To my knowledge, it has never been reported that he led a lecherous life like his father and grandfather. Perhaps it would have been better if he had. Instead, he seems to have remained faithful to his wife Elena. Indeed, it might have been difficult for him to behave otherwise in this respect. He was very short, physically clumsy, unappealing, and probably suffered from a deep inferiority complex. Mussolini must have appeared to him a he-man: strong, robust, courageous, the opposite of what he was. If the king was almost a pygmy in his appearance, he was totally a pygmy in his spiritual dimensions. He did not live up to the oath he took and the commitments he made upon ascending to the throne. Contrary to the wishes of the majority of the Italian people, he permitted Mussolini to form the government, and kept Mussolini in power. The king actually watched him abolish one by one all the democratic institutions of the country without doing anything to stop him. The king was the person who, more easily than anybody else, could have stopped Mussolini, and as the royal guardian of the constitution, he had the duty to do so. Instead, as the nominal chief executive, he put his seal on all the acts of the Fascist regime. He gave to them the regal sanction and the prestige of the monarchy. This was particularly important in relation to the army, many of the officers of which still retained the medieval concept of personal loyalty to the king. Thus, if the king went along with Mussolini, the army must do the same. The king did not make even a gesture of disapproval when Mussolini eliminated civil rights, waged immoral wars, persecuted without any reason small minorities, and even when he took away some prerogatives and rights which, according to the Italian constitution, belonged to the crown. Eventually the power of the king was so greatly diminished that it would not have been possible to get rid of Mussolini without a military defeat. The king at first seemed a gullible admirer of Mussolini or an accomplice for the purpose of retaining power. Then he appeared to be too cowardly to stop him. The king could have deposed Mussolini in 1925 when the dictator was in serious trouble after the murder of the antifascist Matteotti. Finally he seemed entrapped by the Duce's Machiavellian schemes.

But the king always professed great admiration and friendship for Mussolini. It was only when Italy was about to be defeated militarily that the king betrayed Mussolini too and, with the help of Marshal of the Army Badoglio, had him arrested. This abominable king did not do so to help the Italian people (who had needed his help long before) but in a vain attempt to save the crown, which he correctly assumed was in danger. This royal pygmy thus deserves to be studied as a paradigm on three counts.

1. He is a typical example of an evil watcher. He was the most suitable person to stop Mussolini, but he did not. He must be considered second only to Mussolini in bearing the responsibility for the evils which befell Italy.

2. He is a typical example of surplus power given to a single person. According to the Italian constitution, a person like Victor Emmanuel III by accident of birth had the power to appoint as prime minister a psychopathic adventurer like Mussolini.

3. He is a typical example of the role played by personalities as well as by chance and contingency in history. The will of a person like Victor Emmanuel III had the possibility of unchaining a series of events of tremendous proportions and unpredictable ramifications.

It is not implausible that if Mussolini had not had access to power, Hitler, too, would not have gained power. In the first years of organizing the Nazi party, Hitler used Mussolini as his model and inspiration. He was also helped by Mussolini. Franco, too, would not have come to power without the help of Mussolini and Hitler. It can thus be conjectured that if the king of Italy, by an act of his will, had not given power to Mussolini, the course of European history from 1922 on would have been different. I realize that this is only a hypothetical formulation, but this matter deserves to be studied. Another unbelievable thing is that the king was never made to pay for his misdeeds. The French probably would have done to him what they did to Louis XVI or at least to Petain, but the generous Italians did otherwise. The king was allowed to abdicate peacefully and to spend the last year of his life in the warm hospitality offered him by his fellow king, the playboy Farouk of Egypt. His son Humbert II became king. After a month of his reign, Italy voted in a general referendum either to maintain the monarchy or establish a republic. The republic won, amazingly, by a thin margin. In some regions of Italy the majority still wanted the king. The crown had been endocratized by millions.

INVISIBLE POWER IN DEMOCRATIC COUNTRIES

Whereas in both Fascist and Communist countries power is openly exercised, in democratic countries it tends to remain invisible or at least inconspicuous. In a democracy power cannot reach monstrous degrees as in Fascist and Communist countries, but it may nevertheless obtain great proportions. As a matter of fact, in a democracy power is often more effectively exercised "invisibly." After the pioneer work of Gaetano Mosca and later C. Wright Mills, many have shown how power is concentrated in the hands of an elite.

The majority of people in some democratic countries have become so unaware of basic political realities that they don't seem to recognize the existence of unfair accumulations of power. Some people vaguely protest the power of the Establishment, but they don't go any further. Whatever is established has the power conferred by tradition, habits, and consensus. Within the Establishment, however, we must distinguish a *ruling coalition*, which consists of the individuals and institutions which decide how the country is ruled, oriented, and shaped. The ruling coalition generally preserves the status quo which, in its turn, preserves the privileges of its members. The ruling coalition, however, may permit some changes and even developments toward growth, provided again they do not challenge the vested interests and values of its members.

The ruling coalition consists of enclaves of power such as the army, the major political parties, the major banks, the large firms, some churches, the great industries, the lobbies, etc. Some enclaves, like the army, are so strong as to influence the whole country; others affect only a segment of it. Within big corporations there are enclaves of power formed by some executives and officers. All these agglomerations of power have the tendency to centralize the power in a decreasing number of hands.

Many authors in recent years have exposed the power of the corporate society. It is not one of the aims of this book to repeat these exposés. For the sake of continuity and in an effort to focus on what is relevant to our major points, however, I shall summarize some of these findings. Some of these facts have already been mentioned in Chapter 7 in reference to the deformation of the self, but will be reexamined here from the point of view of power.

The 150 largest firms in the United States produce more than half of the country's manufactured goods and control a large segment of the country's economy. Ownership of these corporations is supposed to be divided among the stockholders, but in practice the stockholders have virtually no power. They assume that they do not know much about business, and in practically every case they support the recommendations of the management. Thus power concentrates in a few hands to a much greater extent than people realize. Not only do corporate managers establish the prices that they believe the market will bear with little interference from the government, but they flood the country with new items; they mold the taste of people to fit their own purposes; they constantly promote in people a need for new products. The consumer thus has the illusion of discovering in himself secret needs that the corporate managers enable him to gratify. No new secret needs are really brought to consciousness (need for an electric toothbrush, or a car, or a television set), but in fact new desires are stimulated.

Whereas in previous societies, and especially in those founded on the puritan ethic, the individual learned that virtue consisted in saving and being parsimonious, now he is under a constant persuasion to "buy, buy, buy! consume! consume! consume!" But the puritan ethic has not been completely eliminated from our midst. Thus the individual is in a double bind. He receives two messages at the same time: save and spend. He does not know what to do. If he believes in the puritan ethic he feels corruptible and corrupted when he indulges in material gratification. If he believes that the puritan ethic is hypocritical and irrelevant in an era not characterized by scarcity, then he feels that if he renounces material goods then he, too, becomes hypocritical.

The situation is reminiscent of society's two-faced attitude toward sex. On one side the individual is surrounded by an increasing number of obvious and impelling sexual stimuli. On the other side he is often told to repress or suppress the primitive instinct. A reasonable attitude toward consumerism resembles a reasonable attitude toward sex. The drastic restrictions imposed by a puritan ethic of scarcity are no longer necessary. If more products are available to improve the life of people, this is to the good. But if the mind of the citizen is diverted from most other activities and the only aim is to be a consumer, the other dimensions of life will atrophy. Whereas the puritan ethic preached deferral of gratification and avoidance of indulgence, the corporate society preaches immediate indulgence and ignores spiritual gratification. But if the spiritual gratification is deferred for too long, the person will lose any need for it, and complete immersion in a materialistic life will ensue. We have already seen in Chapter 7 the consequent deformation of the self. Consumerism does not really satisfy the soul. When people go beyond the immediate pleasure, they realize that they are still discontented.

As a result of these trends people are possessed by the desire to possess. They are also possessed by those persons who promote and control this desire. But why is the corporate elite promoting materialistic desires? Ostensibly in order to make money, but in reality the aim is the retention and increase of power. The relation between the corporate elite and the people is based on an exchange: possession for power. The elite gives material goods (such toys for grownups as cars, dresses, and television sets); the people give the elite increased power. Money seems to be the end; actually it is the means. The invisible end, of which even many members of the elite are not conscious, is power.

Marx and the Marxists are correct in saying that a starving person in a capitalistic society is not free because he has to do things that he would not do if he were well fed. Freedom is thus an illusion for the proletariat. But a similar, although not identical, statement could be made for a consumeristic society, which is neither starving nor proletarian. Whereas until recently most people were kept down so that they could be forced to yield power, now only a minority is kept so: those who still belong to the diminishing proletarian class. Most people in advanced Western societies today are swamped with material possessions. Their power as individuals is still taken away and their spiritual needs are diminished. They become the slaves of consumerism and of those who promote consumerism. Consumerism is justified by many with the pretext that it provides jobs. But if the work of these people were diverted to occupations which benefit society (building schools and hospitals, protecting the environment, beautifying cities and countryside, etc.), jobs would not be scarce.

The proof that money or profit are not the ultimate end of this aspect of our society is to be found in the fact that similar phenomena take place in Communist countries, and especially in Russia. Whereas the ostensible aim of productive organizations in capitalistic countries is maximization of profit for the stockholders, in Russia it is maximization of benefit for the state. In both cases there is unequal distribution of power. In the Soviet Union's organization, the state hierarchy, the party bureaucracy, and the managerial elite constitute the ruling coalition which controls power. Although consumerism does not yet endanger Communist countries, unequal distribution of power occurs there as well. In both the Soviet Union and in capitalistic countries people are served by the coalition only in ways which do not jeopardize the elite's power.

Many authors have illustrated accumulation of power in some segments of society. For instance, the scientific community, which once consisted of persons interested only in scientific pursuits, now tends to shift its aim toward retention or accumulation of power, either by working for the corporate elite or for the state.

Society also crystallizes some positions which have unusual attributes of power. Here are a few examples. Some judges have the power to declare an accused person guilty or innocent and to sentence him. While for some crimes some judges give sentences of a few months duration, others give terms of many years. Such variations are determined not by the law or the traditions of the locality but exclusively by the personal point of view of the judge. Some lawyers can predict how a judge will sentence a given person and try to have the client tried by him, or to avoid him, according to whether the judge is deemed favorable or unfavorable. For such an important matter as sentencing a man, the decision of at least a group of men should always be required. It is true that even when decisions are supposed to be made by a group, one person within the group may succeed in dominating the others and have his point of view prevail, but this is not necessarily the case. At least the most obvious cases of unfair sentencing would be eliminated.

In academic life, too, coalitions of power are formed. Certain positions, especially department chairmanships, are not given necessarily to the most meritorious persons but to the person who has been able to accumulate the greatest support. The situation is also complicated by the fact that within the same department power maneuvers take place and intradepartmental tensions develop.

The various departments of medical schools have become huge organizations with many branches. Often the chairman, consciously or unconsciously, imitates the prevailing methods of the corporate state. The chairman is generally an administrator concerned only with smooth organization and with "producing" as much as possible. He must deliver so many well-trained doctors. Thus the school maintains the function of providing professional men, but not that of establishing a climate propitious to academic freedom. In many cases the chairman becomes an increasingly skillful administrator and an increasingly stale clinician, teacher, and researcher. Since he must retain some academic prestige, in some instances he "persuades" other people to do his academic work for him. Thus he asks people to write articles or even books in which the name of the chairman appears (sometimes even as the senior author), although he may have done no work at all or very little. For these services he will reward his collaborators with academic titles, just as kings of old used to ennoble their devoted subjects.

I repeat that these examples of accumulation of power in democracies, although not so terrible as those described in other sections of this chapter, are bad enough to produce deformation, and to a lesser extent, stultification of the self. The fact that these cases are not so obvious or visible adds to their danger.

By sharpening his eye and maintaining a state of alertness the citizen can recognize in the areas of society in which he is involved many situations in which power accumulates to the detriment of the many and to the nonspiritual aggrandizement of the few. It is part of the exercising of one's will to discover these intricate maneuvers and to oppose them to the best of one's ability.

THE DENIAL

In previous sections of this chapter we have seen the reasons, originating from endocratic surplus or from brutal external power, which make people accept even the most unpleasant conditions. An additional reason exists, not only in situations of tyranny, but even in less pronounced conditions of surplus power. This is a psychological defense which psychoanalysts call *denial*.

The individual says to himself, "It is not really so; such power does not exist because if it did exist, it would be too terrible. Such terrible things cannot possibly be." If the chief of a country makes a special law which seems unfair, this law cannot be unfair because it is inconceivable that a chief of a country could make such an unfair law. Similar illogical ways of thinking expand to other areas. If a chief orders an unjust war, that war [Vietnam] cannot be unjust because it is impossible to believe that the greatest authority would require such a war.

Denials and exonerations of all kinds are used to rationalize acceptance of terror or power. If a minority is persecuted, that minority must deserve persecution. If soldiers, in the tumult [Mai Lai] of warfare, have killed civilian population, including children, invalids, and pregnant women, they must be excused. They did not know what they were doing. Excusing these massacres is preferable to accepting a version of facts which would bring dishonor to one's country. In some of these cases a *collective denial* may actually take place, at times reaching absurd proportions. A murderer may be transformed into a hero. *Denial is thus a strong ally of the forces of coercion.* [Calley]

The time is now ripe for many kinds of men to make new contributions to the vast subject of liberation. Novelists, philosophers, and more recently sociologists have done this. Psychiatrists and psychoanalysts should join forces in this important task, for they have been trained to become experts in detecting facts and ideas which have become unconscious or denied in various ways. If these facts and ideas could be brought to consciousness, they would stimulate men to actions which otherwise would or could not be taken. No one should fear that these actions would lead to violence. Better than most men, psychiatrists know the destructive effects of violence. Violence or denial are not psychiatric methods of solving problems.

CHAPTER 10

The Will in Psychiatric Disorders

SOCIETY AND MENTAL ILLNESS

IF MAN'S INHUMANITY TO MAN REACHES THE PROPORTIONS DES-
cribed in the previous chapter, does it not follow that the minds
of many victimized people should succumb to illness? The obvious answer seems to be yes, for one would expect a clear-cut
connection between mental disorder and the brutal exercise of
power. We must restrain our ethical or therapeutic zeal, however, and refrain from claiming causal links unless we have
clearly established them.

To illustrate the relations between sociopsychological factors
and mental illness we shall take as an example the patient suffering from the paranoid type of schizophrenia.

At the beginning of Chapter 5 we saw that, along with basic
trust, each individual experiences basic mistrust; that is, a certain suspicion about the intentions of others. This feeling is
more pronounced in the person likely to become a paranoid
schizophrenic. Such a person develops special attitudes toward

people who appear to him hostile and malevolent. Before the
patient becomes openly psychotic, generally in late adolescence
or early youth, he comes to believe that his future is hopeless
and that the promise of his life will not be fulfilled. More
then that, he feels threatened by hostile powers from all sides,
as if he were in a jungle. It is not a jungle where lions, tigers,
snakes, and spiders are to be found, but a jungle of concepts,
where the threat is not to survival but to the self-image. The
dangers are concept-feelings such as those of being unwanted,
unloved, inadequate, unacceptable, inferior, awkward, clumsy,
not belonging, peculiar, different, rejected, humiliated, guilty,
unable to find one's own way among the different paths of life,
disgraced, discriminated against, kept at a distance, suspected,
etc.

When the patient becomes a full-fledged psychotic, the jungle
is no longer one of concepts. The experience, which before
could be accepted on a metaphorical level, becomes a system of
delusions and often of hallucinations. The patient may really
see and hear human persecutors appearing as lions and tigers,
or as murderers, rapacious monsters, etc.

The usual psychiatric interpretations given to explain this
negative appraisal of the world, first in the prepsychotic and
then in the psychotic experience, are the following:

1. The parents of the patient were poor representatives of the
world. Because of their own hostility, or neurosis or psychosis,
they inflicted psychological traumata on the children, who became unfit for the world and distorted their own experiences.

2. The child's mentality is still under the influence of what
Freud called the primary process. The primary process is a
primitive functioning of the mind seen in the normal person in
his dreams and in the psychotic person in waking life. When the
mind functions in accordance with the primary process, it does
not follow logic but a bizarre and irrational way of thinking.
Whereas the normal child rapidly acquires the ability to think
logically (or according to what Freud called the modality of
the secondary process), the child who was exposed to an unfavorable family environment continues to interpret the world
in a negative way which embodies the primary process. He
responds to the hostility to which he is exposed by magnifying
and distorting it into fantastic forms. This greater use of the
primary process and the experiences which result from it lead
him to a series of events which make him increasingly malad-
justed. Eventually he will become psychotic and then will use

the primary process preponderantly. He will feel, think, and act in waking life as a normal person does in his dreams.

These two hypotheses are fundamentally correct, although they probably do not include all the requirements necessary for the engendering of paranoid schizophrenia. I have devoted most of my studies and therapeutic activities to patients suffering from this condition, and I can assert without hesitation that I have never seen a schizophrenic patient who did not come from an unhappy or psychologically disturbed family.[1] I have never seen a patient who, in his early life, consciously or unconsciously, rightly or wrongly, did not experience some important members of his family as malevolent. In many cases the patient had experienced the whole world as inimical to him.

Many psychodynamically-oriented psychiatrists are nowadays ready to affirm that schizophrenic patients were subjected to poor parental care,[2] or that their relations with their parents were distorted and at times unnatural. Marital discord frequently existed, which caused the parents to be hostile to each other.[3] Full of conflicts themselves, they were unable to devote themselves to their children as normal parents do. But were they as malevolent or hostile as the children perceived them? Were the children perhaps interpreting as malevolence what instead was the expression of parental preoccupation and personal difficulties? Or could it also be that viewing one's family and the world as malevolent was a fantasy of the unconscious of the patient or a distortion of an already sick mind, a distortion which, if not arrested or corrected, becomes worse and finally gives rise to the mental illness?

Some psychiatrists believe that this way of perceiving the environment is already the effect of excessive use of primary process. On the other hand, many psychiatrists follow the lead of Theodore Lidz in believing that there is no distortion in the way the patient gives an account of the family picture. Their studies of the families of schizophrenics seem to confirm what the patients experienced.

Some other psychiatrists, dissatisfied with these two hypotheses, follow the Finn Siirala and the Briton Laing with yet a third theory. For them, not only in the family but in the world at large, hostility prevails. The hostility of society is strictly and directly related causally to the psychiatric condition of the patient. For Laing [4] schizophrenia is not a disease but a broken-down relationship. The environment of the patient is so bad that he has to invent special strategies in order "to live this un-livable situation." The illness is such a strategy. The psychotic does not want to do any more denying. He unmasks himself; he unmasks the others. The psychosis is madness only for us, ordinary human beings; actually it may contain the supreme truth. Laing states that when we label some people as schizo-phrenic, this label is a social fact and the social fact a political event. The implication in reading Laing is that the cause of the patient's difficulties is the same hostile power which will im-prison him in an institution or at least label him psychotic.

Some years before Laing, Siirala,[5] in a book and several arti-cles, discussed what he considers the prophetic value of many apparent delusions of schizophrenics. Siirala sees the patient as a victim and as a prophet to whom nobody listens. He sees the therapist as a person who has the duty to reveal to society the prophecies of these patients. These prophecies consist of insights into our collective sickness, into the murders that we have com-mitted for many generations and which we have buried so that they will not be noticed. He feels that schizophrenia emerges out of a common sort of sickness, a sickness shared by the others, the healthy.

The ideas I have expressed in previous chapters would seem to indicate that I might have immediately accepted Siirala's and Laing's positions. On the other hand, although I recognized that these positions contained part of the truth, I felt something was missing and that their presentations, as wholes, had many gaps. When Laing says that labeling a person as schizophrenic is a political event, he is literally right, but some implications of this affirmation may deceive us. Any labeling—that is, any naming—is a social fact because language is a social medium. I agree with Laing, although not many would, that a social fact is also a political event. We have repeatedly stated in this book that any activity of man which involves an act of will affecting others has a political dimension. But, disagreeing with Laing, I believe that recognizing that a patient suffers from schizophrenia is not only a political event; it is also a medical event. When we call an event also medical and not only political, we make fewer headlines, but we embrace more dimensions.

I do agree that the world is by and large hostile, and, as I shall explain shortly, I recognize that there is a relation between social hostility and the prepsychotic and psychotic experiences. The hostility of the environment and the schizophrenic disorder, however, are two different sets of phenomena. The relations between these two sets are by no means so direct or so simple as some authors visualize them.

Because of his past experiences, the patient is particularly attuned to perceive hostility. He seems to have a psychological radar which enables him to detect and register the world's hostility much more than the average person does. It is easy for him (and for his psychiatrist, too) to link this hostility with his suffering. The patient ignores or cannot become aware of all the psychodynamic factors operating in his condition and so he concentrates on the environmental hostility. Although the hostility is causally related to the psychosis, other predisposing factors enable it to become related. A plausible hypothesis, advanced by many authors, is that a biological predisposition is necessary to make the future patient experience the hostility so devastatingly that it leads to mental disorder. Another hypothesis is that the hostility becomes particularly virulent in the absence of spiritual ideologies which could protect the patient.

I think all these theories contain some truth but are inadequate inasmuch as they either fail to recognize openly (although they implicitly admit it) an ethical element or, as in the case of Siirala, they stress only the ethical element. To call social factors purely social is a method of concealing the way these factors really hit the core of the patient. Psychiatry is replete with studies concerning relations between so-called social factors and mental illness. Most of these works have studied such data as immigration and emigration, economic class (especially poverty), ethnic origin, religion, number of children and order of birth between siblings, marital status, and rural or urban environment in relation to the incidence of mental illness. These studies are very important, but miss the crucial point if they remain purely statistical and do not deal with the unethical dealings of men and the suffering that follows from them. Comte probably would call my suggestion a regression from the positivistic to the metaphysical or even theological stage,[6] but it is not really so. I do not advocate abandoning the scientific method, but instead broadening it to take into consideration the political and ethical ones and seeing how they relate to bring about mental disorder.[7] For instance, inability to endure hostility may be a result of deprivation caused by poor parental care. But it is probable that many people were poor in their parental role because they themselves have been adversely affected by a society which discriminated against them, stultified them, deprived them of basic rights or of basic values, indoctrinated them with false ones, and inflicted on them deformation of the self and endocratic surplus.

Mental illness is more likely to be furthered by a hostility which does not constitute a danger to the physical self or an immediate and obvious great suffering. The most damaging hostility, from a psychiatric point of view, is that which threatens the self-image, the inner self, so that the individual feels unable to determine his life, or else that he is responsible for his own miserable destiny. Then he considers himself the author of his own inadequacy and failure, and the maker of his own defeat. Another way by which hostility may predispose to mental illness is by creating a climate of uncertainty and constant insecurity with no possibility of escaping.

On the other hand, in conditions of obvious great suffering, as in catastrophic military defeat, slavery, or concentration camps, there seems to be no immediate rise in the incidence of schizophrenia. The slave generally develops that severe distortion of the personality that I have called stultification of the self, but he is not schizophrenic. Indeed most slaves were so indoctrinated that they did not experience inner conflict. They could live safely as far as survival was concerned if they accepted their condition and tried to be good slaves. They could even find a certain peculiar kind of peace of mind if they became Uncle Toms. The slave is more liable to become schizophrenic if, without possibility of escaping from his slavery, he does not accept his being a slave. In that case he deserves to be praised, and his risk of becoming schizophrenic is to be evaluated ethically in a positive way. The slave is more likely to become schizophrenic also if he feels a failure even as a slave, since he has been indoctrinated to believe that he should be a good slave.

The victim in a concentration camp suffers horrible tortures but does not consider himself responsible for his predicament unless he is also subjected to brainwashing and self-incriminating procedures.

At this point we must reconsider Siirala's views and see whether we can accept them, even if in a different frame of reference. I still believe that although the paranoid schizophrenic may borrow the scenario of the society-oriented person, his suffering can easily be recognized as a personal one. He cannot be literally called a philosopher, a prophet, an innovator, a dissenter, a revolutionary. Nevertheless, we must acknowledge that the schizophrenic responds more to universal hostility than we do, and crumbles more than we do. The psychological pollution of the world seems to concentrate its effects on him because he was weak, deprived in childhood, or biologically less well equipped to defend himself. He reminds me of those fish which absorb mercury discharged into the ocean; those fish tell us that mercury should not be discharged into the ocean.

To discuss whether the paranoid is delusional or a prophet is like discussing whether a dream represents irrationality or reality. The dream, like a novel, may in a fictitious way reveal a truth which is not easily heard when we are awake.

Although the schizophrenic exaggerates and greatly distorts the world's hostility, he reminds us that such hostility exists, even when it is difficult for us to discover it or when our neurotic compensations and denials convince us that it does not exist. He may help us to become aware that our "normality" requires mental mechanisms whose validity is questionable. Normality presupposes adaptation or capacity for adjustment. At times what is required on our part is callousness toward harmful stimuli. We protect ourselves by denying them, hiding them, becoming insensitive, or finding a thousand ways of rationalizing them or adjusting to them. We become the "silent majority." When the preschizophrenic and the schizophrenic see society as a Darwinian jungle, we must remind ourselves that not the patient but Darwin himself first made the metaphor but in the reverse fashion. After having studied society in Malthus' writings, Darwin in the Galapagos Islands saw the jungle as a reproduction of society: animals could be as ferocious as human beings. Inequality, competition, struggle, and power prevailed in the two situations. Unless checked by human will, power wins out in both society and jungle. The future schizophrenic is certainly *not* the fittest in any jungle. When he becomes psychotic he is not literally a prophet, but like a prophet he reminds us of the inimical powers which most of the time win and say "woe to the vanquished." And yet, in spite of its significance, this voice is most of the time too humble, too weak, too deprived of adaptational value to be heard. We must hear it. In this important respect I join Siirala.

By being so sensitive and so vulnerable the patient counteracts the callousness that our "healthy" capacity for adjustment and adaptation has brought about. His message is, "Do not compromise at the cost of mutilating your soul. Do not become the ally of the hostile powers. Do not become a watcher of evil." Thus, there are some values that we can share with the schizophrenic if we recognize them in spite of the distortions and concealments produced by his illness. As I wrote elsewhere,[8] the sharing of these values may help the therapist in his treatment. The basic value of the schizophrenic is actually the basic value of the human being. He wants to be the sovereign of his will, to be totally himself. He does not succeed. As a matter of fact, he finds sovereigns all over, but not in himself. We have seen in Chapter 3 that he feels other people determine that the world will be as it is, but that he has no part in that determination. Although the patient became ill in order not to renounce his will, and to assert himself in an individualistic way, it will be his illness which eventually will deprive him of his volition.

In the rest of this chapter we shall consider some psychiatric disorders, not just because of the probable causal relation between them and social conditions, but because studying them may help us understand some effects that society has on people in general, not merely on those who become mentally ill. Although practically every mental illness may serve for this purpose, I shall take into consideration only three, excluding the paranoid type of schizophrenia, which I have already discussed. These three other conditions are characterized by specific disorders of the will.

THE PSYCHOPATH

There are different types of psychopaths. I shall first consider that variety which I have called the simple type.[9] The simple psychopath is an individual who cannot say no to himself. He periodically undergoes a strong urge to satisfy immediately his needs and wishes. Although he is a person of at least average and often superior intelligence, he cannot delay the fulfillment of his wishes, even when fulfillment puts him in conflict with society. For instance, if he has a strong craving for an object which he cannot have or buy, he will steal it. The desired object cannot be for him just an object of contemplation or something he can hope for or daydream about; it is something to be possessed immediately. He will do anything to attain that end as soon as possible. The psychopath seems to lack anxiety or guilt over his past or future actions; that is, over the means he has used to attain his ends. He also appears unable to learn from experience that his antisocial behavior is self-defeating, even in his own limited terms.

Thus the antisocial character of his actions appears at first as the psychopath's most salient feature. A Robinson Crusoe could not be a psychopath; that is, a psychopathic condition becomes manifest only in a social environment. If the psychopath does not gratify his needs, he builds up a tension which he experiences as an unbearable discomfort. The person who becomes legally insane gratifies his wishes vicariously by changing his thinking processes; for instance, he may develop the delusion that he is the emperor of China and may act as such. But the psychopath maintains a mask of sanity (Cleckley),[10] and the law considers him sane and responsible for his actions. But he does not care how far he deviates from social norms or how primitively he must act to achieve his ends.

In many instances, the psychopath could satisfy his wishes in a more or less ·distant future if he resorted to the complicated series of actions usually necessary for mature, socially acceptable attainment of goals. But he cannot wait. Future satisfaction of needs is something that he cannot understand and that has no emotional impact on him. He lives emotionally in the present and completely disregards tomorrow. He finds it easier and quicker to steal and forge checks than to work, to rape than to find a willing sexual partner, to falsify a diploma than to complete years in school. If he has to lie in order to obtain what he needs, he lies. In some psychopaths the impelling need consists of a primitive urge to discharge rage or hostility through actions without any apparent gain other than the pleasure of inflicting injury to others. In these cases the patient not only is more hostile than the average person, but, unlike the usual neurotic, is unable to change, repress, postpone, or neutralize this need. Whether such an increased need for hostility is based on constitutional factors or on early environmental experiences is impossible to determine at this stage of research.

Most psychopathic needs are primitive; in a large percentage of them sexual gratification plays a relatively unimportant role. There are, however, a considerable number of psychopaths who act out in the sexual areas—by rape or by seduction, by resorting to unfulfilled promises of marriage, etc. In female psychopaths, sexual behavior is often manifested as promiscuity and prostitution.

Psychopaths are said to have no loyalties for any person, group, or code. They are also said to be unable to identify with others or to take the role of the other person. These statements are correct, but they have to be related to the need for quick gratification. The urge to gratify the need is so impelling that the patient *cannot* respect any loyalty or identify at all with other people—he simply cannot visualize the bad effects that his actions will have on others. The patient may intellectually visualize these future bad effects, but these thoughts are not accompanied by deterring emotions.

Intellectually the psychopath knows that the future exists and that he could obtain his aims in ways which are acceptable to society. But this knowledge has for him only a theoretical reality, and he experiences it only in a vague, faint way. At times the patient is able to visualize all the steps which he would have to go through were he to satisfy his needs in socially acceptable ways. These steps, however, remain indistinct; they have a flavor of unreality, so that he cannot even begin thinking about them. On the other hand, he continues to experience the present needs which urge him toward immediate action. The patient knows that he may be caught in the antisocial act and be punished; but again, this punishment appears to him only a theoretical possibility concerning the future, and therefore he does not experience the idea of it with enough emotional strength to change the course of his present actions. The quick actions which he uses are self-defeating and lead inevitably to complications in spite of attempts to avoid them. For instance, a psychopath may simply want to rape a girl, and he carries out his wish; but then the sudden fear comes to him that the girl may report him to the police. So the quickest way to avoid this complication is to kill the girl; but the killing produces more serious complications.

In attempting to avoid complications or ramifications which have to do with future happenings, the psychopath repeatedly places himself in a web of new dangers. This series of imbroglios is clearly illustrated in the following summary of a short story that a patient wrote. The story does not excel in literary value, but it portrays the predicament of the simple psychopath. Although the patient never acted in such a striking manner as the protagonist, obviously he identified with him.

> A young man, during a boring afternoon at his job, has the urge to step out of the office for a coffee break. While he is out he sees a beautiful new car parked on the other side of the street. He goes up to it and sees that the ignition key has been left in the keyhole. The idea comes to him that it would be pleasant to interrupt working and go for a brief ride in the country in that beautiful afternoon of spring. He starts the car and drives into the country, and the riding is so beautiful that

he keeps going until it becomes dark. Unexpectedly a girl crosses the street. The man hits the girl, but does not stop. He is afraid that if he does and the police come, they will believe that he has stolen the car. He drives farther and farther, and an hour later he hears on the car's radio that a girl, struck by a hit-and-run driver, has just died. The man does not know what to do. He must run away, but he has no money. In order to get money he holds up a jewelry shop. The owner resists, so the man has to kill him.

The story continues in that vein. What has started as an innocent coffee break ends in multiple murders. The story describes a sequence of events similar to those occurring in the lives of psychopaths. By writing this story the patient revealed once more that psychopaths have intellectual insight, though by itself it is not helpful.

We may conceive of the simple psychopath as a person who, at least in the significant episodes of his life, lives in accordance with the pleasure principle described by Freud. If we remember what we have discussed in Chapter 4, the psychopath lives as if his id had been liberated. But the important point is that society has not permitted a liberation of the id. Even if it were to permit an id liberation in the sexual sense of Reich and Marcuse, it would certainly not permit the psychopath's antisocial acts. The psychopath does not think of liberating society from so-called hypocritical restrictions. He is too egocentric to be concerned with the problems of society; as a matter of fact, he ignores society; and he is too sick to listen to the parts of his psyche which are above the id level and which impose respect for morality. It is not that his id has been liberated; his id had never been modulated by the processes of normal maturity or else his ego is too weak to exert inhibition.

Some novelists have glorified the psychopath, or some psychopaths, as the people who do not compromise, who listen to subjective needs and not to objective or impersonal considerations. They are portrayed as the people who grasp immediacy and hate delay, who heroically allow themselves to follow the temptation and disregard the traditional distinction between right and wrong. To them the psychopath is the person who lives authentically, who has overcome the need for approval which continues to plague the mediocre; the psychopath is really the master of his will.

These are rhetorical misrepresentations of the facts. The truth is that the psychopath has not overcome the need for approval. Approval does not even enter the picture. His attention is focused only on the attainment of the end, is restricted to the goal, and the panorama of life is obliterated. Is he really an authentic man when he gives up so much of life for the sake of satisfying his urge? Is he really capable of choosing in a mature way? Does he really will in a normal sense?

At first impression one could think that the simple psychopath is the victim of the so-called "irresistible impulse," and, as a matter of fact, during legal prosecutions psychopaths have defended themselves by declaring that such was the case. If a policeman is nearby, however, the psychopath will not indulge in the antisocial act; he will control himself until a more opportune time comes. Thus the doctrine of the irresistible impulse is shattered to pieces. The psychopathic impulse seems indeed at least in some cases resistible.

The presence of the policeman, as a preventive measure, can give us some clues about the interplay of the interpersonal and the intrapsychic in the symptomatology of the simple psychopath. This individual is in some respects similar to a little child who wants immediate gratification: the breast now, the rattle now, the toy now, being on mother's lap right now. He cannot postpone his pleasure. Mother repeatedly teaches her child what not to do. Many mothers have noticed that between the ages of two and four the child will do the forbidden thing only if mother is not present. If she is absent, the child will follow the urge. Only at the age of four has the maternal sanction become well internalized. The "no," originated interpersonally, has become intrapsychic and endocratic. One might thus conclude that the simple psychopath has reverted to a type of intrapsychic organization which corresponds to that of the child between two and four. This interpretation, however, is not complete. Firstly, we must study how this internalization takes place in normal children and repeat some of the phases that we have described in Chapter 5; secondly, we must see why this mechanism is defective in the psychopath.

Normal children gradually learn to postpone gratification. They learn to do so if they are consistently trained to expect substitute gratification at progressively lengthening intervals. For instance, little George wants a second helping of ice cream. He wants it at all cost; he says he "needs it." But if the mother keeps the child on her lap, caresses him, and says, "No, George, you can't have it now," little George will be able to accept this deprivation because it is immediately compensated for by the tenderness of mother. Later, in similar cases, he will get the approval of mother as a compensation for the deprivation, instead of direct physical tenderness. Still later he will get only a promise; that is, the hope that something good will happen to him as a reward for not responding immediately to impulsive urges. Promises and hopes, although abstract visualizations of things which have not yet materialized, retain the flavor or an echo of mother's approval and tenderness. The mother who used to be only the giver, the helper, the assuager of hunger, thirst, cold, loneliness, immobility, and any other *present* discomfort, from now on becomes also the giver of hopes and promises. She becomes the announcer of the *future*; she opens the door to a mental orientation of optimism for what is yet to come.

It could be that the future simple psychopath did not go through these normal stages. What appeared to the child as deprivation was balanced by no compensations. No benevolent mother was there to help the child to make the transition from immediate gratification to postponement. He did not learn to expect approval and tenderness, to experience hope, and to anticipate the fulfillment of a promise. Frustration remained for him an unpleasant, even unbearable experience. Thus he continued to exercise patterns of behavior which involved only the present and led to quick responses.

This explanation is, in my opinion, correct but incomplete. Inability to modify, suppress, or postpone the need for gratification does not constitute the whole abnormality. Wanting two ice creams right now may be immature, but not necessarily psychopathic; to reveal psychopathic tendencies the child must do something more; for instance, steal the second ice cream.

A person may be desirous of quick gratification, but if he has the ability to experience a sufficient degree of anxiety or of guilt feeling, he will not become a psychopath. In this particular context, anxiety means anxiety about future punishment; guilt feeling means the unpleasant feeling of deserving punishment, irrespective of whether the punishment is actualized or not.

Again, the interpersonal parent-child relationship has a great deal to do with this intrapsychic lack of anxiety or guilt of the psychopath. The mother, and later the father, who are not able to open the door of the future to the child with hope and promise, may not even be able to open the door of anxiety about future punishment. These parents belong to two groups. Those who belong to the first are excessively permissive and put no limitations whatsoever on their children. The second group consists of parents who are very strict, but their strictness consists of *immediate* punishment. Present punishment is experienced by the child immediately and is immediately related to the environment. Future punishment is not yet a reality; it exists only as a threat. It exists only intrapsychically; that is, as a mental representation, as an endocratic force. Both very permissive parents and parents who give immediate punishment do not elicit anxiety or the capacity for anxiety. These words may sound strange. It would seem that, contrary to some psychiatric teaching, we are advocating the promotion of negative emotions. There is nothing wrong or destructive in allowing children to experience a modicum of anxiety and guilt, provided the mother has been able to create a state of basic trust; that is, has made it possible for the child to live in an atmosphere of hope and promise and to orient himself toward life with an attitude of optimistic expectation. If we want to open to the child the door of a future with hope and promise, the toll to be exacted will be paid in anxiety. The anxiety need not be excessive. It should not include endocratic surplus, but it should be the minimum necessary to cope with the complex variables of an uncertain and enlarging world.

Is the simple psychopath obligated to experience base desires and unable to control them? Or is he one who, although capable of choosing and willing, wishes and wills to make what society considers a wrong choice? These questions are of the greatest theoretical and legal importance. It could be that for undetermined biological reasons the psychopath experiences certain primitive desires more strongly than the average person. But this does not seem to be his greatest handicap. His greatest shortcoming is the lack of the inner agent, the inner voice which tells him, "Don't do it; it's wrong." There is no endocracy in him. It is difficult to blame his motivation, which is low and base, or his will, which is weak and unable to forbid him.

As we have seen, the simple psychopath is able to inhibit the low motivation, as in the presence of a policeman. But the inhibition must come totally or partially from an external power, not from an endocratic function. If there is no external control, he acts psychopathically. Therefore, his will is not mature but is weak and diseased. Certainly he is not capable of choosing like others when he responds only to external forces and is deprived of inner control.

The law generally considers psychopaths capable of understanding and of willing their deeds and therefore declares them responsible for their actions. If our interpretation is correct, they are not as capable of willing as normal people are. This assertion should not be interpreted, however, as meaning that society should not use restrictive measures toward them. As a matter of fact, we have seen that unless they recover (and only a very few of them do), external restrictions and immediate punishments are the only measures which prevent them from making the wrong choices. Psychotherapy is generally not successful with them because it does not provide external control.

Another important characteristic of the simple psychopath is that the antisocial plans he puts into effect are devised by him often in flashes of sudden insight. The patient, thinking of ways to solve his problem as quickly as possible, suddenly experiences some kind of "enlightenment" on "how to do it." This quick *psychopathic insight* may appear an act of creativity, and in a certain way it is. Actually it consists chiefly of mechanisms by which it is possible to disregard some factors which, for a normal person, would have an inhibiting influence. Furthermore, the patient tends to resort to the same "solution" again and again, so that after the initial act it can no longer be thought of as psychopathic creativity. Eventually it can even be discussed in terms of stereotyped responses.

Does our description of the simple psychopath remind the reader of our first symbol, Pinocchio—how he refused to work, how with the cat and the fox he tried to find an easy way to make money, how he got into trouble with the police? No, Pinocchio was a naughty boy, not a psychopath. Had he continued in adult life to live as he did during that period of childhood covered by Collodi's book, he might have become a psychopath; but, as the story goes, he was saved. What about the Pinocchians that we have described in Chapter 4, who yield to instinctual demands? Although individual psychopaths may join their group and find themselves at home there more than in the rest of society, they are not psychopaths. They do, however, show tendencies, habits, dispositions similar to those of people clinically diagnosed as psychopaths.

Society and some philosophies of life can indeed promote psychopathiclike tendencies. Although the psychopath becomes sick if he is biologically predisposed and is exposed in his family to the special psychological mechanisms that we have described, society can, in a certain way, imitate the psychopathic family and promote psychopathic behavior. From the study of the psychopath's family we can analogically advance hypotheses on what society does wrong. We must thus adopt a methodology which is the opposite of that generally followed.

A mature society must be oriented also toward the future and not only toward the present; but some aspects of modern life make it less attractive to think of tomorrow and to have a sense of distant purpose. At the same time they subject the individual to an increasing number of increasingly seductive and persuasive stimuli (see Chapter 6). Materialism and consumerism focus on immediate gratification. The individual who becomes almost exclusively a consumer loses sight of distant goals and ideas and may have difficulties in choosing. Ideals are hopes and substitutions for something which cannot be actualized immediately but which require tenacity, perseverance, faith, and desire to grow psychologically.

Space restrictions do not allow us to discuss all types of psychopaths. We shall briefly consider only one other, which I call the complex psychopath. We have seen that the simple psychopath occasionally has an illumination or insight on "how to do it." The insight of the complex psychopath is more involved and can be summarized as "how to do it and get away with it." To this group of pyschopaths belong such groups of people as the "professional" bank robbers and some unscrupulous political leaders.

At first it may seem difficult to explain the mechanisms of the complex psychopath because they do not seem to fit those which have been described. Finding ways to rob a modern bank, and, even more, calculating ways to reach and retain political power seem to imply an ability to conceive high aims and to use complicated mental processes.

We must specify at this point that every mental mechanism has to be considered in relation to an individual's general mental capacity. Although the emotions which motivate the complex psychopath may not be as primitive as those of the simple psychopath, they are relatively simple in comparison with others that he could experience, and they manifest some characteristics of primitive emotions. For instance, such persons' desire for possession retains that quality of immediacy and compelling urgency which characterize primitive emotion. At times this desire for possession becomes desire for extreme degrees of power over others.

Complex psychopaths are very intelligent people, and relative to their intellectual possibilities or to normal ways of reaching goals, the methods they use are quick methods; for example, eliminating political adversaries by murder. Moral considerations are not allowed to delay their urge for gratification. They are able to adopt and endure some relatively time-consuming mental activity in order to avoid still further delays and thus make the gratification possible. Here the rest of the mental functions retain their full effectiveness and are used in the service of the relatively quick gratification. In view of the nature of these cases, the experience that psychiatrists have with them is very limited. I, for one, have not had the opportunity to study them sufficiently to be able to distinguish pyschodynamic factors or the early environmental conditions which differ from those of the simple psychopath.

The philosophy of life of the complex psychopath is different from that of the simple psychopath. The simple psychopath eliminates the conflict between what Freud called the pleasure principle and the reality principle by completely acceding to the pleasure principle and satisfying his id. The complex psychopath operates at a much higher level of motivation. He solves the conflict between self-realization and social morality by following without hesitation what seems to him self-realization. He often deludes himself into thinking that he has a mission in life which he must fulfill at any cost. He believes that he deserves a particular gratification, or that it is congruous with his special personal endowment or with the concept of his own self to seek it. He does not care how he is going to get it; the norms of society are not going to stop him and should not apply to him. The maxim he often invokes is that the end justifies the means. But the end, no matter how rationalized, embellished, or disguised, is the gratification of his primitive emotions, and the means are his quick, unethical methods.

Whereas the simple psychopath can be seen as following a style of life based on the philosophy popularly attributed to Epicurus, the complex psychopath follows a style of life that combines some tenets of Nietzsche and some of Machiavelli. Historical figures like Nero, Cesare Borgia, Stalin, and Mussolini were probably complex psychopaths.

Complex psypchopaths are stubborn people. They resemble the simple psychopath insofar as they do not give up their primitive wishes or grandiose ambitions because of any dictate of conscience or endocratic power. Only external power can stop them. Stalin once asked, "How many divisions has the Pope?" Only military power counted for him and not spiritual. Whenever a glimpse of endocracy reaches the awareness of the complex psychopath, he suppresses it or quiets it down quickly with a thousand different rationalizations. Strangely enough, the complex psychopath who experiences endocracy so weakly himself is able to elicit it in others very strongly. He is very capable in making others feel guilty or in inducing them to become his followers in a party, a plot, or a gang. He deprives weaker psychopaths of that half a conscience they have left and replaces it with his own personal power. Hermann Goering said to Gilbert,[11] "I have no conscience; my conscience is Adolf Hitler."

THE OBSESSIVE-COMPULSIVE

The obsessive-compulsive psychoneurotic is a person in some respects the opposite of the psychopath: he is very much restrained by his inner self. Whereas the psychopath gives vent to his wishes, the obsessive-compulsive "hears" an inner voice which tells him, "Don't, don't, don't do this; you are not allowed." At other times the obsessive-compulsive's voice tells him, "Do this, and only in this particular way!" For instance, "On Monday you must wear this particular suit; you must wash your hands not only when they are dirty but every twenty-five minutes; you must travel to that store by a tortuous route involving nine blocks, although the quickest and most direct route is only four blocks long." Some patients receive dictates as to what to touch and what not to touch, what to eat and what not to eat. They are forced to count series of inconsequential objects like lamp posts, doors, windows, or to memorize useless numbers, like those of license plates of passing cars. These compulsions constitute the so-called rituals, which have to be followed to the most trivial detail. For instance, when a patient prepares himself for going to bed, first he has to take off the right sock, then the left; he must then turn the pillow in a special angle, fold the blanket in a particular way, the sheet in another, and so on. These obsessions and compulsions are the tyrannical laws which cannot be transgressed.

Some obsessions are crippling to an extreme degree. Others permit some freedom. Thus the patient who must wash his hands every twenty-five minutes can enjoy twenty-five subsequent minutes of freedom. The patient becomes the slave of his neurosis, which not only tells him what to do and what not to do, but often how to feel and how not to feel. A patient of mine had the obsessive idea that if some people in the world were sick, she was not allowed to feel well; if some people could not have a good time, she could not have a good time, etc. These alleged laws made her life miserable, as she felt obligated to obey all these internal injunctions but did not know how. Whereas the life of the simple psychopath is dominated by the impulse which cannot be resisted, the life of the obsessive-compulsive is dominated by *compulsions*. Like the psychopath, the obsessive-compulsive is not insane. In almost all cases the patient knows that the compulsions are absurd, but a power stronger than his reason compels him to carry them out. What is the nature of this bizarre power?

Freud interpreted obsessiveness as a derivative of the struggles the child had to face during his toilet training. The little child has the urge to move his bowels, but he must wait until the pot is reached at the right time. If he defecates in his pants or diapers or at the wrong place, mother will be angry and will make him feel guilty. In the words of Rado, "The stage is set for the battle of the chamberpot." "The mother-child conflict provokes in the child a struggle between his own guilty fear and his own defiant rage" (Rado).[12] The conflict derives from the overambition of the mother which demands bowel control from the child who is not ready for it, and from the guilt, fear, and rage that the child develops as a consequence. The ritual is interpreted as a way to atone for the guilt feeling that the mother has initiated. It is debatable whether the original rigidity of the mother concerns only bowel training. In my opinion what is involved is not just the "battle of the chamberpot." It is the battle for a way of living that the mother wants the child to adopt.

The mother communicates two things to the child. The first is that the world is full of dangers and that everything in it is uncertain. The second is that the best way to remove uncertainty and danger is to do what you are supposed to do: the way indicated by mother. Obviously every normal mother has to train her child to control his bowels, to do certain things, and to avoid others. But the mother of the obsessive-compulsive is a very anxious woman who removes anxiety by inflicting strong endocracy on the child. Obedience to the compulsions will remove the uncertainty and the anxiety. Whereas originally it was the mother (or a mother substitute) who required obedience, later it is the neurosis which endocratically imposes obsessions and compulsions.

Psychoanalysis has emphasized the symbolic meaning of these

symptoms. For instance, a mother feels that her child will die unless she bathes herself several times every day. She feels she is a bad mother, and as a consequence of her badness the child will be terribly hurt and may even die unless she cleanses herself in some way. Bathing becomes symbolic of purification. But the important quality of obsessions and compulsions resides in their endocratic power. The patient is theoretically able to resist the symptoms, but the anxiety, the guilt feeling, and the suffering would be atrocious to an extent that he could not tolerate. So he ends up by succumbing to the obsessions and compulsions. His will is paralyzed. A certain number of obsessive-compulsives are not actually paralyzed by neurosis but are compelled to do excessive work. Thus we find some of them who are very successful in business, industry, and professions.

The obsessions of the patient may have nothing to do with his original relations with his parents. The patient may develop a large number of obsessions from an occurrence later in life. For instance, if the day he wore a particular suit an unpleasant event occurred, he will no longer wear that suit. The endocratic law tells him, "If you wear that suit, something bad is going to happen again." The patient intellectually knows that this pseudoinductive evidence is not valid, but he is looking for a guide to his actions in order to avoid a sense of danger which is coming from his inner self. His anxiety is so great that in order to reestablish a modicum of inner security, he is willing to accept the guidance of fallacious, whimsical, pseudoinductive reasoning. In this uncertain and anxiety-ridden world he feels powerless. But now he has found a method to reacquire the power to avoid disaster: he must follow the compulsive command. The fictitiousness of this neurotic structure gives an indication of how profound the patient's sense of powerlessness is.

Obsessive-compulsive patients have diminished in number recently, possibly because of the influence on child rearing of Freud's teachings and of the works of the pediatrician Benjamin Spock. We would have good reason to rejoice if they had not been replaced by an increasing number of psychopaths and juvenile delinquents. The societies in which there has been an increase in the incidence of psychopaths and a decrease in the incidence of obsessive-compulsives seem more inclined to seduce the individual into living in a certain way than to give him direct and harsh commands. The individual may respond to the seduction with *impulsive* (not compulsive) behavior. By and large the tendency in our society to foster obsessive compulsive tendencies has diminished. In times and cultures permeated by religiosity the individual was indoctrinated with commands: "Do this; do not do that." A large part of religious ritual consists of rules that the faithful must follow, and they have been compared to obsessive-compulsive symptoms, by Freud among others.

In Chapter 2 we described how primitive man, when he acts on his own, tends to feel lost or guilty in this mysterious world where he does not know what the next moment will bring. In order to remove anxiety the primitive has to do everything, to the least detail, in accordance with the injunctions of the tribe. His behavior is reminiscent of that of an obsessive-compulsive. He is not free at all, as some romantic writers have in past eras described him. Inasmuch as he obtains approval from his group, however, he does not resent his way of living, which does not appear obsessive-compulsive to him. Similar influences can be detected in our not-so-primitive society. In a democracy the individual generally tends to become a conformist rather than an obsessive-compulsive. It could be, however, that what we call habits are compulsions which originate from the external world, receive collective approval, and generally make our life less difficult. These social compulsions, in order to be experienced as habits and not as tyrannical or absurd commands, must be either useful or at least not grossly disturbing to the individual's welfare or pursuit of happiness. Both the conformist and the obsessive-compulsive have developed their ways (respectively, habits and compulsions) in order to avoid the chaos which they fear. Indeed the psychopath who does not follow these restrictive methods produces chaos in himself and others.

Some psychiatric conditions and the societal influences with which they could be compared show how difficult it is for the human being to navigate in freedom. He veers between the danger of conformism, compulsion, or psychopathic anarchy. The risk is indeed great, and man's determination must unceasingly try to decrease it.

THE CATATONIC

If the predicament of the obsessive-compulsive is serious and cruel, that of the catatonic is even worse. In this type of patient we observe a complete loss of the capacity to will.

This patient has a special type of schizophrenia which fortunately has become much less common in recent years in most parts of the world.[13] At times after a certain period of excitement and agitation, at other times without warning, the patient slows down, reaching sooner or later a state of partial or complete immobility. He may become so stiff, rigid, and incapable of movement that he resembles a statue. He then becomes unable to move around and take care of his physical needs. He cannot dress or undress, does not have the initiative to feed himself in the presence of food or to talk in the presence of other people, nor does he answer questions. At other times the patient is not so severely affected, but his activities are reduced to a minimum. He gives the impression of being paralyzed, but there is nothing wrong with his motor equipment, musculature, nerves, articulation, etc. What is disturbed is his faculty to will. He cannot will and therefore cannot will to move. At times he is very obedient and suggestible because he follows the will of someone else. The examiner may put the body of the patient in the most awkward positions and the patient will remain in those positions for hours.[14] At other times the patient puts himself in an awkward or statuesque position and remains in that position until he is put to bed, to resume the same position the following day. A phenomenon that seems opposite to this suggestibility but is instead related to it is *negativism*. Instead of doing what he is requested to do, the patient does the opposite. For instance, if he is told to show the tongue, he closes the mouth tightly, or turns his face away. If he is told to stand, he assumes a reclining position, etc. In many cases, a few activities remain, but they are carried out in a routine, stereotyped manner.

Why the catatonic should suddenly become so affected is not at all clear. Before becoming acutely ill, the patient generally is confronted with a very important decision to make, or with a challenge for which he was not prepared. Such a task seems gigantic, impossible to cope with, and finally overwhelming to the patient. For instance, a woman was supposed to go to Europe to rejoin her husband, who had been absent for a year. During his absence she had become pregnant by another man and obtained an illegal abortion. On the way to the airport to take the plane for Europe the patient became catatonic. A college student became catatonic while he was considering dropping out of college and going back home. A woman who had just given birth to a baby became catatonic a few days after she saw her baby, and another patient on whom I have reported

in detail elsewhere became catatonic during her honeymoon.
The catatonic patients whom I have studied intensively were
people who, in their early childhood, were not able to develop
confidence in their own actions and reliance on their capacity
to will. The parents or parent substitutes influenced these
patients either not to will or to follow parental decisions. When
the patients later had to make their own choices, they found
themselves unable to act; if they acted, they were criticized
and made to feel guilty. Catatonia is an avoidance of action in
order to remove the panic connected with willed action. The
panic, at first connected with one or a few actions, becomes
generalized. When it is extended to every action, the patient
lapses into a state of complete inability to will and consequent
immobility. At other times it is an obsessive-compulsive anxiety
rather than a definite fear which does not permit the patient to
move. Is it better to move or not to move, to talk or not to talk,
to choose this word or another one? In the midst of this terrifying uncertainty the patient decides not to will at all.

In some cases, as if in answer to an order, the patient starts
a movement but then stops, as if a counterorder had prevented
him from continuing. Having decided to obey, he is then afraid
to will the act involved, and he stops. At other times there is a
series of alternated opposing movements, like a cogwheel movement. In the middle of a movement the patient becomes afraid
of willing that action, decides not to perform it, and arrests his
motion. But to decide not to perform the action is also an act
of will. The patient becomes afraid of it and starts to make the
movement again. To do this is also an act of will, and he is
again afraid. This series of attempted escapes from volition may
go on for a long time. It is a horrifying experience which only
a few patients are able to relate.

The Swiss psychiatrist Christian Muller, professor of psychiatry at the University of Lausanne, told me the following episode. During the Second World War, one of his patients had
been arrested by the Nazis and was to be executed. He was already facing the firing squad when the order came to stay the
execution because the Allies were approaching. Later on the
patient developed catatonic schizophrenia, from which he re-
covered. He was one of the few patients who are able to remember the experiences of the illness, and told Professor Muller
that the agonizing distress he had to endure because of the
Nazis, even when he was about to be executed, was small in
comparison to what he suffered during the catatonic episode.

existential

During the catatonic illness the patient attaches a tremendous
sense of responsibility to any manifestation of his will, even in
reference to actions which are generally considered of little
importance. Every willed movement comes to be seen not as a
function but as a moral issue; every motion is considered not
merely as a fact but as a value. Such an abnormal sense of responsibility reaches the acme of intensity when it becomes associated with delusions of negative cosmic power or negative
omnipotence. The patient comes to believe that a little movement that he can make, by producing a change in the state of
the universe, may be capable of harming his whole community
or even of destroying the whole world. Alas! This conception of
the psychotic mind reminds us that exactly this may come to
pass today, when the pushing of a button may have vast effects.
Only the oceanic responsibility of the catatonic can include this
possibility, which was, until recently, inconceivable for normal
persons.

The fear of the willed action accounts for other characteristics
of catatonia. The patient may not be able to will to act independently, but may still be able to accept commands from
others. He may passively follow orders given by someone else
because the responsibility will not be his: when he obeys, he
substitutes another person's will for his own. When the patient
is put into a given position, the will or responsibilty of someone else is involved. If he wants to change his position, he has
to will the change, and this causes anxiety or guilt. Thus the
passivity to the suggestion of others is not an acceptance of
power from others, as in hypnosis, but a relief from responsibility.

Quite often the reverse seems to occur: the patient will resist
the order, or will do the opposite. This is the phenomenon of
negativism to which we have already referred. Such willed dis-
obedience may be a return to the stage in which will consists
of resisting the will of others (see Chapter 2). At times the
catatonic loses his usual inhibited attitude and acts in an opposite way—that is, as if he were not concerned at all with responsibility, or as if he were defying previous feelings of fear
and responsibility. His behavior consists of a sequence of aimless
acts. This is the state of *catatonic excitement*, during which the
patient may become violent and homicidal.

Theoretically, the catatonic could avoid his difficulties and the
agony of his not willing to will by reverting to the level of the
pleasure principle or to the level of wish fulfillment. Apparently,

however, these simple solutions are not available to him. He cannot become a psychopath or a delusional person in the wish-fulfilling sense. Perhaps the tremendous fear of his own wish for hostility, or the fear of what he is capable of doing in the catatonic excitement, does not permit him to regress to those simple solutions. He can neither will nor indulge in wishing. Although he cannot wish, he can fear. He lives only in the fear of what he could do; and the only choice, which he thinks he is not choosing, is not to do.

There is nothing in any social situation which reproduces the clinical picture of catatonia. It is true that terrorized people decrease their actions. It is also true that prisoners are put in conditions in which their actions are curtailed. Some people, like Trappist monks, put themselves in positions reminiscent of catatonia, and so do people who join organizations which make all the decisions for them.

In spite of these similarities, I repeat that there is no social situation resembling closely the clinical state of catatonia. Nevertheless, even for those who are interested only in social situations and not in psychiatry, it is important to have a picture of catatonia because it shows what happens when man completely loses his will. Although he is not physiologically paralyzed, he is, for practical purposes, petrified. Like a statue he cannot respond to people who touch him, bump into him, smile at him, or caress him. But unlike a statue he hurts in the most atrocious way, having lost something more precious than his eyesight, the most human of his possessions—his will.[15]

CHAPTER 11

The Ethical Aim

FREEDOM AND ETHICS

FREEDOM IS OF TWO KINDS, AS DANTE MAKES CLEAR AT THE BEginning of the *Purgatorio*. In the first canto Virgil explains to Cato, the guardian, why Dante is making the journey in the underworld. He says, "He [Dante] seeks freedom which is so dear, as he knows who gives up life for her!" [1] Virgil refers to Cato himself, who killed himself rather than to submit to the tyranny of Julius Caesar. Cato wanted political freedom, but Dante is seeking a different one: liberation from personal problems in order to be free to pursue eternal truths. A man is free when he has broken the chains of his inner difficulties, or those of his external oppressors. Thus freedom refers to a psychological state of the individual, a relation with oneself in the sense that one's choice is not determined by personal problems. [2] It refers also and unequivocally to a relation with other persons. It is a state in which a man's choice is not imposed or restrained by other men. But the concept of freedom goes much further. It

Fromm

is not only liberation (or freed*om from*) but freedom *to* or *for* something which makes freedom valuable.

Freedom is generally connected with the pursuit of happiness, as it is in the American Declaration of Independence. By some authors, like Bertrand Russell, freedom is defined as the absence of obstacles to the realization of desires. But this concept of freedom is not entirely satisfactory on several counts. An authoritarian society may manipulate the citizens so subtly and successfully that the majority of them end up by desiring what the rulers want. Delgado [3] has recently illustrated how the mind may be controlled by physical methods. A person may believe that his desires are his own when really they have been imposed on him artificially and without his knowledge by an experimenter. Earlier in this book we have seen how the elites of corporate states may lead a large number of people to believe that the pursuit of happiness is best carried out by consuming more.

The type of freedom which seems most worthwhile is the one which leads to the betterment of mankind in general as well as to the betterment of the individual. Since people differ on what betterment consists of, the concept remains controversial.

My own view is that the two most mature aims of free will are:

free will

1. the practice of an ethical life, which we shall discuss in this chapter (what I will and do affects much more than myself).

2. the exercise of individuality and, whenever possible, of creativity, provided it does not interfere with the ethical life. We shall discuss this topic in the next chapter.

These two aims directly or indirectly bring about the highest forms of happiness.

This book is not a treatise on ethics, and therefore we are not to pose such questions as "What ought a man do in order to make his life good?" Nor is this book a treatise on politics, the science of bringing about the greatest good for the community. To start with, I shall focus on the fact that neither the individual nor society has willed to accept the ethical way as one of the highest aims of life. Theoretical politics, especially since Machiavelli, has become the science not of bringing about the common good, but of achieving, retaining, or increasing power. Our century is not only characterized by the appearance of many leaders who did not pursue ethical aims but also by the ideological influence of some thinkers who advocated unethical positions. The most typical example is that of Nietzsche. Also, our century is characterized by misunderstandings of scientific findings used to justify an unethical stand. In this case the most typical example is the misinterpretation of Darwin.

NIETZSCHE AND DARWIN

Most of his detractors and admirers alike have inaccurately evaluated Nietzsche's philosophy, perhaps because the many contradictory sides to this complex man make any final appraisal difficult. Those who see him as responsible for Nazi and Fascist theories are mistaken. It is true that Mussolini admired him, but the Nazis had to expurgate his writings to make him appear their advocate. Nietzsche was an internationalist at heart and strongly opposed nationalism, especially German nationalism. The admirers of Nietzsche see in him either a great existentialist or a metaphysician and are under the spell of his beautiful poetic and aphoristic style. I shall focus only on Nietzsche's political and ethical ideas, and I must say immediately that they are deleterious. His major concern is not with man but with "superman." [4] The masses must endure pain and oppression for the fulfillment of a few great men. Nietzsche hated Judaeo-Christian ethics because it is not on the side of the superman but is rather a "slave morality," a code of rules for the protection of the weak, the feeble, the ignoble, "the slave." In a way that he did not intend, Nietzsche was right in stating that the Judaeo-Christian morality is a slave morality. The Judaeo-Christian morality had its first great stage of development among people who had indeed been slaves and remembered their recent suffering. I am referring to the Jews when they left Egypt and achieved independence under the leadership of Moses. The greatness and significance of the biblical story for all ages lies in the fact that freedom had an aim: the ethical law to be obtained at Sinai, the common good, the good society. Politics was subordinate to ethics. In the biblical context it is impossible to dissociate freedom from the Law of Sinai; and throughout the Old Testament a statement is repeated to serve as a guideline: "Remember that you were slaves in the land of Egypt." Thus Nietzsche is right; at least in its origin, Judaeo-Christian morality is a slave morality. But in being a slave morality lies its greatness, not its shame. God is seen as being on the side of the slaves, those who have suffered from the hands of the oppressor and are therefore in a better position to be inspired by the ideals of justice and ready to strive for their attainment. Because of the intensity of their experiences, people who have suffered greatly, and especially people who have been slaves (perhaps the blacks today), are in a better position than others to make great contributions to ethics if other propitious circumstances are present.

According to almost all ethical writers, the good life entails the opposite of what Nietzsche advocates. It means to stand for justice, equality, and goodness for the largest number of men and not to serve the gratification of the handful of Julius Caesars. But Nietzsche, and not only Nietzsche, would say that equality, justice, and goodness for the largest number of people are unnatural attributes. We have seen in Chapter 9 that Mussolini and Hitler stated that equality is not found in nature and is thus unnatural and to be condemned. Nietzsche called compassion a weakness to be combatted, and Hitler called conscience "a blemish like circumcision."

It is true that ethics does not follow nature, but in transcending nature it becomes uniquely human. The beauty and mystery of nature inspires both poetry and science. Her pristine freshness is a refuge from mundane sophistication. But these qualities should not blind us to the fact that nature is amoral, indifferent to ethics. The "law" of the jungle declares that the stronger wins. Darwin described what he observed in the jungle as biological *facts*; but later, Nietzsche, Mussolini, and Hitler took the Darwinian findings as *values*, as paradigms for human society. In other words, they did not say, "This is how not only animal life but also human life unfortunately is most of the time." They said, "That is how life should be." Ethics requires that *homo sapiens* transcend his biology and embrace the common good as his cause. The cosmos is amoral, but amorality becomes immorality when accepted by man. Some people are born strong and some weak; some healthy and some sick; some beautiful and some ugly; some intelligent and some dull. It is up to human society to do whatever it can to rectify these natural inequalities. Men must use whatever abilities they have to correct the defects with which some are born, or at least try to correct those inequalities which bring about unhappiness. If these inequalities cannot be corrected, they should be minimized, not used as a pretext to defeat or to subjugate the less well endowed. Men and human institutions, however, have generally done the opposite. They have exploited and magnified the meaning of natural differences in order to perpetuate inequalities. The stronger have overpowered the weaker, the intelligent have defeated the dull, political and racial majorities have oppressed minorities, and so on. As if there were not enough natural differences, artificial ones have been created, as in the caste system; and ideological-religious differences have been stressed and given a political status to justify social injustice. A Darwinian type of society is advocated by some who believe that competition is as useful among people as it is in the jungle. Just as in the jungle competition leads to salutary evolution, so in society it will lead to progress because in an effort to compete, people will improve. Conversely, this argument continues, abolition of competition would promote a state of indulgence and social stagnation. But we must distinguish between two possibilities. A competition which aims only at obtaining something that another man will consequently lose reproduces the law of the jungle and should be abolished; for instance, satisfying my hunger at the cost of your life, job, etc. Let us remember that Darwin did not say that the *best* wins in the jungle, but the *fittest*. In a society of human beings it is desirable that the best prevail. In other words, if competition means excellence, that is, not necessarily defeat of others but improvement of one's own faculties for the benefit of oneself and others, then it is a healthy motivation. But it is misnamed. How must we consider the case in which only one position is available and there are many aspirants? Isn't competition necessary in this case? It is if we see this particular circumstance as one where there is one winner and many losers. But if the position is given to the best—that is, to the one who, on account of that position, will benefit the largest possible number of people—the world will win.

PAIN AND EVIL

Ethical life directs the will of man to the elimination of suffering. Suffering is of at least three major types. The first, generally called *pain*, is determined by the facts of nature: disease, hunger, malnutrition, cold, etc. The second sort of suffering, that undeservedly inflicted by man to man, is *evil*. The third is *intrapsychic anguish*, generally the result of various combinations of the first two types of sufferings, in different proportions and multiple ways. In Chapter 10 we discussed some of the most serious forms of intrapsychic anguish, those which appear as mental illnesses. In this section we shall discuss only the first two types, with the help of the biblical Book of Job, which is probably the greatest book ever written on these two aspects of suffering. Whereas the Greek epic dealt with wars, kings, and warriors, the epic of the Old Testament is that of the suffering of a man named Job, from the land of Uz.

The Book of Job is one of the most difficult in the Bible. Generations of men brought up in the Judaeo-Christian tradition have revered the book, interpreted it in different ways, and admitted that they may not have understood it completely.

Job has undergone immense suffering in his life, and three friends, who come to visit him with the intent of consoling him, cause him additional sorrow. They state that God is just and has never inflicted pain on an innocent person. Thus Job must have sinned and is now being punished.

But Job protests and proclaims his innocence. He says that he will defend himself in front of God. He states that the wicked often do prosper and the righteous do suffer and that God does not seem to hear the prayer of the innocent sufferer. He also tells his friends that they do not speak correctly about God and that God will vindicate him. He again speaks to God, reaffirming his innocence:

> *If I have walked with vanity, and my foot hath hasted to deceit . . .*
> *If my step hath turned out of the way,*
> *And my heart walked after mine eyes,*
> *And if any spot hath cleaved to my hands; . . .*
> *If my heart have been enticed unto a woman, and I have lain in wait at my neighbour's door . . .*
> *If I did despise the cause of my man-servant.*
> *Or of my maid-servant, when they contended with me . . .*
> *If I have withheld aught that the poor desired,*
> *Or have caused the eyes of the widow to fail,*
> *Or have eaten my morsel myself alone,*
> *And the fatherless hath not eaten thereof . . .*
> *If I have seen any wanderer in want of clothing,*
> *Or that the needy had no covering; . . .*
> *If I have made gold my hope . . .*
> *If I have rejoiced because my wealth was great . . .*
> *If I rejoiced at the destruction of him that hated me . . .*[5]

It is a crescendo of hypothetical suppositions. These "ifs" mean, "If I had done those misdeeds, You would be right in punishing me; but I am innocent."

At the end of the book God replies to Job from the whirl-wind. God reproaches Job for criticizing Him. He seems to say, "How dare you criticize Me? Were you there when I created the world?" Thereupon God presents a summary of the creation of the universe. This speech of God at the conclusion of the book has left generations of readers perplexed. Yes, the creation of the world reveals the magnificence of God, but what has this to do with Job's suffering?

If my interpretation is correct (and in this interpretation I borrow greatly from the writings of, and my discussions with, Jack Bemporad [6]), God seems to say that suffering was a neces-sary ingredient in the process of creation. Job (or any other man) is not necessarily afflicted by pain because he sinned, but because pain is part of nature—in other words, pain is not punishment, is not necessarily given in retribution, or ordained, but is *caused* inevitably by the laws of nature which rule the cosmos. A disease, an earthquake, a lack of food or water may cause him pain, independently of any moral judgment.

Let us here examine whether pain is necessary in human nature. Biology teaches us that pain is an absolute necessity for the evolution of animal life. As a result of an improbable series of complicated mutations, a revolutionary event occurred in the world which differentiated animal forms from the rest of the universe (plants included)—the appearance of *feeling*.

Feeling is a characteristic unique to the animal world and is the basis of psychological life. Feeling is unanalyzable in its essential nature and defies any attempt at a noncircular defini-tion. Often-used synonyms for feeling are awareness, subjec-tivity, consciousness, experience, felt experience. Although each of these terms stresses a particular quality, all of them refer to a subjective form of experience.

Transmission of information from one part of the organism to another exists even without any subjective experience. For instance, the important information transmitted through some nervous tracts, like the spinocerebellar, never reaches the level of awareness. As long as information is transmitted without awareness, the organism is not too different from an electronic computing machine. When a change in the organism becomes accompanied by awareness, a new phenomenon emerges in the cosmos: experience. Awareness and experience introduce the factor of psyche. Eventually animals become capable of distin-guishing in their private experiences the qualities of pleasure (to be searched for) and pain (to be avoided). A thirsty animal, for instance, is not just thirsty; by its thirst, it is moved to search for water. The animal does not have the concept of dehydration and its danger, but is driven to remove the painful sensation of thirst. If the animal could not experience thirst, it would die of dehydration. It is obvious that species provided with this type of sensation are more likely to survive. Natural selection has thus favored the evolution of feeling.

Unpleasant sensations trigger responses which lead to the removal of the painful feeling: the animal learns to keep away from what hurts. On the contrary, pleasant sensations make the animal search for ways to prolong or renew the pleasant feeling.

In the life of animals a general rule, although one with many exceptions, can be recognized—what is pleasant enhances survival and what is painful decreases the chance of survival. Pleasantness and increased probability of survival thus become associated, and their association is transmitted from generation to generation. Although this association is imperfect and susceptible to many exceptions, it is a statistically favorable one from the viewpoint of the preservation of the species.

Among all the feelings of the organism, pain plays an important role. It is a signal that a discontinuity of the integrity of the organism has occurred and may increase unless the animal moves away or removes the source of pain. Pain is thus a translation of an abnormal state of the organism into a subjective experience. Survival of animal species, other than the simplest, and animal evolution would not be possible without the existence of pain.

The Book of Job remains unclear. If in the order of creation pain is necessary, then God would not seem to be omnipotent, as the Bible states that He is. If God had unlimited capacity and possibilities, He would not have resorted to pain to ensure evolution. The religious man believes that God assigned to man this ethical mission, the relief of pain. Few, whether believers or nonbelievers, would deny that man should try to find ways of conquering pain. Dedicated men, particularly in the field of medicine, have always done that.

Evil is a more complicated phenomenon than physical pain. I shall define it here as any undeserved suffering caused by man, or any suffering which, although preventable, has not been prevented by man. This definition does not satisfy those who include in the concept of evil any cause of sorrow; for instance, the effects of an earthquake. It also does not satisfy many philosophers, some of whom define evil simply as lack of good. The problem then remains of defining what is good.

Our working definition reaffirms the role of man's will in bringing about evil. Evil depends on man's choice, not on his cosmic or biological nature. As a causer of events, his will may determine evil.

Let us return to Job. His suffering was not detemined only by natural causes, like diseases and the storm that killed all his children. Job was also the victim of evil, undeserved suffering inflicted by other men. The Sabeans and the Chaldeans killed his servants and robbed him of everything he had. The Sabeans and the Chaldeans acted in accordance with the law of the jungle, not according to the moral law, and became symbols of man the evildoer.

How does man come to choose evil? We have already discussed this matter in several chapters, especially Chapter 8. It is true that many men prefer to obtain possessions by stealing, fighting, and conquering rather than by working. We have, however, seen that although the desire for possession and in some cases for impermissible sexual pleasure is conducive to evil actions, the desire for power is the prominent incentive. Even the infliction of suffering for sadistic pleasure, as in the case of the Nazis, can be subsumed under the concept of power. Only extreme degrees of power enable some men to indulge in that perversity.

Evil, however, has a much larger role in human life than is generally realized. This lack of recognition occurs to a large extent because we label as "evil" only the most terrible crimes, like those perpetrated by the Nazis. Actually human existence is pervaded by evil to a staggering degree, evil not reaching the criminal stage, but still capable of tragically coloring the life of the individual.

Degrees of evil may exist in personal tragedies, as they exist in the misunderstandings and resulting hostility between parents and children, in the disturbed relations between husband and wife, in the vindictive jealousy between brothers and sisters, business partners, or professional associates, in the heartless behavior between competitors, in academic intrigues, in the loss of jobs after many years of work for a firm, etc. Evil may manifest itself also as inability to feel for other human beings or, as we illustrated in Chapter 9, by our becoming evil watchers and not preventing evil which we could prevent.

Some readers may feel that I assume a purely moralistic and not a psychological position, that I would condemn instead of explain. The truth is that psychology and psychiatry have not studied evil as evil. Neither the well-known psychological dictionary by English and English [7] nor the psychiatric dictionary by Hinsie and Campbell [8] so much as lists the term "evil." [9] I am aware of the psychological determinants which motivate evil actions, and certainly I hope that the conflicts predisposing to evil, whether within the family or in society at large, will be eliminated. Let us remember, however, that with the exceptions of relatively few cases of psychosis, even in the individual who is torn by conflicts or psychologically predisposed to hurtful actions there is a margin of will left. By increasing our awareness of the enormous range of evil and its effects, we may do what psychological methods have not yet achieved. There is no inherent incompatibility between psychology, psychoanalysis, and ethics. They may all work together, all aiming at the betterment of man.

In the first section of Chapter 10, we saw that an ethical element plays an important role in mental illness. We may repeat the same thing about all those interpersonal relations which cause suffering, even if they do not eventuate in mental illness. Although it is true that disturbed interpersonal relations have predominantly psychological components, they are to some extent often determined also by the will of the people involved. When these disturbances are caused by so-called social phenomena, they are also related to the ethical implications of these phenomena.

The Book of Job is not concerned with intrapsychic suffering. If Job's friends had succeeded in making him feel guilty, his suffering would have become intrapsychic also. But Job did not feel guilty, and in this fact lies a large part of his moral greatness. Of course, I do not imply the converse: that people who experience intrapsychical suffering are immoral or cannot achieve moral greatness.

Although Job's friends meant well, they were in error and in some respects can be considered as representatives of all those people, institutions, creeds, and philosophies that make people feel guilty so that they obey or acquiesce in their miserable conditions. False endocracy is a Trojan horse which acts from inside and brings about the doom of the individual. Job's greatness prevented its occurrence in his case.

THE ETHICAL LAW

Man has tried to combat evil and to promote good by means of the *law*. The law, however, is not enough unless it coincides with ethics, unless the common good is made to agree with the personal good.

The greatest philosophers have conceived of ethical states which would establish and enforce the ethical law. Plato has done so in *The Republic*. Plato's conceptions were entirely ideal, however, and had no practical feasibility. Hegel transformed the ethical state into something earthly, or immanent, but associated it with Prussian nationalism. In history, utopias notwithstanding, the ethical law had a relatively slow development, except in the smallest groups of primitive men. In Chapter 8 we saw that in the primordial times of humanity there were two unwritten codes of behavior: the ethical, applied to relations with the members of the same group; and the other, characterized by hostility and the search for power, applied to relations with the other groups. Since a man belonged to only one group and those to which he did not belong were all the others, he found himself surrounded by a world of hostility and terror. When one's group outgrew the size of a clan or a small tribe, hostility, discriminatory practices, and the search for power began to occur also within each group.

The advent of an ethical conception which would be applied to more people than one's own small intimate group was a great accomplishment. In a predominantly unethical world only a few periods in history achieved greatness by making such an advent possible. One of them was the Exodus of the Jews from Egypt, which culminated in the promulgation of the ethical Law at Sinai. Orthodox Jews and fundamentalist Christians believe in the literal truth of the events as they are described in the Bible: the intervention of God in the liberation of the Jews from Pharaoh and the revelation of the Law on Mount Sinai. Since moments of greatness appear so seldom in history, it is easy to understand how divine participation, if not by direct intervention at least by inspiration, is by many considered necessary for their occurrence. In a barbaric world, approximately 1250 years before Christ, the Jews had the inspiration of the ethical law. Whereas nature is cyclical, with an ineluctable repetition of physical laws, the ethical law is linear and progressive.

Nature should be transcended and human history should become ethical history. In ethical progress, mankind should find its greatest source of dignity. Alas! History, too, can be viewed as cyclical; and we can very well understand why many famous historians, from Vico to Spengler and Toynbee, have stressed its cyclical nature. Their interpretations are acknowledgement that the history of mankind was not linear and progressive. As revealed in the Old Testament, Jews did not follow the ethical law for long periods of time. Other people who conceived something similar to an ethical law or, relatively speaking, a good society, soon lost what they had achieved. One of the greatest accomplishments of the Greeks was to set up city governments which guaranteed political liberty to their citizens. For the first time in history, each free citizen had a share in the sovereignty of the state. This experiment with its various vicissitudes lasted in Greece only four hundred years. Today's Greece does not enjoy such government. Four hundred years before Christ, Rome expelled the Tarquins and instituted a similar free democratic government, to be lost again forever with Caesar and the Empire. The French Revolution was an attempt to regain for Western Europe the stage of political achievement of the great Greek period.

But let us go back to the portentous event by which Jews living in a barbaric world in 1250 B.C. could have an ethical law. How can the event be explained historically? Such an understanding can reveal a great deal about ethics. I can only advance some personal hypotheses.

I believe that the Mount Sinai event was the result of the unusual interaction or intersection of three circumstances. The first was that the Jews, when they were slaves in Egypt, were separated from the general population and retained their own clan or tribal organization, as described in the Bible in reference to the patriarchs Abraham, Isaac, and Jacob. The Bible says that that more than 600,000 left Egypt, but this figure is surely a gross exaggeration. Perhaps the Hebrew population in Egypt at its peak did not exceed a few thousand. It is thus conceivable that within this small group the ethical code prevailed, with the best moral principles of cooperation and equality described in Chapter 8 in reference to the primordial small groups of men. Occasional episodes of violence, as epitomized in the biblical story of Joseph and his brothers, occurred; but the overall picture was one of mutual help and moral behavior. The fact that the Jews were persecuted and victimized in Egypt reinforced the ethical principles of cooperation and mutual help among themselves.

The second important circumstance was the exposure of the Jews to the high civilization of Egypt. Inferior to the Jews ethically, the Egyptians had, on the other hand, attained a relatively high cultural level which promoted conceptual thought. The Jews learned from this civilization and therefore could formulate into general principles habits of behavior and norms which were already common practice among them.

The third important circumstance was the state of slavery to which they were subjected and the consequent injustice and suffering. They could compare it with the state of equality and justice which prevailed among them. Their daily experiences made them focus on ethical laws that would be applied not just to a small group, but to their whole community and possibly to the human race.

When Moses guided the people from slavery to freedom, he did not have an army of soldiers but only a purpose and, soon, an ethical law. To be free meant to make use of freedom by following the ethical way. The moral law came to be the foundation of the Hebrew nation. Throughout the Old Testament, the sojourn in Egypt, the land of slavery, is mentioned as an example of suffering and injustice and is a warning against inflicting on others or accepting for oneself a similar fate.

Many great thinkers have conceived of society as based on some kind of all-embracing contract or covenant. According to Hobbes (1651), people made a covenant to obey a human ruler, the sovereign. For Rousseau (1762) men renounced their natural rights and obeyed a social contract by virtue of which the state gives equal rights to all. Thus, Hobbes and Rousseau conceived of the contract in a strictly legal way. Politics came before social ethics; the focus was on power first and on the common good second. But the Jews, long before, believed in another covenant, that made by Abraham with God, later reestablished by Moses. According to this covenant, the Jews are supposed to be a kingdom of priests and a holy nation. If we translate the words of the myth into the language of moral philosophy, the meaning is that the Jews have the obligation to follow the moral law. The first obedience is not to an earthly sovereign, a state, but to ethics, the law of God. Isaiah and Jesus of Nazareth tried to apply to the whole of humanity this ethic of justice and love.

But history was cyclical. The prophets of the Old Testament

were the first to realize that the linear line of progress had not been followed. We must acknowledge that no kind of religion has succeeded in its intent. To fight rather than to cooperate has been the major occupation of man, irrespective of whether the fight was on the battlefield or in the arena of modern business competition.

Great men have expressed different ideas about what should be the essential activity of man. Hegel believed that the idea, or the supremacy of thought, should be the essential activity, and Marx thought that work should be. Now it seems to me that thought and work must have an ethical quality, and must become ethical events. The essential activity of man is the good deed. But here comes the point which the ethical law or politics as common good also must safeguard: the good deed should not require that the person renounce his inalienable rights, the assertion of his own individuality, and, whenever possible, the expression of his creativity.

CHAPTER 12

Individuality
and Creativity

NO MORE HEROES

OFTEN IDEOLOGIES HAVE DEMANDED THAT MAN SACRIFICE HIS FREE-
dom, individuality, or even his life for the common good. No
ideology or sense of duty should extort so much. To the extent
that such sacrifices are requested, inequality and suffering per-
sist. To die for a war of aggrandizement, for loyalty to one's
king, or for an imposed ideology is a barbarous imposition. It is
time now to revise conceptions and attitudes of whose obsoles-
cence Shakespeare was already aware. In *Henry V*, the king in
disguise tries to convince the soldiers to fight.

> *King Henry.*
> . . . Methinks I could not die anywhere so contented as in the
> king's company, his cause being just and his quarrel honorable.
> *Williams* (a soldier). That's more than we know.
> *Bates* (a soldier).
> Ay, or more than we should seek after; for we know enough if

we know we are the king's subjects. If his cause be wrong, our obedience to the king wipes the crime of it out of us.
Williams.
But if the cause be not good, the king himself hath a heavy reckoning to make, when all those legs and arms and heads, chopp'd off in a battle, shall join together at the latter day and cry all, "We died at such a place," some swearing, some crying for a surgeon, some upon their wives left poor behind them, some upon the debts they owe, some upon their children rawly left. I am afeard there are few die well that die in a battle; for how can they charitably dispose of anything, when blood is their argument? Now, if these men do not die well, it will be a black matter for the king that led them to it, who to disobey were against all proportion of subjection.

Many people still agree with Shakespeare's Bates that obedience to the chief of state wipes out the crime of those who commit it. But the other character, Williams, has a more modern view. Later the king, still in disguise, says, "Every subject's duty is the king's; but every subject's soul is his own." What about duty and soul being in conflict? Williams believes that only "few die well in a battle"; but we must say that no one dies well in battle. As long as society requires heroes, society is antihuman and is not morally heroic. To require the sacrifice of others in order to increase one's power, under the pretext of patriotism or loyalty to a past historical role or to obsolete ideologies, must be totally rejected. Certainly an individual may be willing to sacrifice his life to save his children, to defend his country from the invader, or to stop a great evil that engulfs the community. This sacrifice, however, should not be necessary among civilized men at any time. A society which requires heroes must search and find the cause of the evil, which must then be vanquished. The blood of one man is an irreparable injustice for all time, an infamy committed against all men, an injury to the dignity of every human being. To rationalize the deed by saying that the sacrifice was only of one or of a few persons and for the benefit of many is no proper argument. The collectivity is important, of course, but so is the individual. Number is no criterion on which to appraise value. Any system or society which stresses only the collectivity and minimizes the individual is not consistent with the spiritual and physical needs of man.

And yet history, until very recently, has been quite critical of those who were not willing to give their lives for "big issues."

A historical figure who has been so maligned is Galileo, who, instead of reaffirming what he knew was right—that the earth moved around the sun—and thus in all likelihood facing the death penalty at the hands of the church, made a public statement that he had erred. Many generations have been embarrassed by Galileo's recantation. I myself remember feeling during my adolescence that it behooved a great man like Galileo not to give in. He should have stuck bravely to what he knew was the truth despite the consequences. Galileo was absolutely sure that it was the earth that was moving, and was sure too of the truth, unacceptable to the church, of the other observations which he had made with the telescope. But should he have sacrificed his life and deprived the world of his genius simply to oppose the rigid dogma of the ecclesiastic establishment? He knew that whether he recanted his truth or not, the truth would eventually be recognized and accepted by the whole world. By recanting Galileo actually helped the church, for he prevented it from murdering him. He continued his research and studies, and in no way prevented the truth from eventually being recognized. But, most of all, he was true to himself and to the sacredness of his life.

The example of Galileo does not encompass the whole range of the pressure exerted by culture to be heroic because, after all, Galileo was a great man. Since ancient times, society has glorified the hero, and has expected simple citizens either to emulate him or to worship him. Literature concerned only great men and heroes and ignored or had contempt for the average person, who lacked heroic stature. As an example I shall mention an episode in the second book of the *Iliad*, which contrasts with the rest of the Homeric epic.

Thersites, a Greek, bandy-legged, lame in one foot, and "having two rounded shoulders, arched down upon his chest," has been conscripted into the Greek army and has fought for nine years against Troy. Finally he protests. He is not a hero; he wants to go home. He is not even in awe of the heroes and, in a moment of anger, inveighs against the great men Odysseus, Agamemnon, and, to a lesser extent, Achilles. Odysseus has just tried, with beautiful words addressed to the troops, to rekindle their patriotic fervor, to close the ranks behind King Agamemnon, and has urged them to fight for the glory of Greece, for the "heaven-fostered kings," and the honor of Zeus. Thersites does not buy that rhetoric. Alone among the thousands of soldiers he dares to unmask the powerful and the power seekers.

With angry words he says that Agamemnon wants to fight and possess the beautiful captured women and even the gold collected from the enemy. Thersites urges his fellow soldiers to depart and leave Odysseus in Troy "to gorge with deeds of honor." Odysseus then reproaches Thersites for daring to talk in this way about kings, calls him the basest of all those in Agamemnon's army, and threatens to beat him mercilessly. He then proceeds to strike Thersites' back and shoulders with a club. We must be thankful that he stopped at that point. Hitler and Stalin would have had poor Thersites executed.

There is no doubt that Homer is on the side of the kings and the heroes. The whole *Iliad* is an exaltation of the heroic in man. Thersites does not want to fight or die for those who want to become rich and powerful, and could not care less about recapturing *la belle Hélène*. He wants to go home. Thersites is described as a horrible-looking, grotesque human being, as if his physical deformity reflects his antiheroic soul. We can say this for Homer, a propos of Thersites, that the majesty of his poetry caused him to maintain sufficient aesthetic distance to permit us, twenty-eight centuries later, to rehabilitate the character that he created. Hurrah for Thersites! Hurrah for the man who was a precursor of freedom three thousand years ago and dared to unmask the kings! Rather than equate his physical ugliness with his alleged wickedness, we contrast it with his fiery and beautiful spirit. And yet, for almost three thousand years, generations of people educated in the classic tradition have learned to despise Thersites. When he was beaten by Odysseus, the soldiers laughed at him. Thersites "sat down and was amazed, and in pain, with helpless look, wiped away the tear." I am inclined to believe that he did not weep only over his physical pain. He was not a weakling. I revere the tear he shed at seeing his point of view doomed to failure, the truth masked again, the crowd deceived, and the power-crazy heroes continue their mad race.

SPONTANEITY AND ORIGINALITY

Man's final actualization is in his actions, or acts of will, be they ordinary deeds or creative acts. Man's autonomy has its beginning in those spontaneous animal movements described in Chapter 2, but it undergoes a fantastic development. His most important forms of spontaneity manifest themselves as thoughts and feelings. Any choice is at first a choice of some of these thoughts and feelings. From the spontaneous flow of ideas and feelings, certain trends become differentiated which the individual may or may not accept and enact. Classical psychoanalysis has understood this problem, although in a very indirect way, and has based its therapy on the phenomenon of free association. The patient who lies on the couch must allow his ideas to come to the surface without any inhibition or editing and must communicate them to the analyst. The aim of the technique is to remove conscious control and to allow the ideas to come freely to consciousness. From this free flow of ideas patterns emerge which will disclose first the conflicts and then the personality of the analysand.[1]

What seemed at first a reliance on freedom became, in Freud's system, a complete denial of freedom. In fact, Freud found these ideas, seemingly so freely expressed, not to be free at all. Their occurrence is determined by motivational forces which, in their turn, are the result of previous causes, ultimately of instinctual origin. Thus "free" associations are not free but follow a rigid determinism. They are like everything else in the universe, as viewed by nineteenth-century science. The patient who seeks analytic treatment, however, does so voluntarily and chooses to follow the instructions of the analyst and to put himself into the analytic frame of mind. Once he has put himself in that position by an act of choice, ideas emerge spontaneously and he refrains from screening or editing. One patient may start to express ideas about his current problems or life, another patient about childhood experiences, another about ambitions for the future, etc. The uniqueness and the spontaneity of the individual are expressed by the group of emerging ideas.

Spontaneity and uniqueness are largely based on the past— Freud was right. Certainly what seems to be a result of chance is in fact the result of special combinations of biological circumstances and antecedent life experiences. These circumstances are millions of events, and since they are never duplicated in their number, sequence, strength, and other characteristics, their combination is enough to explain the uniqueness of the individual. When spontaneous ideas occur repeatedly or in cycles or special sequences, the analyst helps the patient recognize patterns in them. The patterns existed before; but without the intervention of the analyst, the patient would not have discovered them, or at least would have discovered them only with the greatest difficulty. Thus the will of the involved analyst is important.

As a result of spontaneity, *originality* tends to emerge as a manifestation and implementation of the authenticity, autonomy, and uniqueness of the individual. Nevertheless, originality is by and large repressed by social organizations, be they the family, the school, or the community at large. The individual is under an almost constant pressure to give up his own ways and to adopt those sanctioned by society.

From a statistical point of view, society has some justification for this repressive attitude in spite of the fact that, as we shall see later in this chapter, originality is one of the major ingredients of creativity. Society favors what is good for the majority of people, and is not considerate of the creativity which is restricted to a few gifted persons. What are the faults society sees in originality? Original behavior may hamper the efficiency of standardized society. Let us say that a man wants to follow his inclination to walk in a zigzag way in the street. He would interfere with the traffic. Society intimates that to maintain harmonious relations with the rest of the population the individual must give up a great deal of his originality. Originality may also appear bizarre and repulsive to the aesthetic taste of the majority of people. New things are not necessarily beautiful because they are new. As a matter of fact, most new combinations are unaesthetic. Moreover, the unfamiliar produces in most people a sense of discomfort or even fear: they have to learn how to respond to it. Psychological economy is thus on the side of repeating usual patterns of behavior. Society has consequently resented originality and has labeled its practitioners eccentric, peculiar, bizarre, or even schizophrenic. The result is that, throughout history, most people have found it easier to be conformists, whether the society was based on feudalism, militarism, or the bourgeoisie, corporate capitalism, communism, etc. Now we do not propose that every kind of originality be allowed. Originality which interferes with the inalienable rights of other individuals or with the common good should be prohibited. But we must not confuse intolerance with the common good or inalienable rights. Intolerance is an aversion to the new or different, not because it is harmful but because it is new or different.

Needless to say, society does not need to embrace new ways that seem unaesthetic, bizarre, and repulsive. We must grant to society the right to prefer the old ways. Originality which is not harmful to others, however, should not only be respected, but also encouraged as a precursor of creativity.

Even what seems incongruous should be tolerated. What seems today an apparent incongruity may prove to be an opening to new avenues of understanding or new horizons of experience.

INDIVIDUAL CONFRONTATION

Individual confrontation is a form of originality which expresses itself in challenging the accepted ways, in not taking them for granted because they are transmitted from generation to generation or because society imposes them on the individual. Thus, although nothing new is necessarily created or discovered by confrontation, masks are removed and the individual rids himself of unnecessary burdens. We have already seen in this book how, in some instances, the greatness and courage of people like Pope John XXIII were required to reject the accepted ways. Each era has had its great confronters. For example, the thirteenth century had Francis of Assisi, who confronted the wealthy class of people in which he was born, opposed the social structure of his time, and embraced and preached poverty. But all persons, each in his own way, even if less endowed than Francis and John, can do something in the way of confrontation. We have seen in Chapter 7 how special educational trends predispose some people to confrontation. Everyone, however, with some discipline and practice, could learn not to be overwhelmed by the prevailing mores and ideas but to question their usefulness or validity.

First of all, we must not confuse customs and mores with habits. Even the great psychologist William James defended habits because, by following them, the mind can conserve enough energy to have enough left for progress and intelligent thinking. According to him, "We must make automatic and habitual, as early as possible, as many useful actions as we can." [2] Habits, then, are such activities as table manners, washing, dressing oneself, etc. James is right, provided we are not overpowered by the tendency to act only through habit, and especially provided we distinguish habits from *customs,* which we may accept as habits. A custom is a long-established practice to which a society gives a special meaning. The custom may become as ingrained as a habit. In India, for instance, the almost automatic acceptance of customs as if they were habits has been a misfortune which has plagued the country for many centuries, and to a large extent continues to do so in spite of the great questioners like Mohandas Gandhi, Nehru, and Indira

Gandhi. These mores have great endocratic power. During a period of famine, some Hindus prefer to die of starvation rather than to go against the tradition and use food touched by pariahs. If Brahmins touch pariahs or Westerners they feel contaminated; and in order to purify themselves, they drink the urine of cows, which are considered holy animals. I have mentioned these Indian customs because to Westerners they appear grossly inappropriate; but we have our own, whose equal absurdity we do not recognize.

If we prepare ourselves to listen to our own individuality, autonomy, and authenticity, we become able to reject some of the usual ways which no longer are acceptable; we become able to recognize in them not just habits and customs but masks and hypocrisies. We recognize that often what seemed to be just a psychological *reinforcement* of a habit or custom has become, as we already expressed in Chapter 2, a societal *enforcement*. The challenger may have to pay a big price for not conforming. If he belongs to a political party or to a school of thought (not merely ideological but scientific schools as well) and rejects some of the ideas of the party or the tenets of the school, he may be considered not only eccentric and peculiar but also disloyal. His straightforwardness may be considered brashness and immaturity.

There is indeed a similarity between the bold man, in his confrontation, and the young child who has not yet learned to put on the masks of society and approaches the world with a genuine freshness. When children act in this way, they often elicit laughter; when adults do, they elicit reproach. As an example of this attitude of children I shall always remember a cousin of mine, who was much younger than I, so that when I was in my teens, he was four. Once he and his mother came to visit us for a few days from the city of Bologna, where they lived. On a Sunday afternoon, a lady, a friend of the family, came to visit us and on unexpectedly seeing little Victor, addressed him in an intensely affectionate tone and made the following request:

"Victor, would you give me a little kiss?"

"No," Victor replied firmly.

"Why?" asked the lady, taken aback.

"Because your mouth is crooked, you are ugly, and I don't even know you."

Four-year-old Victor was not only bold; he also happened to be right. The lady was ugly; her mouth was slightly uneven because of a hardly visible facial asymmetry, and it was the first time he had met her.

Victor's visit remained proverbial in my family. One day he had a cold and had to blow his nose. Without hesitation he went to the curtain of the window and blew his nose on the curtain. The maid was horrified. She screamed, "Victor, don't use the curtain to blow your nose!"

Victor replied, "Why not? I have a cold and I have no handkerchief."

It is true that little Victor had not yet been corrupted by society, but he *was* immature. We do not expect an adult to behave like Victor, who, by the way, has grown up to be a very fine person. The adult who practices confrontation is different from the child who has no inhibitions. The adult actually must make an effort to overcome his inhibitions and do what he would do had he not these inhibitions. Thus, instead of apparent immaturity, he may actually have more than the usual degree of maturity. The complicated ways of life seem almost ineluctably to lead to the building of stifling artificialities. Thus confrontation must be permanent if we do not want to be straitjacketed or deformed by them.

But why go through the difficult process of unmasking oneself and society? Would it not be better not to create these masks at all? Do we have to choose only between these three possibilities: the immaturity of the child, the suffocation of the conformist, or the labor of the confronter? Theoretically there is another possibility: to institute and maintain those ideals of genuine, unadulterated life which do not require masks. This certainly should be the aim of any healthy society, but alas, it is only an ideal. Since these masks, false beliefs, and burdensome habits will continue to exist until man has undergone a drastic and not foreseeable improvement, the best we can do is again and again to challenge and remove these fetters. To do so, courage and open-mindedness are necessary.

Before concluding this section, I want to make one further remark. In this chapter I have used the analogy of the mask, which, however, is adequate only in some situations. A mask is something easy to drop. The face is supposed to show its natural aspect once the mask is taken off. In some cases it is so; namely, when we deal only with relatively light masks which, once removed, leave no effects. In many other cases it is not so. In Chapters 5 and 7 we saw that the burden is not a mask but an endocratic surplus which changes the personality. In

Chapter 6 we saw that some societal effects produce a deformation of the self. Thus, rather than comparing these social influences to masks, they should be compared to the old Chinese practice of binding the feet which in turn changed the structure of the body.

IDENTITY THROUGH APPROVAL AND FUSION WITH OTHERS

Need for approval is one of the major factors which induce men to conform and to deny their individuality and autonomy. Why is approval so important for most people? In spite of its apparent simplicity, the question is serious and the answer complicated. To say that a person seeks approval in order to escape anxiety is not a satisfactory answer. Certainly the person who needs approval becomes anxious if he does not get it, but why? What is the origin of this anxiety?

The most important reason for the majority of people is still connected with the experiences of childhood which were described in early chapters. It is based not on the quest for approval but on the quest for love. The child has learned that if mother approves of him, she is more likely to bestow love on him. Later the child extends this attitude to the whole world. The community of which he is part is identified with the mother from whom he wants love. The government, or even the dictator, is identified with father. It requires maturity on the part of the individual to dissociate the need for love from the need for approval.

The need for approval also has other roots, if not in all people, at least in a large number of them. Approval is sought as a *method of contact* with other people, in place of a state of relatedness, trust, or communion, which would be more appropriate but is harder to obtain. The individual feels terribly alone. As we mentioned in Chapter 4, he feels separated from the rest of the world, even from his fellow men. His intellect, instead of helping him in this respect, may increase his doubts. He asks himself, "Am I right in my thoughts and feelings? It seems to me that it is so, and that I should feel in this way, but am I not pretentious in thinking I am right?" He is obsessed by the Cartesian doubt, but not being a Descartes he is not able to answer his own doubts, and so he finds it easier to agree with others.

When he tries to convey his private thoughts and feelings to others, he may find difficulty in communicating them, and often he is misunderstood. People respond not to the totality of him but to a part of him, to that part which may be involved with the present or immediate relation but which does not reflect the whole or even the essential him. Moreover, when he tries to assert himself, he may realize that he is unable to affirm his own identity. He is overcome by the ways of others, by society at large. The need for approval, developed in childhood, is not only not outgrown, but is reinforced by all these doubts about himself. The mature man should be able to overcome this need. He should, of course, welcome the approval that comes spontaneously, but he should not pursue it at the loss of his own individuality and autonomy. If a person does not need approval to make contact with other people; if he feels he has the right to assert himself even though he cannot be absolutely certain of his position; if he feels that even in the event he is not entirely understood, human solidarity will offer him a common ground on which to base a mutuality of feelings and aims, then he will not jeopardize his individuality and autonomy. The individual should be true to himself. Whenever he is led to think that, by adopting values in which he does not believe, he will gain approval and therefore will help himself, he will lose part of himself, perhaps the best part. Many men unfortunately succumb to the quest for approval. This submission is not related to the degree of eminence or even greatness which they may reach in other parts of life. We find some great men who were able to maintain their autonomy and some who, instead, succumbed to others.

As an example of the first, I shall mention Sigmund Freud, who, opposed not only by the prevailing Viennese culture but also by his psychiatric colleagues, was able to stick tenaciously to his ideas and reaffirm his beliefs. So did Galileo. His recantation was purely an external, formal act to save his life, but inside he never gave up his ideas.

In the second category we must unfortunately include the Nobel Prize winner Luigi Pirandello, who is considered the greatest playwright in Italian literature since Alfieri and Goldoni. It would take too long to give an adequate account here of Pirandello's drama: not a drama he wrote but the drama he lived, in which, in spite of his literary genius, he remained a negative protagonist. Possibly because of the circumstances of his life, including the fact that his wife was psychotic, Pirandello was always preoccupied with such problems as truth and illusion, real identity or false identity, being masked or unmasked, being understood or misunderstood. In many of his plays, in ways similar to the Japanese film *Rashomon,* we hear different versions of facts, and the tragedy is that there is no Truth, with a capital "T," because each person has his own truth, equally valid.

In his play *Right You Are If You Think You Are,* we do not know who is crazy—the mother-in-law or the daughter-in-law. In *Henry IV (The Living Mask),* a rich man who developed paranoia after a fall from his horse believes he is the emperor Henry IV. Since he is a rich man, the family has him taken care of in a mansion where he can continue to act as an emperor and be addressed as the emperor. One day the protagonist reacquires sanity; he discovers that after all he is not Henry IV. Nevertheless, he chooses not to go back to the mediocre reality of life and decides to make other people believe that he still believes he is Henry IV.

Pirandello's major novel, *The Late Mattia Pascal,* written long before his famous plays, has a similar subject. People believe that Mattia Pascal has committed suicide and is now dead. Mattia Pascal takes advantage of the situation. Now that everybody believes he is dead, he can start his life again and be free of all the restrictions that society imposes. He assumes the name of Adriano Meis and begins a new existence, only to discover quickly that he is not free at all even in this second trial. All the restrictions repeat themselves and accumulate to an unbearable degree. The protagonist undergoes one disappointment after another, is disgusted with life again, and decides to commit suicide. But while he is in the process of carrying out the fatal act, a brilliant idea occurs to him: Why not kill Adriano Meis and resume the identity of Mattia Pascal? He thus leaves suicidal notes allegedly written by Meis and reappears in the world as Pascal, to find again the same difficulties in this third life.

In *Six Characters in Search of an Author,* the character father says,

> The drama, as I see it, is all here: in the consciousness that I have that each of us believes to be one, but is not; each person is many people, according to the possibilities of being which are in us . . . We become aware of it when, in some of our

actions, for an unfortunate circumstance, we remain suddenly hung or suspended: I mean, we become aware of not being completely in that act, and that thus it would be an atrocious injustice to judge us from that act alone.[3]

In a preface to *Six Characters in Search of an Author,* Pirandello wrote of what for many years had been the travails of his spirit: the deceit of mutual understanding, the potential multiple personality of everyone according to the various possibilities which exist in each of us, and the tragic conflict between constantly moving and changing life and the unchangeable "form" which determines and immobilizes it.

Pirandello denies that individual consciousness can find satisfaction by accepting the mores and laws of society. Life is dynamic and yet static. He and his characters rebel against all these impositions. Up to here we agree with Pirandello, but not further. According to him the idea of freeing oneself is an illusion and the battle will be lost. The tragedy of man is in his own rebellion. There is only one solution: to change the tyranny of democratic living for a real tyranny, which is tragic but heroic, the only truth, the only way to reconcile movement and form. Thus let us welcome tyranny! Let us embrace Fascism! Mussolini is the only possible savior of Italy. Pirandello became an ardent Fascist.[4] We should not believe that his adherence to the party was due to opportunism. He wired Mussolini himself asking him to accept him as a member of the party in September 1924, which time, until 1943, was the only time Fascism was in serious trouble because of Italy's reaction to the murder by Fascists of the democratic leader Matteotti. Pirandello was great enough to become aware of the tragic hazards involved in such problems as the uniqueness of individuality which contrasts with the multiple personality, the aloneness, the misunderstanding from others, the refusal to accept society, and the impossibility of escaping from society. He understood that many people cannot live their lives without a lie. But he did not accept or challenge these hazards; he was afraid of them and tried a clownish solution: to lose his isolation and obtain approval by submerging himself in political tyranny. He did not live with the hazards of life, as Oedipus and Hamlet did, but by accepting a lie, as many of his characters did, he failed both in his art and his life to partake of the ultimate essence of the human predicament, which he had so well individualized.

ON BEING MADE BY ONE'S OWN CHOICES

Only when the individual is in full possession of his will and is fully conscious of it can his self flourish and grow. At times he may have to pay the price of standing alone, but as a result he will be more himself. And by being more himself, he will be able to give more of himself to others. The free man must become aware that although he is partially biologically determined, and although he is also partially determined by sociocultural influences, he is also determined by the choices he himself has made in life. Yes, not totally, but in his most significant human part, he chooses himself. Any important choice determines to a large extent the character of one's subsequent life. As Robert Frost wrote in one of his famous poems, two roads diverge in the wood, and it will "make all the difference" whether we take one or the other. And Dante, in words difficult to translate into English, wrote, "*Cosa fatta capo ha*" ("An accomplished deed is a beginning or lead of things which will follow"). We do not have to be Julius Caesar to cross a Rubicon. All of us have our Rubicons, and our future life will depend on whether we cross them or not.

Psychiatrists and psychoanalysts are in a particularly good position to observe that when people have been true and faithful to themselves, and have made the choices which were consonant with their basic philosophies of life, they have prospered. Even if at times they did not have glamor or success, they had peace of mind and a feeling of integrity. When they succumbed to the demands of their family, society, false values, or to the impositions of their own insecurity, they practiced a nongenuine and at times sterile course of life, even if that life was accompanied by opportunistic gains.

When a man yields to diverting temptations and takes seductive roads, he ends up in blind alleys and will find increasing difficulty in retrieving his true way. In some cases his life may assume a tragically inflexible course, with little hope of return to an acceptable position or a new beginning. The free man must define what he wants to dedicate his life to. He must establish a list of priorities and face the issues involved. He must say yes to the choices which implement his basic aims; he must say no to the choices which lead to false substitutions. To make oneself out of one's own choices requires a fundamental commitment in thinking, feeling, and acting. The choices should not remain hypothetical. The free man should not say, "I should have selected this course of action, but I didn't." Not to act in accordance with one's own choices means to allow oneself to be molded entirely by all the biological, familial, social, and traditional forces; it means not to live in accordance with the capacity to will. It means to give up whatever freedom one has to choose for oneself.

The example of a psychoanalytic patient, Aurora B., can show how people fare when they allow their own individuality and autonomy to have the upper hand and when they do not.

Aurora was born in a small American town in a very conventional family of marginal financial condition. She was the second of four children (two boys and two girls). The father felt that his modest means would allow him to provide an education for the boys, but the girls, because of their sex, did not need to go to college. But the boys did not care about studying. Aurora was the only one who did. She welcomed education and looked forward to the possibility of bypassing the limited horizons of her conventional milieu. By winning many battles against the reluctant father and by going to work, she managed to go to college at her own expense and to graduate. Her aim was to pursue a career in fine arts. When she returned home after college, she felt out of place. She was the educated one; she was cultured, liberal-minded, a stranger. In her little town she had few opportunities for dating. Roy, a professional man, far inferior to her intellectually, courted her and asked her to marry him. The family started a big campaign in favor of this marriage. Aurora knew that Roy was not the man for her; but alas, this time she did not act according to what her self was telling her to do, and eventually she married him. She also allowed her desire to escape from the family to influence her decision. The marriage was an unfortunate one. Soon Roy took to drinking and to seeking the company of other women. Possibly Aurora contributed to Roy's selection of this style of life. She did not have much love or respect for him, and he felt frustrated. On the other hand, his excessive drinking and especially his repeated and scandalous affairs with other women alienated her from him more and more. The marriage became a disaster. The family again insisted she had to put up with it. She did so for fifteen years. By an unforeseeable set of circumstances, Aurora eventually met Rudolph, a divorced man, who showed interest in her. The two confided their individual troubles. Rudolph asked her for a date. Aurora was under strong pressure to say no: her upbringing, her family attitude about relations with the opposite sex were against her meeting Rudolph. On the other hand, something in her was telling her that there was nothing wrong in meeting someone whom she liked and who could help her to overcome her doubts about dissolving her marriage.

On the way to the meeting, Aurora, who was driving her car, had many impulses to turn back; but she resisted the urge. She felt that to go ahead was her choice, her Rubicon. She did. Eventually her marriage with Roy ended in divorce, and she married Rudolph. Her life, which was disturbed by many neurotic symptoms, flourished again. Aurora began to do the things in life she always wanted to do. After many years she started again to devote herself to art, and is now a sculptress of some merit.

CREATIVITY AND ITS CULTIVATION [5]

The supreme achievement of individuality is creativity, which transcends the usual ways of dealing with the world and brings about a desirable enlargement of human experience.

This enlargement may include aesthetic pleasure, as in art, or utility, understanding, and predictability, as in science. At the same time that the creative process opens new dimensions of the universe, it expands man, too, who can enjoy and inwardly retain these new dimensions.

The creative process has an additional important characteristic. It tends to fulfill a longing or a search for a new object or for a state of experience or of existence not easily found or easily attainable. Especially in aesthetic creativity the work often represents not only the new object, but this longing as well, this sustained and yet never completed effort which has either a conscious or an unconscious motivation.

A sharp distinction must be made between the creative process and the creative product. In contrast to what could be said about the creative product, the creative process is not only not new or sublime, but to a considerable extent consists of ancient, obsolete mental mechanisms, generally relegated to special recesses of the psyche. In my book *The Intrapsychic Self* and in other writings I have shown that the creative process is the result of intricate combinations of archaic mental mechanisms, which Freud called the primary process and considered mostly part of the id, and of the usual logical thinking mechanisms, which Freud considered as belonging mostly to the ego and called the secondary process.

It is from appropriate matchings with secondary-process mechanisms that these primitive forms of cognition, generally confined to abnormal conditions or to the unconscious, become innovating elements. I have proposed the term *tertiary process* to designate these special combinations and syntheses which bring about the creative process. In the third part of *The Intrapsychic Self* and in other writings I have described the specific ways by which these matches occur in the various fields of creativity, such as art, poetry, religion, and science.[6] This is a very important topic, but too vast to be illustrated here, and not directly involved with the aim of the present book. It is instead important to examine in this chapter the role of spontaneity, motivation, and will in the creative process, and also to study ways by which we can promote creativity.

The spontaneity of the creative man is unusual, but in at least one respect is reminiscent of the behavior presented by the patient during psychoanalytic treatment. At first ideas occur freely to the creative man, and they come from various, unexpected directions. Contrary to what an ordinary man would do, and like the psychoanalytic patient, the creative man does not discard, repress, or suppress thoughts which appear irrational, inconsequential, or unrelated. He accepts them in the repertory of his consciousness. But he does more than that.

A special selective apparatus puts him in a position to become aware of hidden structures and combinations of the good, the beautiful, and the true, and to recognize the opportunity to externalize such structures. He does not stick to what is, but is receptive to what may appear. He wants to make visible the invisible and audible the inaudible, and thus X-rays and the wireless are invented, and the moon is reached. In works of art and literature he gives form to what was not yet seen or heard before in that particular way, and thus reveals to us some aspects of the unsuspected sensitivity or unknown depth of man. Only the greatest of our kind are able to offer us a Sistine Chapel or a Mona Lisa or a Ninth Symphony; but all of us can make some efforts to pursue truth and beauty.

Concerning the promotion of creativity, we might consider the writings of the anthropologist A. L. Kroeber on the occurrence of genius. In 1944 he wrote:

Inasmuch as even the people possessing higher civilization have produced cultural products of value only intermittently, during relatively small fractions of their time span, it follows that more individuals born with the endowment of genius have been inhibited by the cultural situations into which they were born than have been developed by other cultural situations . . . Genetics leaves only an infinitesimal possibility for the racial stock occupying England to have given birth to no geniuses at all between 1450 and 1550 and a whole series of geniuses in literature, music, science, philosophy, and politics between 1550 and 1650. Similarly with the Germany of 1550–1650 and 1700–1800, respectively, and innumerable other instances in history.[7]

If Kroeber is correct in his conclusions, we must accept that the possibility for the development of a large number of creative people always exists in certain populations. We may add that, in addition to general sociohistorical factors, special personal conditions and attitudes acquired from early childhood through the whole period of adolescence are important in actualizing potential creativity.

It is to be expected that educators and sociologists will resort more and more to child and adolescent psychiatry, school psychology, school psychiatry, and mental hygiene in their efforts to accumulate that body of knowledge which, once applied, could promote creativity and remove inhibiting factors. There is also the possibility, as will appear from what follows, that some characteristics or habits which have so far been considered unhealthy or undesirable may be recognized as favorable to creativity. The reverse may also be true.

Studies made independently by several authors have determined that highly intelligent persons are not necessarily highly creative.[8] Although creative people are intelligent persons, an exceptionally high IQ is not a prerequisite for creativity. On the contrary, it may inhibit the inner resources of the individual because of too rigid self-criticism or a too quick learning of what the cultural environment has to offer. We must add that a great ability to deduce according to the laws of logic and mathematics makes for disciplined thinkers, but not necessarily for creative people.

The science of promoting creativity is in its initial stages. I can suggest only rudimentary and tentative notions, reduced from my psychoanalytic-psychotherapeutic treatment of a relatively large number of creative people. These notions have to be confirmed or disproved by a much vaster collection of findings.

Statistical data are difficult to find because definitional standards are lacking.

Two things now seem established:

1. An inclination toward creativity must be fostered in childhood and/or adolescence, even if it is not revealed until much later in life.

2. As a whole, American culture has not enhanced creativity.

It is urgent that we reexamine our methods of fostering creativity, just as we reexamined our scholastic methods after Sputnik. We must start with the most elementary, hoping that additional studies will increase the list. The first condition promoting creativity is *aloneness*. The person who is alone is not constantly exposed to the conventions and clichés of society. He has more opportunity to listen to his inner self and to come in contact with his inner resources. Aloneness makes it less likely for the others to submerge his autonomy, individuality, and authenticity. But American culture recommends gregariousness, popularity, and togetherness. As the sociologist David Riesman [9] wrote, it has become "other-directed."

Aloneness should not be confused with painful loneliness or with withdrawal or constant solitude. It should only mean being able periodically to remain alone for a few hours. Aloneness, as we have characterized it, should be recommended not only as a preparation for a life of creativity, but also as a state of being when creative work is in process. At the present time, emphasis instead is on teamwork, especially in scientific research. It is more than doubtful that an original idea can come from a team, although teamwork is often useful for expanding and applying the original idea and, more than anything else, for developing the technology by which the original idea is applied to practical uses.

In artistic work teamwork is almost unthinkable, although occasionally resorted to in mediocre productions. One cannot even theoretically imagine that such works as *The Divine Comedy, Hamlet,* or Handel's *Messiah* could be created by more than one person. In science, too, great discoveries and inventions have been made by solitary individuals. When more than one individual has made the same discovery or invention, the innovating ideas were obtained independently (for instance, the cases of Newton and Leibnitz for calculus, of Wallace and Darwin for evolution).

A second condition which seems to promote creativity is one

which is contrary to the present spirit of American culture: *inactivity*.

By inactivity, of course, we do not mean withdrawal or excessive loafing, but the allowing of periods of time during which the person is permitted to do nothing at an overt behavior level. If a person must always focus his attention on external work, he decreases the possibility of expanding his inner resources. Here again American upbringing promotes an opposite attitude: high school and college students are encouraged to work during summer vacations. Any kind of manual work is considered valuable in building the character of the future adult citizen. As a general rule, it is a commendable practice to encourage in young people a willingness to work. It promotes a sense of responsibility and of good citizenship. People with creative tendencies, however, should be recognized and permitted relatively long periods of time for free thinking and feeling when they do not have to attend to schoolwork.

What we have just said about youth could, with some modifications, be repeated for adults who have already shown creative tendencies. Excessive amounts of routine activities stifle mental activity and creativity. Moreover, even a creative career that has already started should be allowed to proceed at its own pace, which may be very slow, irregular, and intermittent.

The third condition is *daydreaming*. Daydreaming is often discouraged as unrealistic or at least as enlarging the discrepancy between the individual's ambitions and his capacities. It is also often discouraged because it is thought of as promoting a vicarious fantasy life which retards the implementing of realistic and adequate behavior. Although it is true that excessive daydreaming may have these results, it is also true that daydreaming becomes a source of fantasy life and may open to the individual new and unforeseeable paths of expansion. It is in daydream-life that the individual permits himself to diverge from the usual ways and to make little excursions into irrational worlds. Daydreaming offers a relief from the conventions of society.

Remembrance and inner replaying of past traumatic conflicts is another important condition. It is generally assumed that once a person has overcome a psychological conflict or the effects of an early trauma, he should try to forget them. Forgetting in these cases would require an act of suppression, not of repression.

Some creative people recognize that this belief is an error, although in turn they fall into another mistake. They believe that the neurotic conflict is a prerequisite for creativity. At times they are reluctant to undergo psychotherapy or psychoanalysis because they are afraid that if they lose their conflicts they will also lose the motivation to create. We must remember that conflicts always exist in the psyche of man and that we must distinguish between nontraumatic conflicts and traumatic or neurotic conflicts. Nontraumatic conflicts need not concern us. On the other hand, traumatic or neurotic conflicts of the creative person should be solved but not ignored after their solution. If the traumatic or neurotic conflicts are not solved, they will remain too deeply felt and too personal. The creative person will not be able to transcend his own subjective involvement, and his work will have no universal significance or general resonance. On the contrary, the solved or almost-solved conflict may be reevoked at the same time with a sense of familiarity and distance and may be more easily transformed into a product of creativity.

Another requirement for the creative person is even more difficult to accept: *gullibility*. This word is used here to mean the willingness to suspend disbelief, or to accept, at least temporarily or until proved wrong, that there are certain underlying orderly arrangements in everything outside us and inside us. Creativity often implies the discovery of these underlying orderly arrangements, more than the inventing of new things. Connected with this special gullibility is the recognition of the significance of apparently unrelated similarities.[10]

The discovery of underlying arrangements may, of course, be part also of paranoiac-paranoid delusion, and the acceptance of a similarity as a significant fact may be part of disturbed thinking in general. The creative person, however, does not accept these findings indiscriminately. He is guillible only to the extent of not discarding them a priori as nonsense. But he does even more than that: he becomes more attuned to these findings. His final acceptance or rejection, however, must depend on his secondary-process mechanisms. This gullibility may seem the opposite of another characteristic above advocated: reluctance to accept uncritically what is transmitted by the environment and by culture, as, for instance, in the phenomenon of confrontation. We must make a distinction: whereas the creative person must always be critical of what comes in from the outside world, he must be more accepting of what comes up from the inside. At least he must do so with an open mind, until his secondary process rejects the newly emerged ideas.

Alertness and *discipline* are other requirements for creativity. Although they are necessary prerequisites for productivity in general, they acquire a particular quality in creativity. Many would-be creative persons, especially in the artistic fields, would like to believe that only such qualities as imagination, intuition, and talent are important. They are reluctant to submit themselves to the rigor of learning technique, discipline, or logical thinking, on the pretext that all these things would stultify their creativity. They ignore the fact that such people as Giotto, Leonardo, Freud, and Einstein had teachers. A humorous remark, which by now has become commonplace but in which there is a great deal of metaphorical truth, is that creativity is 10 percent inspiration and 90 percent perspiration.

All these characteristics, as well as others which will be discovered in future studies, facilitate the new combinations of primary and secondary processes which lead to the tertiary process. By this statement I do not mean that a process of creativity is just a "recombination" of already existing elements. From the new combination unexpected, at times completely new, entities emerge.

In the midst of all these conditions that genetics, history, and chance put together, the autonomous will of man emerges as the synthesizer of motivation, knowledge, selectivity, and inexplicable subjectivity. Innovation results. With the attainment of desirable enlargement of human experience, creativity is responsible for progress. What starts as the highest expression of individuality becomes the dispenser of the common good and acquires an ethical quality. The two great aims of the individual thus converge and combine, provided, of course, the products of creativity are used for good purposes.

PRIVACY, COMMUNION, AND PEACE

Another condition related to individuality and autonomy is privacy. Privacy is neither indifference to others nor a barricading of oneself from the rest of the world, but the capacity and right to be periodically in touch with only oneself, and to have feelings, thoughts, and habits which one need not share with others. Privacy, as a state of being freely at one with oneself, does not make us more distant from others. It is a respectful recognition of that part of ourselves which emerged when we became beings endowed with feelings and ideas. In their subjective quality, our feelings, like joy and pain, cannot be shared. We can communicate the idea of them and an emotional echo of them to others, but as private experiences they will remain our own. If we are aware of the element of aloneness associated with this subjectivity, we become also aware that at least occasionally we can overcome it. One way of overcoming it was described in Chapter 4, in reference to the sexual act accompanied by love. Another way will be described shortly.

A healthy society permits privacy and condemns all the methods, such as wiretapping, mail inspection, the keeping of personal dossiers, etc., which infringe upon it. A healthy society also allows the individual to be secretive about his own private matters and ideas unless knowledge of them is necessary for the common good.

Secrecy, as part of human life, must be accepted. We can distinguish three types of secret. The first type consists of secrets kept between people; that is, secrets that other people want to keep from us and those we want to keep from them. For the reasons mentioned above, we must respect people's secrecy and our own unless they endanger the common good. At the same time we should feel free to share our secrets with people who are close and dear to us.

The second type of secret, secrets kept from oneself, is of particular interest to the psychoanalyst. Do we want privacy also from ourselves? Are there things which we need to conceal from ourselves? Freud was the first to demonstrate that if we remove repression and become aware of our secret unconscious life, we shall be able to live more appropriately and we shall have less chance of becoming neurotic. But the amount of unconscious material is enormous and we must accept the fact that some part of us will always remain a secret to us.[11]

There is a third type of secret that the individual can never uncover: the one he shares with the cosmos, about his being here. Man can face this secret in two ways. He may accept the unknowable. He and his fellow men will continue to light candles, but the great night will still embrace us all. And if his greatest urge is to light these candles, his greatest dignity will derive from accepting the night, a night not ending in dawn. But he has another choice for this secret: faith. Faith lightens the burden; faith lightens the night. Whichever of these two choices he makes, he ennobles himself. But he can go further.

He can feel united to his fellow men, who share the endless night. While we are here in the dark and grope and feel our way, let us give each other a sustaining hand. In the short and tortuous path in which we make our unsteady and almost blind steps, let us not push some higher up and others down. Just as individuality is one of the pinnacles of our will, the other is the state of communion which comes after we have striven for the common good. Then Mr. Nobody will be Mr. Somebody, Mr. Everybody, Mr. Man.

autonomy plus heteronomy

Communion, together with love, may compensate for that inherent aloneness that we find in ourselves. Communion includes basic trust (described in Chapter 5), which to a large extent we lose early in life. Let us try to reacquire it, not with the naive inexperience of the infant, but with the depth of a mature adulthood. Then your fellow man will not be a person who has the power to use or exploit you, but a peer in a limited and unpredictable reality. Help him and he will help you. Go toward him and he will come toward you. Make him feel happy he has met you. You will be happy you have met him. His hand will not hold a knife; it is open to meet your palm. His eye will not pierce your privacy or invade your rights or watch you with reprobation. He recognizes his friend and peer. His peace will be your peace, and yours will be his. Peace will be the ultimate aim and result of individuality, common good, and state of communion. Peace inside of yourself; peace between you and the other, whether the other is a person or a whole country. Peace, something which history shows to be more difficult to obtain than love. Peace, under which, in a circular process, the will of man can renew individuality and creativity, common good and communion.

And now that I have come to the end of this work, I must clearly express my opinion that what defines man is not only his nature but also his ability to transcend his nature. What characterizes him is not only his origin, but also his aims. The most important of them are the striving toward autonomy, the assertion of individuality, and the practice of the common good. The degree of maturity attained by man depends on the extent to which he realizes these aims. Certainly he meets many obstacles of different nature. Most biological functions which he shares with other animals tend to keep him an animal. His conceptual life, originated from his family and from society, and the emotions which are connected with the network of concepts enable him to go beyond his animal status. These concepts make his life uncertain, conflictful, and they themselves originate many conditions which cannot be solved. In trying to overcome or ignore these conflicts man often allows himself to be dominated by dictators, overburdened and stultified by stagnant sociocultural environments, programmed by technological developments, and persuaded by some psychological thinkers who deny he has any possibility for autonomy and teach that he is or should be an automaton or a computer. As was stated at the beginning of this book, man is not an automaton or a computer, but may come close to being one. Man is not fully autonomous and may never become so, but we can always strive toward increasing autonomy. To be a whole man requires resisting all the obstacles which interfere with our attempts to enlarge our margin of will. We must will to be human.

HAVE I CONVEYED A MESSAGE?

My readers, my peers, I have come to the end of my discourse. I wish I had offered a straight and easy road toward autonomy, assertion of individuality, common good, communion, and peace. I have not. By clarifying some issues, I have made an attempt to bring a message. In going over these pages, and especially the last few, I find that the dispassionate and tranquil style of the scientist has not always flowed from my pen, but rather that I have written with the fervor of a person who wants to bring a message to a new Nineveh! I ask indulgence. Yes, it is clear now to me, in writing this very last page, what must have been already clear to you, readers, for a long time. I identify with the prophet Jonah, by whom I have been inspired since, at the age of three or four, I heard in my mother's voice Pinocchio's version of his story. And my father's reproach made me hear later the echo of Jonah. Since then I have not allowed myself to become a supporter or a silent watcher of the oppressor. Because of my training and experience I have tried to explain the mixed impact of psychological and sociological events on the thwarting of man's will, and, whenever possible, I have indicated what seem to me the ways of liberation.

Lest I be considered too presumptuous, I hurry to stress that I believe every human being should identify with Jonah, the smallest of all the prophets and therefore the most similar to us. All of us should have a day of atonement and convey a message. To those who are discouraged, let us remember that Nineveh was not destroyed.

If we accept the endlessness of the night as well as our possibilities, we shall not stop lighting candles, we shall not desist from learning, we shall not accept inequality, injustice, or whatever infringes upon our freedom and individuality. When the invisible speck, tossed by the waves of time and the result of incalculable combinations, became endowed with the spontaneous movements that culminated in the will of man, the possibility was open for breaking the chains, for spreading our wings.

NEW YORK AND
VILLASIMIUS, SARDINIA
1970–1971

NOTES

Chapter One

1. Fromm, E., *Man for Himself* (New York, 1947).
2. Skinner, B. F., *Beyond Freedom and Dignity* (New York, 1971).

Chapter Two

1. Von Holst called these movements autorhythmic (in *Arch. ges. Physiol.* 237, 356, 1936, and in *Naturwissenschaften* 25, 625–31, 641–47, 1937).
2. See Thorpe, W. H., *Learning and Instinct in Animals* (Cambridge, 1956). It is doubtful that we could consider imitative the behavior of some animals when they follow so-called "pioneer animals" that are nearby.
3. Yerkes, R. M., *Chimpanzees: A Laboratory Colony* (New Haven, 1943).
4. Hayes, K. J., and Hayes, C., The Intellectual Development of a Home-raised Chimpanzee. *Proc. Am. Phil. Soc.* 95, 105–9, 1951.
5. Asch, S. E., *Social Psychology* (New York, 1952).
6. This osmotic and imitative relation constitutes the basis of what

later on develops into a real "identification"; that is, taking as a model the behavior and directives of another person.

7. The anatomy and physiology of the mechanism of inhibition at various levels of development are in some aspects still uncertain. See the monograph by Diamond, S., Balvin, R. S., and Diamond, F. R., *Inhibition and Choice* (New York, 1963).

8. According to Parsons action requires: (1) an agent or doer (in our case, the baby); (2) a goal or a future state of affairs toward which the process of action is oriented (in our case, to please mother, or to elicit in mother a pleasant attitude); (3) that the initial situation be different from the terminal (in our case, at first the need to defecate; at the end, defecation at the proper time and place); (4) a unity between different parts (at first, retention of feces until the toilet is reached; then defecation and the act of pleasing mother). Parsons, T., *The Structure of Social Action* (Glencoe, 1949).

9. This transformation from imperative to indicative occurs when the object is no longer what Werner calls a thing of action, something to react to, but an object of contemplation, or something which may be seen at a distance independent of the immediate involvement of the individual with it. Werner, H., *Comparative Developmental Psychology* (New York, 1947). See also my book, *The Intrapsychic Self* (New York, 1967).

10. Although the evidence is only analogic, we may postulate as a working hypothesis, which needs more investigation, that hypnosis is an artificial reproduction (and perhaps exaggeration) in adult persons of this stage of receptivity, imitation, and suggestibility which occurs spontaneously at an early stage of child development. The hypnotized person, like the child who is extremely receptive to the will of others, does not remember who gave the instructions or suggestions (Arieti, Volition and Value, *Comprehensive Psychiatry* 2, 74, 1961). (Spiegel, H., Hypnosis and Transference, *A.M.A. Arch. Gen. Psych.* 1, 634, 1954). Meares has advanced his atavistic theory of hypnosis, which is similar to this one (*A System of Medical Hypnosis*, Philadelphia, 1960). In other words, he believes that similar phenomena have occurred at a phylogenetic level, with the primordial races of men.

11. Diamond, A. S., *The History and Origin of Language* (London, 1959).

12. See also Chapter 8 for mutual help among primitive groups.

13. Most neurologists agree that there is a direct relationship between handedness and language centers. In right-handed people the language centers are in the left cerebral hemisphere, and in left-handed people they are in the right cerebral hemisphere. The movements of the preferred hand awaken the language center of the cerebral hemisphere of the opposite side.

14. See Arieti, S., *Interpretation of Schizophrenia* (New York, 1955).

15. The author who has made a pioneer and profound study of children's negativism is David M. Levy [see, for instance, Oppositional

Syndromes and Oppositional Behavior in Hock, P., and Zubin, Z. (eds.), *Psychopathology of Childhood* (New York, 1955)].

16. See David Levy (cf. note 15).

17. Kelsen has illustrated very well the relation between *to do* and *to be guilty* in the primitive, as well as the relation between guilt and cause. The concepts of guilt and cause are confused in many primitive languages. Even in early Greek, which certainly is not a primitive language, the word *aitia* (from which is derived the English word "etiology") has both the meaning of guilt, cause, and responsibility (Kelsen, H., *Society and Nature* (Chicago, 1943).

18. Lorenzini, P., Il Collodi e il Suo Figliolo di Legno in Collodi, C., *Le Avventure di Pinocchio* (Florence, 1947).

19. Up to the present day, Jewish collectivities have retained some of their maternal roles. Their philanthropic institutions are among the best. In each family, however, the individual mother has maintained, at a personal level, a protective role toward her children, who, she believes with some historical justification, have been exposed to the hostility of the world. This is perhaps the origin of the role of the overprotective Jewish mother which some novelists, for instance, Philip Roth in *Portnoy's Complaint*, have portrayed.

20. Skinner, B. F., *Beyond Freedom and Dignity* (New York, 1971), p. 198.

21. *Ibid.*, p. 42.

22. Ayllon, T., and Azzin, N. H., The Measurement and Reinforcement of Behavior of Psychotics. *J. Exper. Anal. Behav.* 8, 357–83, 1965.

23. We must also consider that most patients treated by Ayllon and Azzin with token therapy were also on phenothiazine treatment.

Chapter Three

1. I shall enumerate in this note only those steps which are of particular relevance to the theme of this book.

When confronted with the possibility of making an action, a mature individual goes through six major steps: (1) the evaluation of several possible courses of action (for instance, in the morning, to stay in bed and sleep; to stay in bed and read; to get up and go to work; etc.); (2) the choice of one of these possibilities (for instance, he may choose going to work); (3) the planning of the chosen possibility (dressing; taking the bus to go to work); (4) the determination to carry out the planned choice (I must really do it!); (5) the ability to inhibit the nonchosen forms of action (I must inhibit my desire to sleep or read in bed); (6) the execution of the chosen action (making the actual movements necessary to dress, to take the bus, to go to work, etc.).

2. At this point we must briefly clarify two possible points of confusion. The content of a wish is not necessarily contrary to what the

best judgment suggests: it may be concordant or discordant. Secondly, what do we define as best judgment? Even an attempt to formulate a working definition would evoke numerous discussions of controversial points. Best judgment according to whom? Society, the authority, or the individual himself? As a tentative working definition we shall call best judgment that which suggests the course of action that has the most beneficial (or the least harmful) effect on the individual and his environment. We do not refer only to immediate effect, but to lasting, and perhaps ultimate effect.

3. See Arieti, S., *The Intrapsychic Self* (New York, 1967), chapter 3.

4. English, H. B., and English, A. C., *A Comprehensive Dictionary of Psychological Terms* (New York, 1958).

5. A wish may seem to be elicited directly by a perception, and not by an image or symbol. For instance, beautiful objects, like diamonds, fur coats, etc., displayed in shop windows, have the purpose of eliciting wishes in the passerby. The emotions involved in these examples are wishes and not appetites, in spite of the fact that the objects are perceived; that is, immediately presented to the mind and not represented symbolically. This is because the perception leads to other mental processes: imagining how pleasant it would be to have that given object; debating with oneself whether it is advisable or not, because of one's economic circumstances, to buy it.

6. According to the Freudian school, such concept-feelings are only displacements, detours, or rationalizations which cover instinctual drives. Although this is true in some cases, to think that it is so in all or most cases is a reductionist point of view.

7. May, R., *Love and Will* (New York, 1969).

8. Farber, L., *The Ways of the Will* (New York, 1966).

9. May, R. (see note 7).

10. Arieti, S., *The Intrapsychic Self* (New York, 1967). Also The Structural and Psychodynamic Role of Cognition in the Human Psyche in Arieti, S., *The World Biennial of Psychiatry and Psychotherapy* (New York, 1970).

11. Knight, R. P., Determinism, "Freedom" and Psychotherapy in Knight, R. P., and Friedman, C. R. (eds.), *Psychoanalytic Psychiatry and Psychology* (New York, 1954).

12. May, R. (see note 7, pp. 197–98).

13. An example of this type of thinking was that of Loeb, a biologist who had a great influence on people who accepted a completely materialistic explanation of life. Loeb studied tropisms, or movements of animals and plants in response to environmental stimuli. For instance, leaves and trees grow and bend toward light; roots respond to the force of gravity by growing downward, etc. From similar studies he reached analogically the conclusion that will, too, like everything else in nature, is totally controlled by outside forces and is therefore not free. (Loeb, J., *The Mechanistic Conception of Life* (Cambridge, 1912).

14. Capek, M., *The Philosophical Impact of Contemporary Physics* (New York, 1964).
15. Reichenbach, H., *The Rise of Scientific Philosophy* (Berkeley, 1951).
16. Capek, M., The Development of Reichenbach's Epistemology, *Review of Metaphysics* 9, 42–67, 1957.

Chapter Four

1. In 1938 Volkmann discovered how the vagus nerve inhibits a frog's heart. Since then a large number of neurophysiologists have discovered numerous mechanisms of inhibition.
2. Morgan, 1891, p. 459; quoted by Diamond, S., Balvin, R. S., and Diamond, F. R., *Inhibition and Choice* (New York, 1963), p. 147.
3. English, H. B., and English, A. C., *A Comprehensive Dictionary of Psychological Terms* (New York, 1958), p. 262.
4. Diamond, Balvin, and Diamond (1963), p. 394.
5. Freud probably acquired the concept of the structure of the psyche and of hierarchical inhibition from his famous contemporary, the neurologist John Hughlings Jackson (1835–1911). Jackson divided the central nervous system into three hierarchical levels. The middle level inhibits the lowest, and the highest inhibits the middle. Hughlings Jackson's ideas have since undergone revisions. The nervous system is no longer seen exclusively as a series of horizontally organized centers. In addition to horizontal organization there are vertical transactions between the different centers. In the realm of the psyche, the various parts are not to be conceived only in the sense of inhibiting one another, but of influencing one another in various ways. Other authors, influenced by psychoanalysis, have tried to understand the problem of inhibition in a general psychological frame of reference. Klopfer (1924), quoted by Diamond, Balvin, and Diamond (1963, p. 172), felt that inhibition "is not only essential for the phenomenon of attention, but also for those of personality development, including the maintenance of personal individuality in the face of social environmental influences."
6. Reich, W., *Character Analysis* (New York, 1949).
7. Marcuse, H., *Eros and Civilization* (Boston, 1955).
8. To my knowledge the first author who has tried to explain why incest should be forbidden is Augustine (*The City of God*, Book XV, Chapter 16). This great thinker gives a rather naive interpretation of why people have prohibited incest since ancient times. He writes, ". . . it is very reasonable and just that men, among whom concord is honourable and useful, should be bound together by various relationships, and that one man should not himself sustain many relationships, but that the various relationships should be distributed among several, and should thus serve to bind together the greatest

number in the same social interests" (translation by Marcus Dods, New York, Modern Library). Thus, if a man marries his sister, his sister is also his wife; his father is also his father-in-law; his children would have only one grandfather and one grandmother, etc. The various relationships would not be distributed among several persons.
9. Concepts like those of force and energy can be used metaphorically to indicate psychological phenomena having the ability to produce certain effects. These terms should not be used literally, in the way they are generally applied to physical energies, hydraulic, thermal, or electric. Motivation, as a tendency to seek pleasure and to avoid pain, is certainly a fundamental psychological phenomenon and is based on the feelings of the organism; that is, on sensation, emotion, and other physiological experiences. Physiologists have repeatedly stated that it is not necessary to postulate the existence of "investments" of libido to explain the occurrence of motivation (Lashley, 1957, in Lashley and Colby, 1957). The libido theory is considered by some to be derived from Freud's need to remain in a biological frame of reference. Actually, the libido theory is not a biological theory; it is an application to the psyche of concepts borrowed from the field of inorganic physics. But concepts which are applicable to the inorganic world (at least, as it was seen by nineteenth-century physicists) are not necessarily relevant to biological science. In the libido theory, general biology and neurophysiology are bypassed. The leap is from inorganic physics to psychology.
10. Maslow, A. H., Cognition of Being in the Peak Experiences, *J. Genet. Psychol.* 94, 43–66, 1959.
11. Lorenz, K., *On Aggression* (New York, 1966).
12. Ardrey, R., *The Territorial Imperative* (New York, 1966).
13. Storr, A., *Human Aggression* (New York: Atheneum, 1968).
14. Arieti, S., *The Intrapsychic Self* (New York, 1967).

Chapter Five

1. For a good evaluation of Buber's contribution, see Friedman, M. S,. *Martin Buber: The Life of Dialogue* (Chicago, 1955).
2. Buber, M., *I and Thou* (Edinburgh, 1937).
3. Erikson, E. H., Growth and Crises of the Healthy Personality in Kluckhohn, C. *et al.*, *Personality* (New York, 1953).
4. Horney, K., *Our Inner Conflicts* (New York, 1943).
5. If we follow a behavioristic terminology, we may state that these variables include reinforcement or extinction. They have, however, other characteristics.
6. Arieti, S., The Structural and Psychodynamic Role of Cognition in the Human Psyche in Arieti, S., *The World Biennial of Psychiatry and Psychotherapy* (New York, 1970).
7. In hypnosis the hypnotized person returns to a primitive psychological level (Meares, A., *A System of Medical Hypnosis*, Phila-

delphia, 1960). He attributes a quality of omnipotence to the hypnotist and a quality of complete impotence to himself.

8. Chapter 7, page 122.

9. Mussolini, B., The Doctrine of Fascism in Chandler, A. R. (ed.), *The Clash of Political Ideals* (New York, 1949).

10. Durkheim, E. *The Rules of Sociological Method* (Glencoe, 1938).

11. White, L., Cultural Determinants of Mind in White, L. A., *The Science of Culture* (New York, 1969).

12. Fromm, E., *Man for Himself* (New York, 1947).

13. Arieti, S., *The Intrapsychic Self* (New York, 1967), chapter 9.

14. Horney, K., *Neurosis and Human Growth* (New York, 1950).

15. See Chapter 7 for further analysis of this phenomenon.

Chapter Six

1. Roszak, T., *The Making of a Counter Culture* (New York, 1969).

2. Keniston, K., *The Uncommitted: Alienated Youth in American Society* (New York, 1965). Also *Young Radicals* (New York, 1968).

3. Subsequent sociologists have made a distinction between a rationality which could be put to good use and deals with desirable results and a rationality which, although perfectly logical, and goal-directed in its substeps, leads to technocracy and to undesirable effects. Mannheim called the first "substantive rationality" and the second "formal rationality." We must conclude that the growth of science requires on the part of citizens an increased sense of alertness to prevent "formal rationality." (Mannheim, K., *Man and Society in an Age of Reconstruction*, New York, 1951).

4. Bourguignon, E., (1968), World Distribution and Patterns of Possession States in Prince, R. (Montreal, 1968).

5. Keniston, K., *The Uncommitted: Alienated Youth in American Society* (New York, 1965).

6. Arieti, S., *The Intrapsychic Self* (New York, 1967); The Structural and Psychodynamic Role of Cognition in the Human Psyche in Arieti, S., *The World Biennial of Psychiatry and Psychotherapy* (New York, 1970).

7. Marcuse, H., *One-dimensional Man* (Boston, 1964).

8. Riesman, D., *et al. The Lonely Crowd* (New Haven, 1950).

9. It is a new kind of depression. It is not the usual depression which makes people feel guilty, self-accusatory, unable to sleep and eat. This new form of depression is characterized by constant demands and claims on others (Arieti), and the experiencing of deep sadness when no praise or admiration is received from others (Bemporad). (Arieti, S., The Psychotherapeutic Approach to Depression, *Am. J. Psychotherapy*, 16, 397–406, 1962). (Bemporad, Jules, New Views on the Psychodynamics of the Depressive Character in Arieti, S., *The World Biennial of Psychiatry and Psychotherapy* (New York, 1970).

10. Guntrip, H., *Schizoid Phenomena, Object-Relations and the Self* (New York, 1968).

11. Bridgman, P. W., *The Logic of Modern Physics* (New York, 1928).

12. Von Bertalanffy, L., *Robots, Men and Minds: Psychology in the Modern World* (New York, 1967).

13. Keniston, K., *Young Radicals* (New York, 1968).

14. The recent trend toward natural childbirth is an attempt to check this indulgence and to return to acceptance of genuine feelings.

Chapter Seven

1. This fact may have induced Marcuse to reinterpret the Freudian theory of the parricide, as described in *Totem and Taboo*. (See Chapter 4 of this book.)

2. Plumb, J. H., *The Death of the Past* (Boston, 1970), pp. 83–84.

3. Arieti, S., Anti-Psychoanalytic Cultural Forces in the Development of Western Civilization. *Am. J. Psychotherapy*, 63–78, 1952.

4. Keniston, K., *The Uncommitted* (New York, 1965).

5. Here are a few important exceptions. Max Weber (1864–1920) demonstrated that Calvinistic ethics had a great deal to do with the development of capitalism. The American sociologist Robert Merton has three decades later continued Weber's direction by showing how the endocratic power of Calvinism has influenced the development of pure science. The French sociologist Emile Durkheim (1858–1917) has predominantly studied the socialization of the individual as a continuous process, but has not assessed the psychological price that the individual has to pay for it. His book on suicide is a classic in the field of sociology, but does not clarify the individualistic or psychiatric import of the problem.

For the American George Herbert Mead (1863–1931) society controls the individual through "the generalized other," a synthesis of the others which the person makes in his own mind. The generalized other resembles more a benevolent teacher than a harsh superego.

Chapter Eight

1. Russell, B., *Power* (New York, 1962), p. 25.

2. Lorenz, K., *On Aggression* (New York, 1966).

3. Pioneer in this respect is the work of Nathan Ackerman. See especially *The Psychodynamics of Family Life* (New York, 1958).

4. See, for instance, *Understanding Human Nature* (New York, 1927). The original references to power in Adler are in *Über den Nervösen Charakter* (Munich, 1912). In the fourth edition they can be found on pp. 15, 16, 19, 24, 43.

5. Keith, A., *Evolution and Ethics* (New York, 1946).

6. See Arieti, S., *The Intrapsychic Self* (New York, 1967), especially chapters 9 and 14.

7. Gouldner, A. W., *The Coming Crisis of Western Civilization* (New York,1970), pp. 31–33, 46–48.

8. Darwin, C., *The Descent of Man* (1871); quoted by Keith. See note 5.

9. Kropotkin, P., *Mutual Aid: A Factor in Evolution* (1902); quoted by Keith. See note 5.

10. Darwin, C., *The Descent of Man* (1871), quoted by Keith. See note 5.

Chapter Nine

1. Machiavelli, N., *The Prince,* chapter 26.

2. *Ibid.*, chapter 26. The exact quotation in Latin from Livy is *Iustum est bellum quibus necessarium, et pia arma quibus nulla nisi in armis relinquitur spes.* Machiavelli, trying to quote from memory, was not accurate.

3. *Ibid.*, chapter 7.

4. Mussolini, B., *Preludio al Principe, Gerarchia,* vol. 3, no. 4, April 1924.

5. Machiavelli, N., *The Prince,* chapter 17. Also in *Discourses upon the First Decade of Titus Livius.* It is worthwhile to note that Machiavelli considers the citizen more interested in his property than in the life of his father and brother but not of his mother. Even Machiavelli bows to the filial love for one's mother.

6. Mussolini, B., *Preludio al Principe, Gerarchia,* vol. 3, no. 4, April, 1924.

7. Marx, K., and Engels, F., *Manifesto of the Communist Party,* 1847.

8. I obtained this information from Berlin, I., *Four Essays on Liberty* (New York, 1970).

9. Lenin, V. I., *State and Revolution,* 1917.

10. Stalin, J., *The Foundation of Leninism* (1924). Reprinted in Cohen, C., *Communism, Fascism and Democracy* (New York, 1962).

11. Khrushchev, N. (1956), Crimes of the Stalin Era in Special Report to the 20th Congress of the Communist Party of the Soviet Union. Closed Session February 24–25, 1956. Reprinted in Carl Cohen, *Communism, Fascism, Democracy* (New York, 1962).

12. Stalin, J., in *State and Revolution.* Reprinted in Cohen, C., (New York, 1962), p. 173.

13. Conquest, R., *The Great Terror* (New York, 1968), especially Appendix A, pp. 525–35.

14. There are many theories which attempted to explain why Russian political prisoners confessed crimes they could not have committed. The explanation given by Koestler in *Darkness at Noon* was that the prisoners felt that it was good to confess for the sake of the party.

If the prisoners had not confessed, they would have felt guilty. The inquisitors would be effective, according to Koestler's theory, by exerting what in the present book is called endocratic power. According to Guerriero (pp. 136–42. *Epoca,* 1970) the reason is an old one. Since ancient times even mentally healthy people have "confessed" in order to avoid being tortured. Even being declared guilty is better than to be subjected to horribly inhuman, indescribable atrocities. In some cases the accused people were also afraid of retaliation against members of their family. According to Guerriero the threat was external, not endocratic.

15. Rocco, A., "The Political Doctrine of Fascism." Reprinted in Cohen, C. (New York, 1962), pp. 333–49.

16. Mussolini, B. (1932), "The Doctrine of Fascism." Reprinted in Cohen, C. (New York, 1962), pp. 349–64.

17. Mussolini, B. *Preludio al Principe, Gerarchia,* vol. 3, no. 4, April 1924.

18. This and the following excerpts from Hitler's speeches are from Prange, G. W. (ed.), *Hitler's Words* (Washington, D.C., n.d.) and reprinted in Cohen (New York, 1962).

19. The excerpts from Huber are from *Constitutional Law of the Greater German Reich* (1939), reprinted in Cohen, C., (New York, 1962).

20 Fromm, E., *Escape from Freedom* (New York, 1941).

21. Berle, A. A., *Power* (New York, 1969).

22. Zeigarnik, B. V., *The Pathology of Thinking* (New York, 1965), p. 24.

23. Lenin, quoted by Zeigarnik (*ibid.*)

24. Marx, quoted by Zeigarnik (*ibid.*)

25. Zeigarnik, B. V., *The Pathology of Thinking* (New York, 1965), p. 24.

26. See chapter 7 of this book.

27. Earlier in the history of the United Nations the Belgian government tried to enlarge the concept of colonialism to include in it discriminatory attitudes against ethnic minorities by a country's majority. The UN rejected the proposal.

28. Fanon, F., *The Wretched of the Earth* (New York, 1969).

29. Weld, T. D., *American Slavery as It Is* (1839). Reprinted by Arno Press and *The New York Times,* 1969.

30. Elkins, S. M., *Slavery* (Chicago, 1963).

31. *Ibid.,* p. 59.

32. *Ibid.,* p. 54.

Hitler is quoted in Louis Lochner's *What About Germany?* (New York, 1942). Marjorie Housepian reproduces the quotation in her article "The Unremembered Genocide" published in *Commentary* (Sept. 1966, pp. 55–61). Housepian is also the author of a remarkable book on the Armenian massacre, *The Smyrna Affair* (New York, 1971).

Chapter Ten

1. See the first edition of my book *Interpretation of Schizophrenia*, published in 1955. Further elaboration of these ideas appeared in other articles and books (Arieti, S., Schizophrenia in *American Handbook of Psychiatry*, New York, 1959).

2. Important in this respect are the pioneer works of H. S. Sullivan and John Rosen.

3. Theodore Lidz is the author who has made the largest contribution to the study of the family of the schizophrenic. Other important authors are Nathan Ackerman, Don Jackson, and Lyman Wynne.

4. Laing, R. D., *The Politics of Experience* (New York, 1967).

5. Siirala, M. *Die Schizophrenie* (Gottingen, 1961); Schizophrenic Human Situation, *Am. J. Psychoanalysis*, 23, 39, 1963.

6. See also chapter 6 of this book.

7. Thomas Szasz is one of the few authors who, in his various writings, takes into consideration moral issues in reference to psychiatric disorders. While I admire him for this stand, I cannot accept his removal of them from the medical field. At the same time that he becomes aware of a neglected dimension, he removes another one.

8. Lecture presented at Turku, Finland, Aug. 4, 1971 (in press).

9. Arieti, S. *The Intrapsychic Self.* Chapter 15. (New York, 1967).

10. Cleckley, H. M., *The Mask of Sanity* (St. Louis, 1955).

11. Gilbert, G. M., *The Psychology of Dictatorship* (New York, 1950).

12. Rado, S., Obsessive Behavior in Arieti, S. (ed.), *American Handbook of Psychiatry* (New York, 1959).

13. Catatonics continue to be relatively numerous in a few areas like the state of Mississippi in the United States and the island of Sardinia in Italy.

14. This phenomenon is called "waxy flexibility."

15. For a complete description and explanation of catatonic phenomena, see Arieti, S., *Interpretation of Schizophrenia* (New York, 1955).

Chapter Eleven

1. Dante, *Purgatory*, canto 1, lines 71–72.

2. See chapter 10 of this book.

3. Delgado, J. M. R., *Physical Control of the Mind* (New York, 1969).

4. Nietzsche is not the only writer concerned with superman. Another one is the composer Richard Wagner, by whom Nietzsche was inspired at an early period of his life. Later Nietzsche became critical of the composer.

Another writer concerned with superman is the Italian Gabriele d'Annunzio, especially in his novel *The Virgins of the Rocks*, published in 1895. There is evidence, however, that D'Annunzio was influenced by Nietzsche since the early 1890s. For D'Annunzio's role as precursor of Fascism, see chapter 9 of this book, page 166.

5. Translation from *Book of Job*. Commentary by Solomon B. Freehof (New York, 1958), Union of American Hebrew Congregations.

6. Bemporad, Jack, *Man, God and History: A Study in Origins* (in press).

7. English, H. B., and English, A. C., *A Comprehensive Dictionary of Psychological Terms* (New York, 1958).

8. Hinsie, L. E., and Campbell, R. J., *Psychiatric Dictionary* (New York, 1960).

9. The only evil mentioned in Hinsie and Campbell's dictionary is "St. John's Evil," which is an old term for epilepsy.

Chapter Twelve

1. Strangely, this method was devised by Freud to replace the method of hypnosis, which was in some respects the opposite. Hypnosis had been used by Breuer to force the patient to remember connections between forgotten incidents and symptoms. Freud replaced hypnotic coercion with spontaneity.

2. James, W., *The Principles of Psychology* (New York, 1890).

3. All works of Pirandello are included in *Opera Omnia*, published by Mondadori, Milan.

4. For an excellent account of this problem see Gian Franco Venè: *Pirandello Fascista* (Milan, 1971).

by Mondadori, Milan. Translation mine.

5. For this section I have liberally drawn from my chapter "Creativity and Its Cultivation" in *American Handbook of Psychiatry*, edited by S. Arieti, vol. 3, (New York, Basic Books, 1966).

6. Arieti, S., *The Intrapsychic Self* (New York, 1967).

7. Kroeber, A. L., *Configurations of Culture* (Berkeley, 1944).

8. See the study by Getzel, J. W., and Jackson, P. W., *Creativity and Intelligence* (London, 1962).

9. Riesman, D., *et al.*, *The Lonely Crowd* (New York, 1950).

10. The importance of recognition of similarities in the process of creativity is fully explained in my book *The Intrapsychic Self*, part 3.

11. In chapter 3 of this book we have seen that repression became a necessity with the expansion of man's symbolic processes.

BIBLIOGRAPHY

ADLER, A. *Über den Nervösen Charakter.* 4th ed. Munich: Verlag J. F. Bergmann, 1912.

———. *Understanding Human Nature.* New York: Greenberg, 1927.

ARDREY, R. *The Territorial Imperative.* New York: Atheneum, 1966.

ARIETI, S. "Anti-Psychoanalytic Cultural Forces in the Development of Western Civilization," *Am. J. Psychotherapy,* 6 (1952), 63–78.

———. *Interpretation of Schizophrenia.* New York: Brunner, 1955.

———. "Schizophrenia." In ARIETI, S. (ed.). *American Handbook of Psychiatry.* New York: Basic Books, 1959.

———. "Volition and Value: A Study Based on Catatonic Schizophrenia," *Comprehensive Psychiatry,* 2 (1961a), 74.

———. "The Psychotherapeutic Approach to Depression," *Am. J. Psychotherapy,* 16 (1962), 397–406.

———. *The Intrapsychic Self.* New York: Basic Books, 1967.

———. "The Structural and Psychodynamic Role of Cognition in the Human Psyche." In ARIETI, S. *The World Biennial of Psychitry and Psychotherapy,* Vol. 1. New York: Basic Books, 1970.

ASCH, S. E. *Social Psychology.* New York: Prentice-Hall, 1952.

AUGUSTINE. *The City of God.* Translated by Marcus Dods, 1950. New York: Modern Library, George Wilson, and J. J. Smith.

AYLLON, T., and AZZIN, N. H. "The Measurement and Reinforcement of Behavior of Psychotics," *J. Exper. Anal. Behavior,* 8 (1965), 357–83.

BEMPORAD, JACK. *Man, God and History: A Study in Origins.* In press.

BEMPORAD, JULES R. "New Views on the Psychodynamics of the Depressive Character." In ARIETI, S., (ed.) *The World Biennial of Psychiatry and Psychotherapy,* Vol. 1. New York: Basic Books, 1970.

BERLE, A. A. *Power.* New York: Harcourt, Brace & World, 1969.

BERLIN, I. *Four Essays on Liberty.* New York: Oxford Univ. Press, 1970.

BOURGUIGNON, E. "World Distribution and Patterns of Possession States." In PRINCE, R. (ed.), *Trance and Possession States.* Montreal: R. M. Bucke Memorial Society, 1968.

BRIDGMAN, P. W. *The Logic of Modern Physics.* New York: Macmillan, 1928.

BUBER, M. *I and Thou.* Edinburgh: Clark, 1937.

CAPEK, M. "The Development of Reichenbach's Epistemology," *Review of Metaphysics,* IX (1957), 42–67.

————. *The Philosophical Impact of Contemporary Physics.* New York: Van Nostrand, 1964.

CLECKLEY, H. M. *The Mask of Sanity.* St. Louis: Mosby, 1955.

COHEN, C. *Communism, Fascism, Democracy: The Theoretical Foundations.* New York: Random House, 1962.

CONQUEST, R. *The Great Terror.* New York: Macmillan, 1968.

DARWIN, C. *The Descent of Man.* London: 1871.

DELGADO, J. M. R. *Physical Control of the Mind: Toward a Psychocivilized Society.* New York: Harper & Row, 1969.

DIAMOND, A. S. *The History and Origin of Language.* London: Methuen, 1959.

DIAMOND, S., BALVIN, R. S., and DIAMOND, F. R. *Inhibition and Choice: A Neurobehavioral Approach to Problems of Plasticity in Behavior.* New York: Harper & Row, 1963.

DURKHEIM, E. *The Rules of Sociological Method.* Glencoe: Free Press, 1938.

ELKINS, S. M. *Slavery: A Problem in American Institutional and Intellectual Life.* Chicago: Univ. of Chicago Press, 1968.

ENGLISH, H. B., and ENGLISH, A. C. *A Comprehensive Dictionary of Psychological and Psychoanalytical Terms.* London: Longmans, Green, 1958.

ERIKSON, E. H., "Growth and Crises of the Healthy Personality." In KLUCKHOHN, C., MURRAY, H. A., and SCHNEIDER, D. M. *Personality.* New York: Knopf, 1953.

FANON, F. *The Wretched of the Earth.* New York: Grove Press, 1966.

FARBER, L. *The Ways of the Will: Essays Toward a Psychology and Psychopathology of the Will.* New York: Basic Books, 1966.

FRANKL, V. E. *Man's Search for Meaning: An Introduction to Logotherapy.* Boston: Beacon Press, 1963.

FRIEDMAN, M. S. *Martin Buber: The Life of Dialogue.* Chicago: Univ. of Chicago Press, 1955.

FROMM, E. *Escape from Freedom.* New York: Rinehart, 1941.

————. *Man for Himself.* New York: Rinehart, 1947.

GETZELS, J. W., and JACKSON, P. W. *Creativity and Intelligence: Explorations with Gifted Children.* New York: Wiley, 1962.

GILBERT, G. M. *The Psychology of Dictatorship.* New York: Ronald, 1950.

GOULDNER, A. W. *The Coming Crisis of Western Civilization.* New York: Basic Books, 1970.

GUERRIERO, A. "Perchè Stalin Uccise Milioni di Uomini," *Epoca,* 21 (May 24, 1970), 136–42.

GUNTRIP, H. *Schizoid Phenomena, Object Relations and the Self.* New York: International Universities Press, 1968.

HAMMER, E. F. *Creativity.* New York: Random House, 1961.

HAYES, K. J., and HAYES, C. "The Intellectual Development of a Home-raised Chimpanzee," *Proc. Am. Philo. Soc.,* 95 (1951), 105–9.

HINSIE, L. E., and CAMPBELL, R. J. *Psychiatric Dictionary.* New York: Oxford Univ. Press, 1960.

HORNEY, K. *Our Inner Conflicts.* New York: Norton, 1943.

————. *Neurosis and Human Growth.* New York: Norton, 1953.

HOUSEPIAN, M. "The Unremembered Genocide." *Commentary,* 42 (Sept. 1966), 55–61.

HOUSEPIAN, M. *The Smyrna Affair.* New York: Harcourt, Brace, Jovanovitch, 1971.

HUBER, E. "Constitutional Law of the Greater German Reich, 1939." Quoted in U.S. Department of State, *National Socialism.* Washington, D.C.: Government Printing Office, 1943.

JAMES, W. *The Principles of Psychology.* New York: Holt, 1890.

KEITH, A. *Evolution and Ethics.* New York: Putnam, 1946.

KELSEN, H. *Society and Nature. A Sociological Inquiry.* Chicago: Univ. of Chicago Press, 1943.

KENISTON, K. *The Uncommitted: Alienated Youth in American Society.* New York: Harcourt, Brace & World, 1965.

————. *Young Radicals: Notes on Committed Youth.* New York: Harcourt, Brace & World, 1968.

KNIGHT, R. P. "Determinism, 'Freedom,' and Psychotherapy." In KNIGHT, R. P., and FRIEDMAN, C. R. (eds.). *Psychoanalytic Psychiatry and Psychology,* Vol. 1. New York: International Universities Press, 1954.

KROEBER, A. L. *Configurations of Culture Growth.* Berkeley and Los Angeles: Univ. of California Press, 1944.

KROPOTKIN, P. *Mutual Aid: A Factor in Evolution.* (1902) (Quoted by Keith, 1946.)

KHRUSHCHEV, N. "Special Report to the 20th Congress of the Communist Party of the Soviet Union, February 24-25, 1956." Reprinted in Cohen, 1967.

LAING, R. D. *The Politics of Experience.* New York: Pantheon, 1967.

LASHLEY, K. S., and COLBY, K. M. "An Exchange of Views on Psychic Energy and Psychoanalysis," *Behavioral Science,* 2 (1957), 230–40.

LENIN, V. I. *State and Revolution.* Moscow: Foreign Languages Publishing House, 1917.

———. "Filosofskie Tetradi." In *Works,* Vol. 38. (Quoted by Zeigarnik, 1965.)

LEVY, D. M. "Oppositional Syndromes and Oppositional Behavior." In HOCH, P., and ZUBIN, Z. (eds.), *Psychopathology of Childhood.* New York: Grune & Stratton, 1955.

LOEB, J. *The Mechanistic Conception of Life.* Cambridge: Harvard Univ. Press, 1912.

LORENZ, K. *On Aggression.* New York: Harcourt, Brace & World, 1966.

LORENZINI, P. "Il Collodi e il Suo Figliolo di Legno" (1940). In Collodi, C. *Le Avventure di Pinocchio.* Florence: Nerbini, 1947.

MANNHEIM, K. *Man and Society in an Age of Reconstruction.* New York: Harcourt, Brace & World, 1951.

MARCUSE, H. *Eros and Civilization: A Philosophical Inquiry into Freud.* Boston: Beacon, 1955.

———. *One-Dimensional Man: Studies in the Ideology of Advanced Industrial Society.* Boston: Beacon, 1964.

MASLOW, A. H. "Cognition of Being in the Peak Experiences," *J. Genet. Psychol.,* 94 (1959), 43–66.

MAY, R. *Love and Will.* New York: Norton, 1969.

MEARES, A. *A System of Medical Hypnosis.* Philadelphia: Saunders, 1960.

MORGAN, C. L. *Animal Life and Intelligence.* Boston: Ginn, 1891. (Quoted by DIAMOND, BALVIN, and DIAMOND, 1963.)

MUSSOLINI, B. "The Doctrine of Fascism." (1922) In CHANDLER, A. R. (ed.) *The Clash of Political Ideals.* New York: Appleton-Century-Crofts, 1949.

———. "Preludio al Principe," *Gerarchia,* vol. 3, no. 4, April 1924.

PARSONS, T. *The Structure of Social Action.* Glencoe: Free Press, 1949.

PLUMB, J. H. *The Death of the Past.* Boston: Houghton Mifflin, 1970.

POINCARE, H. "Mathematical Creation" (1913). In *The Foundations of Science.* Lancaster: Science Press, 1946.

PRANGE, G. W. (ed.). *Hitler's Words: The Speeches of Adolph Hitler from 1923–1943.* Washington, D.C.: Public Affairs Press, 1944.

RADO, S. "Obsessive Behavior." In ARIETI, S., *American Handbook of Psychiatry,* Vol. 1. New York: Basic Books, 1959.

REICH, W. *Character Analysis.* New York: Orgone Institute Press, 1949.

REICHENBACH, H. *The Rise of Scientific Philosophy.* Berkeley: Univ. of California Press, 1951.

RIESMAN, D., DENNEY, R., and GLAZER, N. *The Lonely Crowd: A Study of the Changing American Character.* New Haven: Yale Univ. Press, 1950.

ROCCO, A. "The Political Doctrine of Fascism." From *Readings on Fascism and National Socialism* (Philosophy Department of the University of Colorado), Denver: Alan Swallow, 1925.

ROSZAK, T. *The Making of a Counter Culture: Reflections on the Technocratic Society and Its Youthful Opposition.* New York: Doubleday, 1969.

RUSSELL, B. *Power.* New York: Barnes & Noble, 1962. London: Allen & Unwin.

SIIRALA, M. *Die Schizophrenie—des Einzelnen und der Allgemeinheit.* Göttingen: Vandenhoeck Ruprecht, 1961.

_____. "Schizophrenia: A Human Condition," *Am. J. Psychoanalysis,* 23 (1963), 39.

SKINNER, B. F. *Beyond Freedom and Dignity.* New York: Knopf, 1971.

SPIEGEL, H. "Hypnosis and Transference: A Theoretical Formulation," *A.M.A. Arch. Gen. Psychiatry,* 1 (1959), 634.

STALIN, J. *The Foundations of Leninism.* Moscow: Foreign Languages Publishing House, 1924.

STORR, A. *Human Aggression.* New York: Atheneum, 1968.

THORPE, W. H. *Learning and Instinct in Animals.* Cambridge, Mass.: Harvard University Press, 1956.

VOLKMANN, A. W. "Von dem Baue unl den Verrichtungen der Kopfnerven der Frosches," *Arch. Anal. Physiol. u. Wissensch. Med.,* 15 (1838), 70–89.

VON BERTALANFFY, L. *Robots, Men and Minds: Psychology in the Modern World.* New York: Braziller, 1967.

VON HOLST, E. "Vom Dualismus der motorischen und der automatisch-rhythmischen Funktion im Rückenmark und vom Wesen des automatischen Rhythmus Pflüg," *Arch. ges. Physiol.,* 237 (1936), 356.

_____. "Vom Wesen der Ordnung im Zentralnervensystem," *Naturwissenschaften,* 25 (1937), 625–31; 641–47.

WELD, T. D. *American Slavery as It Is* (1839). Reprinted by Arno Press and *The New York Times,* 1969.

WERNER, H. *Comparative Developmental Psychology.* New York: International Universities Press, 1947.

WHITE, L. A. "Cultural Determinants of Mind." In WHITE, L. A. *The Science of Culture*. New York: Farrar, Strauss, 1949.

YERKES, R. M. *Chimpanzees: A Laboratory Colony*. New Haven: Yale Univ. Press, 1943.

ZEIGARNIK, B. V. *The Pathology of Thinking*. New York: Consultants Bureau, 1965.

Index